Jean Webster

Just Patty & When Patty Went to College

Sharp Ink 2024

Jean Webster

Just Patty & When Patty Went to College

Sharp Ink, 2024
Contact: info@sharpinkbooks.com

ISBN: 978-80-283-7245-3

Contents

Just Patty

Chapter I Reform

It's a shame!" said Priscilla.

"It's an outrage!" said Conny.

"It's an insult!" said Patty.

"To separate us now after we've been together three years —"

"And it isn't as though we were *awfully* bad last year. Lots of girls had more demerits."

"Only our badness was sort of conspicuous," Patty admitted.

"But we were *very* good the last three weeks," reminded Conny.

"And you should see my new room-mate!" wailed Priscilla.

"She can't be any worse than Irene McCullough."

"She is! —Her father's a missionary, and she was brought up in China. Her name is Keren-happuch Hersey, after Job's youngest daughter. And she doesn't think it's funny!"

"Irene," said Conny gloomily, "gained twenty pounds through the summer. She weighs —"

"But you should see mine!" cried Patty, in exasperation. "Her name is Mae Mertelle Van Arsdale."

"Keren studies every second; and expects me to walk on tiptoe so she can concentrate."

"You should hear Mae Mertelle talk! She said her father was a financier, and wanted to know what mine was. I told her he was a reform judge, and that he spent his time putting financiers in prison. She says I'm an impertinent child," Patty grinned feebly.

"How old is she?"

"She's nineteen, and has been proposed to twice."

"Mercy! Whatever made her choose St. Ursula's?"

"Her father and mother ran away and got married when they were nineteen, and they're afraid she inherited the tendency. So they picked out a good, strict, church school. Mae doesn't know how she's ever going to fix her hair without a maid. She's awfully superstitious about moonstones. She never wears anything but silk stockings and she can't stand hash. I'll have to teach her how to make a bed. She always crosses on the White Star Line."

Patty scattered these details at random. The others listened sympathetically, and added a few of their own troubles.

"Irene weighs a hundred and fifty-nine pounds and six ounces, not counting her clothes," said Conny. "She brought two trunks *loaded* with candy. She has it hidden all over the room. The last sound I hear at night, is Irene crunching chocolates-and the first sound in the morning. She never says anything; she simply chews. It's like rooming with a cow. And I have a sweet collection of neighbors! Kid McCoy's across the hall, and she makes more noise than half-a-dozen cowboys. There's a new French girl next door-you know, the pretty little one with the two black braids."

"She looks rather desirable," said Patty.

"She might be if she could talk, but she only knows about fifty words. Harriet Gladden's rooming with her, as limp and mournful as an oyster, and Evalina Smith's at the end of the corridor. You know what a *perfect* idiot Evalina is."

"Oh, it's beastly!" they agreed.

"Lordy's to blame," said Conny. "The Dowager never would have separated us if she hadn't interfered."

"And I've got her!" wailed Patty. "You two have Mam'selle and Waddams, and they're nice, sweet, unsuspicious lambs; but the girls in the East Wing simply can't sneeze but Lordy—"

"Sh!" Conny warned. "Here she comes."

The Latin teacher, in passing, paused on the threshold. Conny disentangled herself from the mixture of clothes and books and sofa cushions that littered the bed, and politely rose to her feet. Patty slid down from the white iron foot-rail, and Priscilla descended from the top of the trunk.

"Ladies don't perch about on the furniture."

"No, Miss Lord," they murmured in unison, gazing back from three pairs of wide, uplifted eyes. They knew, from gleeful past experience, that nothing so annoyed her as smiling acquiescence.

Miss Lord's eyes critically studied the room. Patty was still in traveling dress.

"Put on your uniform, Patty, and finish unpacking. The trunks go down to-morrow morning."

"Yes, Miss Lord."

"Priscilla and Constance, why aren't you out of doors with the other girls, enjoying this beautiful autumn weather?"

"But we haven't seen Patty for such a long time, and now that we are separated—" commenced Conny, with a pathetic droop of her mouth.

"I trust that your lessons will benefit by the change. You, Patty and Priscilla, are going to college, and should realize the necessity of being prepared. Upon the thorough foundation that you lay here depends your success for the next four years-for your whole lives, one might say. Patty is weak in mathematics and Priscilla in Latin. Constance *could* improve her French. Let us see what you can do when you really try."

She divided a curt nod between the three and withdrew.

"We are happy in our work and we dearly love our teachers," chanted Patty, with ironical emphasis, as she rummaged out a blue skirt and middy blouse with "St. U." in gold upon the sleeve.

While she was dressing, Priscilla and Conny set about transferring the contents of her trunk to her bureau, in whatever order the articles presented themselves-but with a carefully folded top layer. The overworked young teacher, who performed the ungrateful task of inspecting sixty-four bureaus and sixty-four closets every Saturday morning, was happily of an unsuspicious nature. She did not penetrate below the crust.

"Lordy needn't make such a fuss over my standing," said Priscilla, frowning over an armful of clothes. "I passed everything except Latin."

"Take care, Pris! You're walking on my new dancing dress," cried Patty, as her head emerged from the neck of the blouse.

Priscilla automatically stepped off a mass of blue chiffon, and resumed her plaint.

"If they think sticking me in with Job's youngest daughter is going to improve my prose composition —"

"I simply *can't* study till they take Irene McCullough out of my room," Conny echoed. "She's just like a lump of sticky dough."

"Wait till you get acquainted with Mae Mertelle!" Patty sat on the floor in the midst of the chaos, and gazed up at the other two with wide, solemn eyes. "She brought five evening gowns cut low, and all her shoes have French heels. And she *laces* —my dears! She just holds in her breath and pulls. But that isn't the worst." She lowered her voice to a confidential whisper. "She's got some red stuff in a bottle. She says it's for her finger nails, but I *saw* her putting it on her face."

"Oh! —not really?" in a horrified whisper from Conny and Priscilla.

Patty shut her lips and nodded.

"Isn't it dreadful?"

"Awful!" Conny shuddered.

"I say, let's mutiny!" cried Priscilla. "Let's *make* the Dowager give us back our old rooms in Paradise Alley."

"But how?" inquired Patty, two parallel wrinkles appearing on her forehead.

"Tell her that unless she does, we won't stay."

"That would be sensible!" Patty jeered. "She'd ring the bell and order Martin to hitch up the hearse and drive us to the station for the six-thirty train. I should think you'd know by this time that you can't bluff the Dowager."

"There's no use threatening," Conny agreed. "We must appeal to her feeling of-of—"

"Affection," said Patty.

Conny stretched out a hand and brought her up standing.

"Come on, Patty, you're good at talking. We'll go down now while our courage is up. —Are your hands clean?"

The three staunchly approached the door of Mrs. Trent's private study.

"I'll use diplomacy," Patty whispered, as she turned the knob in response to the summons from within. "You people nod your heads at everything I say."

Patty did use all the diplomacy at her command. Having dwelt touchingly upon their long friendship, and their sorrow at being separated, she passed lightly to the matter of their new room-mates.

"They are doubtless very nice girls," she ended politely, "only, you see, Mrs. Trent, they don't match us; and it is extremely hard to concentrate one's mind upon lessons, unless one has a congenial room-mate."

Patty's steady, serious gaze suggested that lessons were the end of her existence. A brief smile flitted over the Dowager's face, but the next instant she was grave again.

"It is very necessary that we study this year," Patty added. "Priscilla and I are going to college, and we realize the necessity of being prepared. Upon the thorough foundation that we lay here, depends our success for the next four years-for our whole lives you might say."

Conny jogged her elbow warningly. It was too patently a crib from Miss Lord.

"And besides," Patty added hastily, "all my things are blue, and Mae has a purple screen and a yellow sofa cushion."

"That is awkward," the Dowager admitted.

"We are used to living in Paradise Al—I mean, the West Wing-and we shall-er-miss the sunsets."

The Dowager allowed an anxious silence to follow, while she thoughtfully tapped the desk with her lorgnette. The three studied her face with speculative eyes. It was a mask they could not penetrate.

"The present arrangement is more or less temporary," she commenced in equable tones. "I may find it expedient to make some changes, and I may not. We have an unusual number of new girls this year; and instead of putting them together, it has seemed wisest to mix them with the old girls. You three have been with us a long time. You know the traditions of the school. Therefore —" The Dowager smiled, a smile partially tinged with amusement —"I am sending you as missionaries among the newcomers. I wish you to make your influence felt."

Patty straightened her back and stared.

"Our influence?"

"Your new room-mate," Mrs. Trent continued imperturbably, "is too grown-up for her years. She has lived in fashionable hotels, and under such conditions, it is inevitable that a girl should become somewhat affected. See if you cannot arouse in Mae an interest in girlish sports.

"And you, Constance, are rooming with Irene McCullough. She is, as you know, an only child, and I fear has been a trifle spoiled. It would please me if you could waken her to a higher regard for the spiritual side of life, and less care for material things."

"I —I'll try," Conny stammered, dazed at so suddenly finding herself cast in the unfamiliar rôle of moral reformer.

"And you have next to you the little French girl, Aurelie Deraismes. I should be pleased, Constance, if you would assume an oversight of her school career. She can help you to a more idiomatic knowledge of French-and you can do the same for her in English.

"You, Priscilla, are rooming with —" She adjusted her lorgnette and consulted a large chart. —"Ah, yes, Keren Hersey, a very unusual girl. You two will find many subjects of mutual interest. The daughter of a naval officer should have much in common with the daughter of a missionary. Keren bids fair to become an earnest student-almost, if such a thing were possible, too earnest. She has never had any girl companions, and knows nothing of the give and take of school life. She can teach you, Priscilla, to be more studious, and you can teach her to be more, shall I say, flexible?"

"Yes, Mrs. Trent," Priscilla murmured.

"And so," the Dowager finished, "I am sending you out in my place, as moral reformers. I want the older girls to set an example to the newcomers. I wish to have the real government of the school a strong, healthy Public Opinion. You three exert a great deal of influence. See what you can do in the directions I have indicated-and in others that may occur to you as you mix with your companions. I have watched you carefully for three years, and in your fundamental good sense, I have the greatest confidence."

She nodded dismissal, and the three found themselves in the hall again. They looked at one another for a moment of blank silence.

"Moral reformers!" Conny gasped.

"I see through the Dowager," said Patty, "She thinks she's found a new method of managing us."

"But I don't see that we're getting back to Paradise Alley," Priscilla complained.

Patty's eyes suddenly brightened. She seized them each by an elbow and shoved them into the empty schoolroom.

"We'll do it!"

"Do what?" asked Conny.

"Pitch right in and reform the school. If we just keep at it-steady-you'll see! We'll be back in Paradise Alley at the end of two weeks."

"Um," said Priscilla, thoughtfully. "I believe we might."

"We'll commence with Irene," said Conny, her mind eagerly jumping to details, "and make her lose that twenty pounds. That's what the Dowager meant when she said she wanted her less material."

“We'll have her thin in no time,” Patty nodded energetically. “And we'll give Mae Mertelle a dose of bubbling girlishness.”

“And Keren,” interposed Priscilla, “we'll teach her to become frivolous and neglect her lessons.”

“But we won't just confine ourselves to those three,” said Conny. “The Dowager said to make our influence felt over the whole school.”

“Oh, yes!” Patty agreed, rising to enthusiasm as she called the school roll. ”Kid McCoy uses too much slang. We'll teach her manners. Rosalie doesn't like to study. We'll pour her *full* of algebra and Latin. Harriet Gladden's a jelly fish, Mary Deskam's an awful little liar, Evalina Smith's a silly goose, Nancy Lee's a telltale —”

“When you stop to think about it, there's something the matter with everybody,” said Conny.

“Except us,” amended Priscilla.

“Y —yes,” Patty agreed in thoughtful retrospection, “I can't think of a thing the matter with us —I don't wonder they chose us to head the reform!”

Conny slid to her feet, a bundle of energy.

“Come on! We'll join our little playmates and begin the good work-Hooray for the great Reform Party!”

They scrambled out of the open window, in a fashion foreign to the dictates of Thursday evening manner class. Crowds of girls in blue middy blouses were gathered in groups about the recreation ground. The three paused to reconnoiter.

“There's Irene, still chewing.” Conny nodded toward a comfortable bench set in the shade by the tennis courts.

“Let's have a circus,” Patty proposed. “We'll make Irene and Mae Mertelle roll hoops around the oval. That will kill 'em both with one stone-Irene will get thin, and Mae Mertelle girlish.”

Hoop-rolling was a speciality of St. Ursula's. The gymnasium instructor believed in teaching girls to run. Eleven times around the oval constituted a mile, and a mile of hoop-rolling freed one for the day from dumb-bells and Indian clubs. The three dived into the cellar, and returned with hoops as tall as themselves. Patty assumed command of the campaign and issued her orders.

”Conny, you take a walk with Keren and shock her as much as possible; we must break her of being precise. And Pris, you take charge of Mae Mertelle. Don't let her put on any grown-up airs. If she tells you she's been proposed to twice, tell her you've been proposed to so many times that you've lost count. Keep her snubbed all the time. I'll be elephant trainer and start Irene running; she'll be a graceful gazelle by the time I finish.”

They parted on their several missions. St. Ursula's peace had ended. She was in the throes of reform.

* * * * *

On Friday evening two weeks later, an unofficial faculty meeting was convened in the Dowager's study. “Lights-out” had rung five minutes before, and three harried teachers, relieved of duty for nine blessed hours while their little charges slept, were discussing their troubles with their chief.

“But just what have they done?” inquired Mrs. Trent, in tones of judicial calm, as she vainly tried to stop the flood of interjections.

“It is difficult to put one's finger on the precise facts,” Miss Wadsworth quavered. “They have not broken any rules so far as I can discover, but they have-er-created an atmosphere —”

“Every girl in my corridor,” said Miss Lord, with compressed lips, “has come to me separately, and begged to have Patty moved back to the West Wing with Constance and Priscilla.”

”Patty! *Mon Dieu!*” Mademoiselle rolled a pair of speaking eyes to heaven. “The things that child thinks of! She is one little imp.”

“You remember,” the Dowager addressed Miss Lord, “I said when you suggested separating them, that it was a very doubtful experiment. Together, they exhaust their effervescence on each other; separated —”

"They exhaust the whole school!" cried Miss Wadsworth, on the verge of tears. "Of course they don't mean it, but their unfortunate dispositions —"

"Don't mean it!" Miss Lord's eyes snapped. "Their heads are together planning fresh escapades every moment they are not in class."

"But what have they done?" persisted Mrs. Trent.

Miss Wadsworth hesitated a moment in an endeavor to choose examples from the wealth of material that presented itself.

"I found Priscilla deliberately stirring up the contents of Keren's bureau drawers with a shinny stick, and when I asked what she was doing, she replied without the least embarrassment, that she was trying to teach Keren to be less exact; that Mrs. Trent had asked her to do it."

"Um," mused the Dowager, "that was not my precise request, but no matter."

"But the thing that has really troubled me the most," Miss Wadsworth spoke diffidently, "is a matter almost a blasphemy. Keren has a very religious turn of mind, but an unfortunate habit of saying her prayers out loud. One night, after a peculiarly trying day, she prayed that Priscilla might be forgiven for being so aggravating. Whereupon Priscilla knelt before her bed, and prayed that Keren might become less self-righteous and stubborn, and more ready to join in the sports of her playmates with gen erosity and openness of spirit. They carried on-well, really, one might almost call it a praying match."

"Shocking!" cried Miss Lord.

"And little Aurelie Deraismes-they have been drilling the child in-er-idiomatic English. The phrase that I overheard her repeating, seemed scarcely the expression that a lady would use."

"What was it?" inquired the Dowager, with a slightly expectant note.

"I'll be *gum-swizzled!*"

Miss Wadsworth colored a deep pink. It was foreign to her nature even to repeat so doubtful an expression.

The Dowager's lips twitched. It was a fact, deplored by her assistants, that her sense of humor frequently ran away with her sense of justice. A very naughty little girl, if she managed to be funny, might hope to escape; whereas an equally naughty little girl, who was not funny, paid the full penalty of her crime. Fortunately, however, the school at large had not discovered this vulnerable spot in the Dowager's armor.

"Their influence," it was Miss Lord who spoke, "is demoralizing the school. Mae Van Arsdale says that she will go home if she has to room any longer with Patty Wyatt. I do not know what the trouble is, but —"

"I know it!" said Mademoiselle. "The whole school laughs. It is touching the question of a *sweetch.*"

"Of what?" The Dowager cocked her head. Mademoiselle's English was at times difficult. She mixed her languages impartially.

"A sweetch-some hair-to make pompadour. Last week when they have tableaux, Patty has borrowed it and has dyed it with blueing to make a beard for Bluebeard. But being yellow to start, it has become green, and the color will not wash out. The sweetch is ruin-entirely ruin-and Patty is desolate. She has apologize. She thought it would wash, but since it will not wash, she has suggest to Mae that she color her own hair to match the sweetch, and Mae lose her temper and call names. Then Patty has pretend to cry, and she put the green hair on Mae's bed with a wreath of flowers around, and she hang a stocking on the door for crape, and invite the girls to come to the funeral, and everybody laugh at Mae."

"It's just as well," said the Dowager, unmoved. "I do not wish to favor the wearing of false hair."

"It's the principle of the thing," said Miss Lord.

"And that poor Irene McCullough," Mademoiselle continued the tale, "she dissolves herself in tears. Those three insist that she make herself thin, and she has no wish to become thin."

"They take away her butter-ball," corroborated Miss Wadsworth, "before she comes to the table; they make her go without dessert, and they do not allow her to eat sugar on her oatmeal. They keep her exercising every moment, and when she complains to me, they punish her."

"I should think," the Dowager spoke with a touch of sarcasm, "that Irene were big enough to take care of herself."

"She has three against her," reminded Miss Lord.

"I called Patty to my room," said Miss Wadsworth, "and demanded an explanation. She told me that Mrs. Trent thought that Irene was too fat, and wished them to reduce her twenty pounds! Patty said that it was hard work, they were getting thin themselves, but they realized that they were seniors and must exert an influence over the school. I really think she was sincere. She talked very sweetly about moral responsibility, and the necessity of the older girls setting an example."

"It is her impudence," said Miss Lord, "that is so exasperating."

"That's —just Patty!" the Dowager laughed. "I must confess that I find all three of them amusing. It's good, healthy mischief and I wish there were more of it. They don't bribe the maids to mail letters, or smuggle in candy, or flirt with the soda-water clerk. They at least can be trusted."

"Trusted!" gasped Miss Lord.

"To break every minor rule with cheerful unconcern," nodded the Dowager, "but never to do the slightest thing dishonorable. They have kind hearts and the girls all love them —"

A knock sounded on the door with startling suddenness, and before anyone could reply, the door burst open and Keren-happuch appeared on the threshold. She was clutching with one hand the folds of a brilliant Japanese kimono, the other she reserved for gestures. The kimono was sprinkled with fire-eating dragons as large as cats; and to the astonished spectators, Keren's flushed face and disheveled hair seemed to carry out the decorative scheme. The Dowager's private study was a sacred spot, reserved for interviews of formality; never had a pupil presented herself in such unceremonious garb.

"Keren!" cried Miss Wadsworth. "What has happened?"

"I want a new room-mate! I can't stand Priscilla any longer. She's been having a birthday party in my room —"

"I want a new room-mate"

"A birthday party?" Mrs. Trent turned questioningly to Miss Wadsworth.

She nodded unhappily.

"Yesterday was Priscilla's birthday, and she received a box from her aunt. This being Friday night, I gave her permission—"

"Certainly." The Dowager turned to the tragic figure in the center of the floor. "It is Priscilla's room as much as yours and—"

Keren plunged into a sea of words. The four leaned forward in a strained endeavor to pluck some sense from the torrent.

"They used my bed for a table because it wasn't against the wall, and Patty tipped a pot of chocolate over in the middle of it. She said it was an accident-but she did it on purpose—I know she did! And because I objected, Priscilla said it wasn't polite to notice when a guest spilled anything, and she tipped a glass of current jelly on my pillow, to make Patty feel comfortable.

That was the polite thing for a hostess to do, she said; they learned it last year in manner class. And the chocolate soaked right through, and Conny Wilder said it was fortunate I was thin, because I could sleep in a curve around it; if it had happened to Irene McCullough, she would have had to sleep in it, because she's so big she takes up the whole bed. And Priscilla said I could be thankful to-morrow's Saturday when we get clean sheets; it might have happened so that I would have had to sleep in that puddle of chocolate a whole week. And then the "Lights-out" rang, and they left me to clean up, and the housekeeper's gone to bed, and I can't get any fresh bed clothes, and I *won't* sleep that way! I'm not used to sleeping in chocolaty sheets. I don't like America and I *hate* girls."

Tears were dripping from Keren's cheeks onto the fire-breathing dragons below. The Dowager, without comment, rose and rang the bell.

"Katie," she said, as the maid on duty appeared at the door, "some fresh sheets for Miss Keren, please, and remake her bed. That will do for to-night, Keren. Get to sleep as quickly as possible, and don't talk. You mustn't disturb the other girls. We can see about changing room-mates to-morrow."

Katie and the outraged dragons withdrew.

A silence followed, while Miss Wadsworth and Mademoiselle exchanged glances of despair, and Miss Lord buckled on her war armor.

"You see!" she said, with a suggestion of triumph, "when they get to the point of persecuting a poor little—"

"In my experience of school life," said Mrs. Trent judicially, "it is a girl's own fault when she is persecuted. Their methods are crude, but to the point. Keren is a hopeless little prig—"

"But at least you can't allow her to suffer—"

"Oh, no, I shall do what I can toward peace. To-morrow morning, Keren can move in with Irene McCullough, and Patty and Conny and Priscilla go back to their old rooms in the West Wing. You, Mademoiselle, are somewhat inured—"

"I do not mind them together. They are just-what you say? —exhilarating. It is when they are spread out that it is difficult."

"You mean," Miss Lord stared—"that you are going to *reward* their disgraceful conduct? It is exactly what they have been working for."

"You must acknowledge," smiled the Dowager, "that they have worked hard. Perseverance deserves success."

* * * * *

The next morning, Patty and Conny and Priscilla, their arms running over with dresses and hats and sofa cushions, gaily two-stepped down the length of "Paradise Alley" while a relieved school assisted at the flitting. As they caught sight of Miss Lord hovering in the offing, they broke into the chorus of a popular school song:

"We like to go to chapelAnd listen to the preachers,
We are happy in our work,
And we dearly love our teachers.
Daughters of Saint Ur-su-la!"

Chapter II The Romantic History of Cuthbert St. John

The Dowager" had a very sensible theory that boarding-school girls should be kept little girls, until their school life was over, and they stepped out, fresh and eager and spontaneous, to greet the grown-up world. Saint Ursula's was a cloister, in fact, as in name. The masculine half of the human species was not supposed to count.

Sometimes a new girl was inclined to turn up her nose at the youthful pastimes that contented her companions. But in the end she would be drawn irresistibly into the current. She would learn to jump rope and roll hoops; to participate in paper chases 'cross country; to skate and coast and play hockey on winter afternoons, to enjoy molasses-candy pulls and popcorn around the big open fire on Saturday nights, or impromptu masquerades, when the school raided the trunks in the attic for costumes. After a few weeks' time, the most spoiled little worldling lost her consciousness of calls outside of "bounds," and surrendered to the spirit of the youthful sisterhood.

But the girls in their teens answer readily to the call of romance. And occasionally, in the twilight hour between afternoon study and the dressing bell, as they gathered in the window-seat with faces to the western sky, the talk would turn to the future-particularly when Rosalie Patton was of the group. Pretty, dainty, inconsequential little Rosalie was preëminently fashioned for romance; it clung to her golden hair and looked from her eyes. She might be extremely hazy as to the difference between participles and supines, she might hesitate on her definition of a parallelopiped, but when the subject under discussion was one of sentiment, she spoke with conviction. For hers was no mere theoretical knowledge; it was gained by personal experience. Rosalie had been proposed to!

She confided the details to her most intimate friends, and they confided them to their most intimate friends, until finally, the whole school knew the entire romantic history.

Rosalie's preëminence in the field of sentiment was held entirely fitting. Priscilla might excel in basket-ball, Conny Wilder in dramatics, Keren Hersey in geometry and Patty Wyatt in-well, in impudence and audacity-but Rosalie was the recognized authority in matters of the heart; and until Mae Mertelle Van Arsdale came, nobody thought of questioning her position.

Mae Mertelle spent an uncomfortable month shaking into place in the school life. The point in which she was accustomed to excel was *clothes*, but when she and her four trunks arrived, she found to her disgust that clothes were not useful at St. Ursula's. The school uniform reduced all to a dead level in the matter of fashion. There was another field, however, in which she might hope for supremacy. Her own sentimental history was vivid, compared to the colorless lives of most, and she proceeded to assert her claims.

One Saturday evening in October, half-a-dozen girls were gathered in Rosalie's room, on piled-up sofa cushions, with the gas turned low and the light of the hunter's moon streaming through the window. They had been singing softly in a minor key, but gradually the singing turned to talk. The talk, in accordance with the moonlight and flying clouds, was in a sentimental vein; and it ended, naturally, with Rosalie's Great Experience. Between maidenly hesitations and many promptings she retold the story-the new girls had never heard it, and to the old girls it was always new.

The stage setting had been perfect—a moonlit beach, and lapping waves and rustling pine trees. When Rosalie chanced to omit any detail, her hearers, already familiar with the story, eagerly supplied it.

"And he held your hand all the time he was talking," Priscilla prompted.

"Oh, Rosalie! Did he?" in a shocked chorus from the newcomers.

"Y—yes. He just sort of took hold of it and forgot to let go, and I didn't like to remind him."

"What did he say?"

"He said he couldn't live without me."

"And what did you say?"

"I said I was awfully sorry, but he'd have to."

"And then what happened?"

"Nothing happened," she was obliged to confess. "I s'pose something might have happened if I'd accepted him, but you see, I didn't."

"But you were very young at the time," suggested Evalina Smith. "Are you sure you knew your own mind?"

Rosalie nodded with an air of melancholy regret.

"Yes. I knew I couldn't ever love him, because, he-well, he had an awfully funny nose. It started to point in one direction, and then changed its mind and pointed in the other."

Her hearers would have preferred that she had omitted this detail; but Rosalie was literal-minded and lacked the story-teller's instinct for suppression.

"He asked if there wasn't any hope that I would change," she added pensively. "I told him that I could never love him enough to marry him, but that I would always respect him."

"And then what did he say?"

"He said he wouldn't commit suicide."

A profound hush followed, while Rosalie gazed at the moon and the others gazed at Rosalie. With her gleaming hair and violet eyes, she was entirely their ideal of a storybook heroine. They did not think of envying her; they merely wondered and admired. She was crowned by natural right, Queen of Romance.

Mae Van Arsdale, who had listened in silence to the recital, was the first to break the spell. She rose, fluffed up her hair, straightened her blouse, and politely suppressed a yawn.

"Nonsense, Rosalie! You're a silly little goose to make such a fuss over nothing. —Good-night, children. I'm going to bed now."

She sauntered toward the door, but paused on the threshold to drop the casual statement. "*I've* been proposed to three times."

A shocked gasp arose from the circle at this *lèse-majesté*. The disdainful condescension of a new girl was more than they could brook.

"She's a horrid old thing, and I don't believe a word she says!" Priscilla declared stoutly, as she kissed poor crushed little Rosalie goodnight.

This slight *contretemps* marked the beginning of strained relations. Mae Mertelle gathered her own adherents, and Rosalie's special coterie of friends rallied to the standard of their queen. They intimated to Mae's followers that the quality of the romance was quite different in the two cases. Mae might be the heroine of any number of commonplace flirtations, but Rosalie was the victim of a *grande passion*. She was marked with an indelible scar that she would carry to the grave. In the heat of their allegiance, they overlooked the crookedness of the hero's nose and the avowed fact that Rosalie's own affections had not been engaged.

But Mae's trump card had been withheld. Whispers presently spread about under the seal of confidence. She was hopelessly in love. It was not a matter of the past vacation, but of the burning present. Her room-mate wakened in the night to hear her sobbing to herself. She had no appetite-her whole table could testify to that. In the middle of dessert, even on ice-cream nights, she would forget to eat, and with her spoon half-raised, would sit staring into space. When reminded that she was at the table, she would start guiltily and hastily bolt the rest of the meal. Her enemies unkindly commented upon the fact that she always came to before the end, so she got as much as anybody else.

The English classes at St. Ursula's were weekly drilled in the old-fashioned art of letter writing. The girls wrote letters home, minutely descriptive of school life. They addressed imaginary girl friends, and grandmothers and college brothers and baby sisters. They were learning the great secret of literary forcefulness-to suit their style to their audience. Ultimately, they arrived at the point of thanking imaginary young men for imaginary flowers. Mae listened to the somewhat stilted phraseology of these polite and proper notes with a supercilious smile. The class, covertly regarding her, thrilled anew.

Gradually, the details of the romance spread abroad. The man was English-Mae had met him on the steamer-and some day when his elder brother died (the brother was suffering from an incurable malady that would carry him off in a few years) he would come into the title; though just what the title was, Mae had not specifically stated. But in any case, her father was a staunch American; he hated the English and he hated titles. No daughter of his should ever marry a foreigner. If she did, she would never receive a dollar from him. However, neither Mae nor Cuthbert cared about the money. Cuthbert had plenty of his own. His name was Cuthbert St. John. (Pronounced Sinjun.) He had four names in all, but those were the two he used the most. He was in England now, having been summoned by cable, owing to the critical condition of his brother's health, but the crisis was past, and Cuthbert would soon be returning. Then-Mae closed her lips in a straight line and stared defiantly into space. Her father should see!

Before the throbbing reality of this romance, Rosalie's poor little history paled into nothing.

Then the plot began to thicken. Studying the lists of incoming steamers, Mae announced to her room-mate that he had landed. He had given his word to her father not to write; but she knew that in some way she should hear. And sure enough! The following morning brought a nameless bunch of violets. There had been doubters before-but at this tangible proof of devotion, skepticism crumbled.

Mae wore her violets to church on Sunday. The school mixed its responses in a shocking fashion-nobody pretended to follow the service; all eyes were fixed on Mae's upturned face and far-off smile. Patty Wyatt pointed out that Mae had taken special pains to seat herself in the light of a stained-glass window, and that occasionally the rapt eyes scanned the faces of her companions, to make sure that the effect was reaching across the footlights. But Patty's insinuation was indignantly repudiated by the school.

Mae was at last triumphantly secure in the rôle of leading lady. Poor insipid Rosalie no longer had a speaking part.

The affair ran on for several weeks, gathering momentum as it moved. In the European Travel Class that met on Monday nights, "English Country Seats" was the subject of one of the talks, illustrated by the stereopticon. As a stately, terraced mansion, with deer cropping grass in the fore ground, was thrown upon the screen, Mae Mertelle suddenly grew faint. She vouchsafed no reason to the housekeeper who came with hot-water bottles and cologne; but later, she whispered to her room-mate that that was the house where he was born.

Violets continued to arrive each Saturday, and Mae became more and more *distrait*. The annual basket-ball game with Highland Hall, a near-by school for girls, was imminent. St. Ursula's had been beaten the year before; it would mean everlasting disgrace if defeat met them a second time, for Highland Hall was a third their size. The captain harangued and scolded an apathetic team.

"It's Mae Mertelle and her beastly violets!" she disgustedly grumbled to Patty. "She's taken all the fight out of them."

The teachers, meanwhile, were uneasily aware that the atmosphere was overcharged. The girls stood about in groups, thrilling visibly when Mae Mertelle passed by. There was a moonlight atmosphere about the school that was not conducive to high marks in Latin prose composition. The matter finally became the subject of an anxious faculty meeting. There was no actual data at hand; it was all surmise, but the source of the trouble was evident. The school had been swept before by a wave of sentiment; it was as catching as the measles. The Dowager was inclined to think that the simplest method of clearing the atmosphere would be to pack Mae Mertelle and her four trunks back to the paternal fireside, and let her foolish mother deal with the case. Miss Lord was characteristically bent upon fighting it out. She would stop the nonsense by force. Mademoiselle, who was inclined to sentiment, feared that the poor child was really suffering. She thought sympathy and tact-But Miss Sallie's bluff common-sense won the day. If the sanity of Saint Ursula's demanded it, Mae Mertelle must go; but she thought, by the use of a little diplomacy, both St. Ursula's sanity and Mae Mertelle might be preserved. Leave the matter to her. She would use her own methods.

Miss Sallie was the Dowager's daughter. She managed the practical end of the establishment-provided for the table, ruled the servants, and ran off, with the utmost ease, the two hundred acres of the school farm. Between the details of horseshoeing and haying and butter-making, she lent her abilities wherever they were needed. She never taught; but she disciplined. The school was noted for unusual punishments, and most of them originated in Miss Sallie's brain. Her title of "Dragonette" was bestowed in respectful admiration of her mental qualities.

The next day was Tuesday, Miss Sallie's regular time for inspecting the farm. As she came downstairs after luncheon drawing on her driving gloves, she just escaped stepping on Conny Wilder and Patty Wyatt who, flat on their stomachs, were trying to poke out a golf ball from under the hat-rack.

"Hello, girls!" was her cheerful greeting. "Wouldn't you like a little drive to the farm? Run and tell Miss Wadsworth that you are excused from afternoon study. You may stay away from Current Events this evening, and make it up."

The two scrambled into hats and coats in excited delight. A visit to Round Hill Farm with Miss Sallie, was the greatest good that St. Ursula's had to offer. For Miss Sallie-out of bounds-was the funniest, most companionable person in the world. After an exhilarating five-mile drive through a brown and yellow October landscape, they spent a couple of hours romping over the farm, had milk and ginger cookies in Mrs. Spence's kitchen; and started back, wedged in between cabbages and eggs and butter. They chatted gaily on a dozen different themes-the Thanksgiving masquerade, a possible play, the coming game with Highland Hall, and the lamentable new rule that made them read the editorials in the daily papers. Finally, when conversation flagged for a moment, Miss Sallie dropped the casual inquiry:

"By the way, girls, what *has* got into Mae Van Arsdale? She droops about in corners and looks as dismal as a molting chicken."

Patty and Conny exchanged a glance.

"Of course," Miss Sallie continued cheerfully, "it's perfectly evident what the trouble is. I haven't been connected with a boarding-school for ten years for nothing. The little idiot is posing as the object of an unhappy affection. You know that I never favor talebearing, but, just as a matter of curiosity, is it the young man who passes the plate in church, or the one who sells ribbon in Marsh and Elkins's?"

"Neither." Patty grinned. "It's an English nobleman."

"What?" Miss Sallie stared.

"And Mae's father hates English noblemen," Conny explained, "and has forbidden him ever to see her again."

"Her heart is broken," said Patty sadly. "She's going into a decline."

"And the violets?" inquired Miss Sallie.

"He promised not to send her any letters, but violets weren't mentioned."

"H'm, I see!" said Miss Sallie; and, after a moment of thought, "Girls, I am going to leave this matter in your hands. I want it stopped."

"In our hands?"

"The school can't be stirred up any longer; but the matter's too silly to warrant the teachers taking any notice of it. This is a thing that ought to be regulated by public opinion. Suppose you see what you can do —I will appoint you a committee to bring the school back to a solid basis of common sense. I know that I can trust you not to talk."

"I don't exactly see what we can do," said Patty, dubiously.

"You are usually not without resourcefulness," Miss Sallie returned with a flickering smile. "You may have a *carte blanche* to choose your own methods."

"And may we tell Priscilla?" Conny asked. "We must tell her because we three —"

"Hunt together?" Miss Sallie nodded. "Tell Priscilla, and let it stop at that."

The next afternoon, when Martin drove into the village to accomplish the daily errands, he dropped Patty and Priscilla at the florists, empowered by the school to purchase flowers for the rector's wife and new baby. They turned inside, their minds entirely occupied with the rival merits of red and white roses. They ordered their flowers, inscribed the card, and then waited aimlessly till Martin should return to pick them up. Passing down the counter, they came upon a bill-sticker, the topmost item being, "Violets every Saturday to Miss Mae Van Arsdale, St. Ursula's School."

They stopped and stared for a thoughtful moment. The florist followed their gaze.

"Do you happen to know the young lady who ordered them vi'lets?" he inquired. "She didn't leave any name, and I'd like to know if she wants me to keep on sending 'em. She only paid up to the first, and the price is going up."

"No, I don't know who it was," said Patty, with well-assumed indifference. "What did she look like?"

"She-she had on a blue coat," he suggested. As all sixty-four of the St. Ursula girls wore blue coats, his description was not helpful.

"Oh," Patty prompted, "was she quite tall with a lot of yellow hair and —"

"That's her!"

He recognized the type with some assurance.

"It's Mae herself!" Priscilla whispered excitedly.

Patty nodded and commanded silence.

"We'll tell her," she promised. "And by the way," she added to Priscilla, "I think it would be nice for us to send some flowers to Mae, from our-er-secret society. But I'm afraid the treasury is pretty low just now. They'll have to be cheaper than violets. What are your cheapest flowers?" she inquired of the man.

"There's a kind of small sunflower that some people likes for decoration. 'Cut-and-come-again' they're called. I can give you a good-sized bunch for fifty cents. They make quite a show."

"Just the thing! Send a bunch of sunflowers to Miss Van Arsdale with this card." Patty drew a blank card toward her, and in an upright back hand traced the inscription, "Your disconsolate C. St. J."

She sealed it in an envelope, then regarded the florist sternly.

"Are you a Mason?" she asked, her eye on the crescent in his buttonhole.

"Y—yes," he acknowledged.

"Then you understand the nature of an oath of secrecy? You are not to divulge to anyone the sender of these flowers. The tall young lady with the yellow hair will come in here and try to make you tell who sent them. You are not to remember. It may even have been a man. You don't know anything about it. This secret society at Saint Ursula's is so very much more secret than the Masonic Society, that it is even a secret that it exists. Do you understand?"

"I—yes, ma'am," he grinned.

"If it becomes known," she added darkly, "I shall not be responsible for your life."

She and Priscilla each contributed a quarter for the flowers.

"It's going to be expensive," Patty sighed. "I think we'll have to ask Miss Sallie for an extra allowance while this committee is in session."

Mae was in her room, surrounded by an assemblage of her special followers, when the flowers arrived. She received the box in some bewilderment.

"He's sending flowers on Wednesdays as well as Saturdays!" her room-mate cried. "He must be getting desperate."

Mae opened the box amid an excited hush.

"How perfectly lovely!" they cried in chorus, though with a slightly perfunctory undertone. They would have preferred crimson roses.

Mae regarded the offering for a moment of stupefied amazement. She had been pretending so long, that by now she almost believed in Cuthbert herself. The circle was waiting, and she rallied her powers to meet this unexpected crisis.

"I wonder what sunflowers mean?" she asked softly. "They must convey some message. Does anybody know the language of flowers?"

Nobody did know the language of flowers; but they were relieved at the suggestion.

"Here's a card!" Evalina Smith plucked it from among the bristling leaves.

Mae made a motion to examine it in private, but she had been so generous with her confidences heretofore, that she was not allowed to withdraw them at this interesting point. They leaned over her shoulder and read it aloud.

"'Your disconsolate C. St. J.'—Oh, Mae, think how he must be suffering!"

"Poor man!"

"He simply couldn't remain silent any longer."

"He's the soul of honor," said Mae. "He wouldn't write a real letter because he promised not to, but I suppose—a little message like this—"

Patty Wyatt passing the door, sauntered in. The card was exhibited in spite of a feeble protest from Mae.

"That handwriting shows a lot of character," Patty commented.

This was considered a concession; for Patty, from the first, had held aloof from the cult of Cuthbert St. John. She was Rosalie's friend.

The days that followed, were filled with bewildering experiences for Mae Mertelle. Having accepted the first installment of sunflowers, she could not well refuse the second. Once having committed herself, she was lost. Candy and books followed the flowers in horrifying profusion. The candy was of an inexpensive variety-Patty had discovered the ten-cent store-but the boxes that contained it made up in decorativeness what the candy lacked; they were sprinkled with Cupids and roses in vivid profusion. A message in the same back hand accompanied each gift, signed sometimes with initials, and sometimes with a simple "Bertie." Parcels had never before been delivered with such unsuspicious promptitude. Miss Sallie was the one through whose hands they went. She glanced at the outside, scrawled a "deliver," and the maid would choose the most embarrassing moments to comply-always when Mae Mertelle was surrounded by an audience.

Mae's Englishman, from an object of sentiment, in a few days' time became the joke of the school. His taste in literature was as impossible as his taste in candy. He ran to titles which are supposed to be the special prerogative of the kitchen. "Loved and Lost," "A Born Coquette," "Thorns among the Orange Blossoms." Poor Mae repudiated them, but to no avail; the school had accepted Cuthbert-and was bent upon eliciting all the entertainment possible from his British vagaries. Mae's life became one long dread of seeing the maid appear with a parcel. The last straw was the arrival of a complete edition-in paper-of Marie Corelli.

"He-he never sent them!" she sobbed. "Somebody's just trying to be funny."

"You mustn't mind, Mae, because they aren't just the sort that an American man would choose," Patty offered comfort. "You know that Englishmen have queer tastes, particularly in books. *Everybody* reads Marie Corelli over there."

The next Saturday, a party of girls was taken to the city for shopping and the matinée. Among other errands, the art class visited a photograph dealer's, to purchase some early Italian masters. Patty's interest in Giotto and his kind was not very keen, and she sauntered off on a tour of inspection. She happened upon a pile of actors and actresses, and her eye brightened as she singled out a large photograph of an unfamiliar leading man, with curling mustache and dimpled chin and large appealing eyes. He was dressed in hunting costume and conspicuously displayed a crop. The picture was the last word in Twentieth Century Romance. And, most perfect touch of all, it bore a London mark!

Patty unobtrusively deflected the rest of the committee from a consideration of Fra Angelico, and the three heads bent delightedly over the find.

"It's perfect!" Conny sighed. "But it costs a dollar and fifty cents."

"We'll have to go without soda water *forever!*" said Priscilla.

"It is expensive," Patty agreed, "but—" as she restudied the liquid, appealing eyes—"I really think it's worth it."

They each contributed fifty cents, and the picture was theirs.

Patty wrote across the front, in the bold back hand that Mae had come to hate, a tender message in French, and signed the full name, "Cuthbert St. John." She had it wrapped in a plain envelope and requested the somewhat wondering clerk to mail it the following Wednesday morning, as it was an anniversary present and must not arrive before the day.

The picture came on the five-o'clock delivery, and was handed to Mae as the girls trooped out from afternoon study. She re ceived it in sulky silence and retired to her room. Half a dozen of her dearest friends followed at her heels; Mae had worked hard to gain a following, and now it couldn't be shaken off.

"Open it, Mae quick!"

"What do you s'pose it is?"

"It can't be flowers or candy. He must be starting something new."

"I don't care what it is!" Mae viciously tossed the parcel into the wastebasket.

Irene McCullough fished it out and cut the string.

"Oh, Mae, it's his photograph!" she squealed. "And he's per-fect-ly beau-ti-ful!"

"Did you ever see such eyes!"

"Does he curl his mustache, or it is natural?"

"Why didn't you tell us he had a dimple in his chin?"

"Does he always wear those clothes?"

Mae was divided between curiosity and anger. She snatched the photograph away, cast one glance at the languishing brown eyes, and tumbled it, face downward, into a bureau drawer.

"Don't ever mention his name to me again!" she commanded, as, with compressed lips, she commenced brushing her hair for dinner.

On the next Friday afternoon-shopping day in the village-Patty and Conny and Priscilla dropped in at the florist's to pay a bill.

"Two bunches of sunflowers, one dollar," the man had just announced in ringing tones from the rear of the store, when a step sounded behind them, and they faced about to find Mae Mertelle Van Arsdale, bent on a similar errand.

"Oh!" said Mae, fiercely, "I might have known it was you three."

She stared for a moment in silence, then she dropped into a rustic seat and buried her head on the counter. She had shed so many tears of late that they flowed automatically.

"I suppose," she sobbed, "you'll tell the whole school, and everybody will laugh and-and —"

The three regarded her with unbending mien. They were not to be moved by a few tears.

"You said that Rosalie was a silly little goose to make such a fuss over nothing," Priscilla reminded her.

"And at least he was a live man," said Patty, "even if he did have a crooked nose."

"Do you still think she was a silly goose?" Conny inquired.

"N —no!"

"Don't you think you've been a great deal more silly?"

"Y —yes."

"And will you apologize to Rosalie?"

"No!"

"It will make quite a funny story," Patty ruminated, "the way we'll tell it."

"I think you're perfectly horrid!"

"Will you apologize to Rosalie?" Priscilla asked again.

"Yes-if you'll promise not to tell."

"We'll promise on one condition-you're to break your engagement to Cuthbert St. John, and never refer to it again."

Cuthbert sailed for England on the *Oceanic* the following Thursday; St. Ursula's plunged into a fever of basket-ball, and the atmosphere became bracingly free of Romance.

Chapter III The Virgil Strike

I'm tired of Woman's Rights on Friday afternoons," said Patty disgustedly. "I prefer soda water!"

"This makes the third time they've taken away our holiday for the sake of a beastly lecture," Priscilla grumbled, as she peered over Patty's shoulder to read the notice on the bulletin board, in Miss Lord's perpendicular library hand.

It informed the school that instead of the usual shopping expedition to the village, they would have the pleasure that afternoon of listening to a talk by Professor McVey of Columbia University. The subject would be the strike of the women laundry workers. Tea would be served in the drawing-room afterwards, with Mae Van Arsdale, Harriet Gladden, and Patty Wyatt as hostesses.

"It's not my turn!" objected Patty, as she noted the latter item. "I was hostess two weeks ago."

"That's because you wrote an essay on the 'Eight Hour Day.' Lordie thinks you will ask the professor-man intelligent questions; and show him that St. Ursula's is not a common boarding-school where only superficial accomplishments are taught, but one in which the actual problems of—"

"And I did want to go shopping!" Patty mourned. "I need some new shoe-strings. I've been tying a knot in my old ones every day for a week."

"Here she comes," whispered Priscilla. "Look happy or she'll make you translate the whole-Good morning, Miss Lord! We were just noticing about the lecture. It sounds extremely interesting."

The two smiled a perfunctory greeting, and followed their teacher to the morning's Latin.

Miss Lord was the one who struck the modern note at St. Ursula's. She believed in militant suffragism and unions and boycotts and strikes; and she labored hard to bring her little charges to her own advanced position. But it was against a heavy inertia that she worked. Her little charges didn't care a rap about receiving their rights, in the dim future of twenty-one; but they were very much concerned about losing a present half-holiday. On Friday afternoons, they were ordinarily allowed to draw checks on the school bank for their allowances, and march in a procession —a teacher forming the head and tail-to the village stores, where they laid in their weekly supply of hair ribbons and soda water and kodak films. Even had one acquired so many demerits that her weekly stipend was entirely eaten up by fines, still she marched to the village and watched the lucky ones disburse. It made a break in the monotony of six days of bounds.

But every cloud has its silver lining.

Miss Lord preceded the Virgil recitation that morning by a discussion of the lecture to come. The laundry strike, she told them, marked an epoch in industrial history. It proved that women, as well as men, were capable of standing by each other. The solidarity of labor was a point she wished her girls to grasp. Her girls listened with grave attention; and by eagerly putting a question, whenever she showed signs of running down, they managed to stave off the Latin recitation for three quarters of an hour.

The professor, a mild man with a Van Dyke beard, came and lectured exhaustively upon the relations of employer and employed. His audience listened with politely intelligent smiles, but with minds serenely occupied elsewhere. The great questions of Capital and Labor, were not half so important to them, as the fact of the lost afternoon, or the essays that must be written for to-morrow's English, or even that this was ice-cream night with dancing class to follow. But Patty, on the front seat, sat with wide, serious eyes fixed on the lecturer's face. She was absorbing his arguments-and storing them for use.

Tea followed according to schedule. The three chosen ones received their guests with the facility of long-tried hostesses. The fact that their bearing was under inspection, with marks to follow, did not appreciably diminish their case. They were learning by the laboratory method, the social graces that would be needed later in the larger world. Harriet and Mae presided at the tea table, while Patty engaged the personage in conversation. He commented later, to Miss Lord, upon the students' rare understanding in economic subjects.

Miss Lord replied with some complaisance that she endeavored to have her girls think for themselves. Sociology was a field in which lessons could not be taught by rote. Each must work out her own conclusions, and act upon them.

Ice-cream and dancing restored the balance of St. Ursula's, after the mental exertions of the afternoon. At half-past nine-the school did not retire until ten on dancing nights-Patty and Priscilla dropped their goodnight courtesy, murmured a polite "*Bon soir, Mam'selle,*" and scampered up stairs, still very wide awake. Instead of preparing for bed with all dispatch, as well-conducted school girls should, they engaged themselves in practising the steps of their new Spanish dance down the length of the South Corridor. They brought up with a pirouette at Rosalie Patton's door.

Rosalie, still in the pale blue fluffiness of her dancing frock, was sitting cross-legged on the couch, her yellow curls bent over the open pages of a Virgil, tears spattering with dreary regularity on the lines she was conning.

The course of Rosalie's progress through senior Latin might be marked by blistered pages. She was a pretty, cuddling, helpless little thing, deplorably babyish for a senior; but irresistibly appealing. Everyone teased her, and protected her, and loved her. She was irrevocably predestined to bowl over the first man who came along, with her ultra feminine irresponsibility. Rosalie very often dreamed-when she ought to have been concentrating upon Latin grammar-of that happy future state in which smiles and kisses would take the place of gerunds and gerundives.

"You silly little muff!" cried Patty. "Why on earth are you bothering with Latin on a Friday night?"

She landed herself with a plump on Rosalie's right, and took away the book.

"I have to," Rosalie sobbed. "I'd never finish if I didn't begin. I don't see any sense to it. I can't do eighty lines in two hours. Miss Lord always calls on me for the end, because she knows I won't know that."

"Why don't you begin at the end and read backwards?" Patty practically suggested.

"But that wouldn't be fair, and I can't do it so fast as the others. I work more than two hours every day, but I simply never get through. I know I shan't pass."

"Eighty lines is a good deal," Patty agreed.

"It's easy for you, because you know all the words, but—"

"I worked more than two hours on mine yesterday," said Priscilla, "and I can't af ford it either. I have to save some time for geometry."

"*I just simply can't do it,*" Rosalie wailed. "And she thinks I'm stupid because I don't keep up with Patty."

Conny Wilder drifted in.

"What's the matter?" she asked, viewing Rosalie's tear-streaked face. "Cry on the pillow, child. Don't spoil your dress."

The Latin situation was explained.

"Oh, it's awful the way Lordie works us! She would like to have us spend every moment grubbing over Latin and sociology. She—"

"Doesn't think dancing and French and manners are any good at all," sobbed Rosalie, mentioning the three branches in which she excelled, "and I think they're a lot more sensible than subjunctives. You can put them to practical use, and you can't sociology and Latin."

Patty emerged from a moment of revery.

"There's not much use in Latin," she agreed, "but I should think that something might be done with sociology. Miss Lord told us to apply it to our everyday problems."

Rosalie swept the idea aside with a gesture of disdain.

"Listen!" Patty commanded, springing to her feet and pacing the floor in an ecstasy of enthusiasm. "I've got an idea! It's perfectly true. Eighty lines of Virgil is too much for anybody to learn-particularly Rosalie. And you heard what the man said: it isn't fair to gage the working day by the capacity of the strongest. The weakest has to set the pace, or else he's left behind.

That's what Lordy means when she talks about the solidarity of labor. In any trade, the workers have got to stand by each other. The strong must protect the weak. It's the duty of the rest of the class to stand by Rosalie."

"Yes, but how?" inquired Priscilla, breaking into the tirade.

"We'll form a Virgil Union, and strike for sixty lines a day."

"Oh!" gasped Rosalie, horrified at the audacity of the suggestion.

"Let's!" cried Conny, rising to the call.

"Do you think we can?" asked Priscilla, dubiously.

"What will Miss Lord say?" Rosalie quavered.

"She can't say anything. Didn't she tell us to listen to the lecture and apply its teaching?" Patty reminded.

"She'll be delighted to find we have," said Conny.

"But what if she doesn't give in?"

"We'll call out the Cicero and Cæsar classes in a sympathetic strike."

"Hooray!" cried Conny.

"Lordy does believe in Unions," Priscilla conceded. "She ought to see the justice of it."

"Of course she'll see the justice of it," Patty insisted. "We're exactly like the laundry workers-in the position of dependents, and the only way we can match strength with our employer, is by standing together. If Rosalie alone drops back to sixty lines, she'll be flunked; but if the whole class does, Lordie will *have* to give in."

"Maybe the whole class won't want to join the union," said Priscilla.

"We'll make 'em!" said Patty. In accordance with Miss Lord's desire, she had grasped some basic principles.

"We'll have to hurry," she added, glancing at the clock. "Pris, you run and find Irene and Harriet and Florence Hissop; and Conny, you route out Nancy Lee-she's up in Evalina Smith's room telling ghost stories. Here, Rosalie, stop crying and dump the things off those chairs so somebody can sit down."

Priscilla started obediently, but paused on the threshold.

"And what will you do?" she inquired with meaning.

"I," said Patty, "will be labor leader."

The meeting was convened, and Patty, a self-constituted chairman, outlined the tenets of the Virgil Union. Sixty lines was to constitute a working day. The class was to explain the case to Miss Lord at the regular session on Monday morning, and politely but positively refuse to read the last twenty lines that had been assigned. If Miss Lord proved insistent, the girls were to close their books and go out on strike.

The majority of the class, hypnotized by Patty's eloquence, dazedly accepted the program; but Rosalie, for whose special benefit the union had been formed, had to be coerced into signing the constitution. Finally, after a wealth of argument had been expended, she wrote her name in a very wobbly hand, and sealed it with a tear. By nature, Rosalie was not a fighter; she preferred gaining her rights by more feminine methods.

Irene McCullough had also to be forced. She was a cautious soul who looked forward to consequences. One of the most frequently applied of St. Ursula's punishments was to make the culprit miss desserts. Irene suffered keenly under this form of chastisement; and she carefully refrained from misdemeanors which might bring it upon her. But Conny produced a convincing argument. She threatened to tell that the chambermaid was in the habit of smuggling in chocolates —and poor harassed Irene, threatened with the two-fold loss of chocolates and dessert, sullenly added her signature.

"Lights-out" rang. The Virgil Union adjourned its first meeting and went to bed.

* * * * *

Senior Latin came the last hour of the morning, when everyone was tired and hungry. On the Monday following the founding of the Union, the Virgil class gathered outside the door, in growing perturbation as the actual time for the battle approached. Patty rallied them in a brief address.

"Brace up, Rosalie! Don't be a cry-baby. We'll help you out if the last lines come to you. And for goodness' sake, girls, *don't* look so scared. Remember you're suffering, not only for yourselves, but for all the generations of Virgil classes that come after you. Anyone who backs down now is a coward!"

Patty established herself on the front seat, directly in the line of the fire, and a slight skirmish occurred at the outset. Her heavy walking boots were conspicuously laced with pale blue baby ribbon, which caught the enemy's eye.

"That is scarcely the kind of shoe laces that a lady adopts. May I ask, Patty—?"

"I broke my other laces," Patty affably explained, "and since we didn't go shopping on Friday, I couldn't get any more. I don't quite like the effect myself," she conceded, as she stuck out a foot and critically surveyed it.

"See that you find some black ones immediately after class," Miss Lord acidly suggested. "Priscilla, you may read the first ten lines."

The lesson progressed in the usual manner, except that there was a visible tightening of nerves as each recitation was finished, and they waited to hear the next name called. Conny's turn ended with the sixtieth line. No one had gone beyond that; all ahead was virgin jungle. This was the point for the Union to declare itself; and the burden, true to her forebodings, fell upon poor trembling little Rosalie.

She cast an imploring glance toward Patty's sternly waiting countenance, stammered, hesitated, and miserably plunged into a sight translation. Rosalie never had the slightest luck at sight translations; even after two hours of patient work with a dictionary, she was still extremely hesitant as to meanings. Now, she blindly forged ahead,—amid a profound hush-attributing to the Pious Æneas a most amazing set of actions. She finished; and the slaughter commenced. Miss Lord spent three minutes in obliterating Rosalie; then passed the lines to Irene McCullough.

Irene drew a deep breath-she felt Conny encouragingly patting her on the back, while Patty and Priscilla, at either hand, jogged her elbow with insistent touch. She opened her mouth to declare the principles that had been foisted upon her over night; then she caught the cold gleam of Miss Lord's eye. Rosalie's sobs filled the room. And she fell. Irene was fairly good at Latin-her sight translation was at least intelligible. Miss Lord's comment was merely sarcastic, as she passed to Florence Hissop. By this time the panic had swept through the ranks. Florence would like to have been true to her pledged troth, but the instinct of self-preservation is strong. She improved on Irene's performance.

"Take the next ten lines, Patty, and endeavor to extract a glimmering of sense. Please bear in mind that we are reading poetry."

Patty raised her head and faced her superior in the manner of a Christian martyr.

"I only prepared the first sixty lines, Miss Lord."

"Why did you not finish the lesson that I gave out?" Miss Lord inquired sharply.

"We have decided that eighty lines are more than we can do in a day. It takes too much time away from our other lessons. We are perfectly willing to do sixty lines, and do them thoroughly, but we can't consider any more."

Miss Lord for a moment simply stared. Never had she known such a flagrant case of insubordination. And it was purely insub ordination, for Patty was the most capable person in the class.

"What do you mean?" she gasped at last.

"We have formed a Virgil Union," Patty gravely explained. "You, Miss Lord, will appreciate the fairness of our demands better than any of the other teachers, because you believe in unions. Now, the girls in this class feel that they are overworked and underpa-er-that is, I mean the lessons are too long."

Patty fetched a deep breath and started again.

"Eighty lines a day doesn't leave us any time for recreation, so we have determined to join together and demand our rights. We occupy the position of skilled laborers. You can get all the girls you want for Cæsar and beginning Latin, but you can't find anybody but us to read Virgil. It's like the laundry trade. We are not just plain boilers and starchers; we are fancy ironers. If you want to have a Virgil class, you have *got* to have us. You can't call in scab labor. Now, we aren't trying to take advantage because of our superior strength. We are perfectly willing to do an honest day's work, but we can't allow ourselves to be-er-to be —"

Patty fumbled a moment for her word, but in the end she brought it out triumphantly.

"We can't allow ourselves to be exploited. Singly, we are no match for you, but together, we can dictate our own terms. Because two or three of us can keep up the pace you set, is no reason why we should allow the others to be overworked. It is our duty to stand by one another against the encroachments of our employer. We women are not so advanced as men. But we are learning. Upon the solidarity of labor depends the life of Rosalie. In case you refuse to meet our demands, the Virgil class will be obliged to go out on strike."

Patty pronounced her ultimatum, and leaned back with folded arms.

A moment of silence followed. Then Miss Lord spoke. The class went down in hopeless, abject terror before the storm. Miss Lord's icy sarcasm was, in moments of intensity, lightened by gleams of fire. She had Irish ancestors and red hair. Patty alone listened with head erect and steely eyes. The red blood of martyrs dyed her cheeks. She was fighting for a cause. Weak, helpless, little Rosalie, sniffling at her elbow, should be saved-the cowardice of her comrades put to shame. She, single-handed, would fight and win.

Miss Lord finally drew breath.

"The class is dismissed. Patty will remain in the schoolroom until she has translated perfectly the last twenty lines. I will hear her read them after luncheon."

The girls rose and pressed in a huddled body toward the hall, while Patty turned into the empty schoolroom. On the threshold she paused to hurl one contemptuous word over her shoulder:

"Scabs!"

* * * * *

The lunch bell rang, and Patty at her desk in the empty schoolroom heard the girls laughing and talking, as they clattered down the tin-covered back stairs to the dining-room. She was very tired and very hungry. She had had five hours of work since breakfast, with only a glass of milk at eleven o'clock. Even the pleasurable sensation of being abused did not quite offset the pangs of hunger. She listlessly set about learning the morrow's lesson in French History. It dealt with another martyr. Louis the Ninth left his bones bleaching on the plains of Antioch. The cause was different, but the principle remained. If she was not to be fed until she learned the Latin-very well-she would leave her bones bleaching in the schoolroom of St. Ursula's.

An insistent tapping sounded on the window. She glanced across an angle, to find Osaki, the Japanese butler, leaning far out from his pantry window, and extending toward her a dinner plate containing a large, lone slab of turkey.

"Leave plate in wastebasket, Missy," he whispered hoarsely.

Patty, for an instant, struggled with dignity and martyrdom, but hunger and a love of intrigue triumphed. She tiptoed over and received the offering. There was no knife or fork, but primitive methods suffice in a case of real starvation. She finished the turkey and buried the plate beneath a pile of algebra papers. It was Osaki's daily business to empty the wastebasket; the plate in due course would be restored to its shelf.

A few moments later a scurrying footfall sounded at the door, and a little Junior A. darted to Patty's side. She cast a conspiratorial glance over her shoulder as she drew from a bulging blouse two buttered rolls.

"Take 'em quick!" she panted. "I must hurry back, or they'll suspect. I asked to be excused to get a handkerchief. Keep up your courage. We won't let you starve. It's splendid!"

She thrust the rolls into Patty's lap and vanished.

Patty found it comforting to know that the school was with her. The attractions of martyrdom are enhanced by the knowledge of an audience. Also, the rolls were a grateful addition to the turkey; her five-hour appetite was still insistent. She finished one of them and was about to begin on the second, when furtive footfalls sounded behind her, and one of the maids slipped a paper plate over her shoulder.

"Here's some fresh gingerbread, Miss Patty. Cook says—"

The sound of a closing door startled her, and she scurried off like a detected thief.

Patty placed her second roll in the wastebasket in company with the turkey plate, and was just starting on the gingerbread, when a scrambling sounded at the end window. A blue hat appeared momentarily over the sill, its owner boosted from below, and an unidentified hand sent an orange rolling down the center aisle. Patty hastily intercepted its course and dropped it into the wastebasket. Luncheon would be over momentarily, and a visit from Miss Lord was imminent. This influx of supplies was growing embarrassing.

She heard the rising flood of talk as the girls poured from the dining-room. She knew that sympathetic groups were viewing her from the open doors behind. Judging from the ceaseless shuffle of footsteps, all Saint Ursula's had errands that led past the schoolroom door. Patty did not cast a glance behind, but with rigid shoulders stared into space. Presently a rattling sounded above her head. She raised startled eyes to a register set in the ceiling, and saw Irene McCullough's anxious face peering through the opening.

"You can live for days on chocolates," came in a stage whisper. "I'm awfully sorry there's only half a pound; I ate the rest last night."

The register was lifted out, and a box was swiftly lowered by a string. Irene was chief of the scabs.

"Thank you, Irene," Patty returned in a haughty stage whisper. "I do not care to accept any—"

Miss Lord's voice became audible in the hall.

"I thought, young ladies, that afternoon recreation was to be spent out of doors?"

Patty just had time to snatch the box

Patty just had time to snatch the box and drop it in her lap, with an open essay book above, when Miss Lord advanced into the room. Patty's face assumed an air of suffering stoicism, as she stared ahead, in the profound hope that Irene would have sense enough to remove eight feet of dangling string. Miss Lord was followed by Osaki, carrying a tray with two slices of dry bread and a glass of water.

"Have you finished your Latin, Patty?"

"No, Miss Lord."

"Why not?"

"I am going to do to-morrow's lesson in afternoon study hour."

Patty's tone was respectful, but her meaning was clear. She emphasized slightly the word "to-morrow."

"You will do the twenty lines immediately."

A speaking silence from Patty.

"Do you hear me?"

"Yes, Miss Lord."

"Well?" The monosyllable was sharp enough to cut.

"I stand by my principles," said Patty. "I am not a scab."

"You may sit here until those twenty lines are finished."

"Very well, Miss Lord."

"I do not wish you to suffer. Here is bread and water."

She motioned Osaki to set down the tray.

Patty waved it aside.

"I am not a convict," she said with dignity. "I refuse to eat until I am served properly at the dining-room table."

A fleeting grin replaced for a moment Osaki's Oriental calm. Miss Lord set the bread on a neighboring desk, and the two withdrew.

All through recreation and afternoon study, Patty sat at her desk, the plate of bread conspicuously untouched at her elbow. Then the five-o'clock bell rang, and the girls trooped out and dispersed on their various businesses. The hour between afternoon study and dressing bell, was the one hour of the day entirely their own. Patty could hear them romping up the back stairs, and racing through the corridors. Kid McCoy was conducting a pillow fight in Paradise Alley above her head. Groups passed the schoolroom window with happy calls and laughter. Pepper and Tabasco, the two riding horses, were saddled and brought out. She could see the girls taking turns in galloping around the oval, while Martin, as ringmaster, waved his whip and urged them on. Martin now was bent with rheumatism, but in his far-off reckless youth he had been a cowboy, and when he taught the girls to ride, it was with a disregard of broken bones that dismayed even the adventurous gymnasium teacher. Patty was his star pupil; she could stick on Red Pepper's back with nothing but a blanket to hold her. It was only very occasionally, when Martin was in a propitious mood, that the horses were saddled for mere public amusement. Patty's heart was sore as she watched Priscilla and Conny, her two dearest friends, disport themselves regardless of their incarcerated mate.

It grew dusk; nobody came to furnish a light, and Patty sat in the semi-darkness, her head bent wearily on her arms. Finally she heard footsteps in the hall, and Miss Sallie entered and closed the door behind her. Patty braced herself anew; one needed keen wits to match the "Dragonette."

Miss Sallie had been talking with Miss Lord, and she was inclined to think that Patty needed chastisement of a rare sort; but it was her practice to hear both sides. She drew up a chair, and commenced with business-like directness.

"See here, Patty, what is the meaning of all this nonsense?"

Patty raised reproachful eyes.

"Nonsense, Miss Sallie?"

"Yes, nonsense! Miss Lord says that you refused to learn the lesson that she assigned, and that you incited the rest of the girls to mutiny. You are one of the most able pupils in the class, and your failure to finish the lesson is nothing in the world but stubbornness. If it were Rosalie Patton now, there might be some sense in it."

"I don't think you understand," said Patty gently.

"It might be well for you to explain," suggested Miss Sallie.

"I must stand by my principles."

"By all means!" Miss Sallie affably agreed. "And what are your principles?"

"To hold out for sixty lines of Virgil. It isn't because I *want* to strike, Miss Sallie. It would be much easier for me to do the eighty lines, but that wouldn't be fair to Rosalie. The working day should not be gaged by the capacity of the strongest. Miss Lord will flunk Rosalie if the rest of us don't take care of her. Upon the solidarity of labor depends the welfare of the individual worker. It is the fight of the oppressed against the encroachments of-of-er-organized authority."

"Um —I see! —I really begin to believe that you listened to that lecture, Patty."

"Of course I listened," Patty nodded, "and I must say that I am awfully disappointed in Miss Lord. She *told* us to apply our knowledge of sociology to the problems of our daily lives, and when we do, she backs down. But anyway, we intend to maintain the strike, until she is ready to meet our just demands. It isn't through selfish motives that I am acting, Miss Sallie. I should a lot rather have something to eat and go horseback riding. I am fighting for the cause of my suffering sisters."

The ceiling above shook at the impact, as four of her suffering sisters came down on top of one another, while the walls resounded with their shrieks and laughter.

Miss Sallie's lip twitched, but she controlled herself and spoke with serious gravity.

"Very well, Patty, I am glad to know that this unprecedented behavior is caused by charitable motives. I am sure that when Miss Lord fully understands the case she will feel gratified. Suppose I act as intermediary and lay the matter before her? We may be able to arrive at an-er-compromise."

The half hour that followed dinner was usually devoted to dancing in the big square hall, but to-night the girls were inclined to stand about in groups with furtive glances toward the schoolroom. A conference was going on inside. Miss Lord, the Dowager and the Dragonette had passed in and shut the door. Kid McCoy, returning from Paradise Alley, where she had been stretched on her stomach with her face to the register, reported that Patty had fainted through lack of food, that the Dowager had revived her with whiskey, and that she had come to, still cheering for the Union. Kid McCoy's statements, however, were apt to be touched by imagination. The school was divided in its opinion of Patty's course. The scabs were inclined to make light of her achievement, but Conny and Priscilla staunchly fanned enthusiasm.

Finally, the schoolroom door opened, and the faculty emerged and passed into the Dowager's private study, while the dancing commenced with sudden fervor. No one to-day liked to be caught by Miss Lord whispering in a corner.

Patty followed alone. Her face was pale, and there were weary circles about her eyes, but in them shone the light of victory.

"Patty!"

"Are you dead?"

"How'd it come out?"

"It was perfectly splendid!"

"Was she furious?"

"What did she say?"

"We arbitrated the question and have settled on a compromise," Patty replied with quiet dignity. "Hereafter the lesson will be seventy lines. The Virgil strike is declared off."

They pressed about her eager for details, but she separated herself, and kept on toward the dining-room door. There was an aloofness about her, an air of having experienced the heights alone. She was not quite ready to rub shoulders with common humanity.

The school settled itself to evening study, and Patty to her dinner. They could see her across the court, through the lighted window, as she sat in state at the end of a long table. Osaki on one side, tendered preserved strawberries, and Maggie on the other, frosted cakes. The rewards of martyrdom, in Patty's case, were solidly substantial.

Chapter IV The Third Man from the End

Oh, Patty! Did you bring us some wedding cake?"

"Did you have any adventures?"

Conny and Priscilla, with the dexterity of practice, sprang upon the rear step of the hearse as it turned in at the school gate, and rolled up the curving drive to the porte-cochère. The "hearse" was the popular name for the black varnished wagonette which conveyed the pupils of St. Ursula's from church and station. It was planned to accommodate twenty. Patty and her suit-case, alone in the capacious interior, were jolting about like two tiny peas in a very big pod.

"Adventures!" she called back excitedly. "*Wait till you hear!*"

As they came to a stop, they were besieged by a crowd of blue-coated girls. It was afternoon recreation, and the whole school was abroad. The welcome that she received, would have led an onlooker to infer that Patty had been gone three months instead of three days. She and her two postilions descended, and Martin gathered up his reins.

"Come on, youse! All who wants a ride to the stables," was his hospitable invitation.

It inundated him with passengers. They crowded inside-twice as many as the hearse would hold-they swarmed over the driver's seat and the steps; and two equestriennes even perched themselves on the horses' backs.

"What's the adventure?" demanded Conny and Priscilla in a breath, as the cavalcade rattled off.

Patty waved her hand toward the suit-case.

"There it is. Take it upstairs. I'll be with you as soon as I've reported."

"But that isn't your suit-case."

Patty shook her head mysteriously.

"If you tried a thousand years you'd never guess who owns it."

"Who?"

Patty laughed.

"Looks like a man's," said Conny.

"It is."

"Oh, Patty! Don't be so exasperating. Where'd you get it?"

"Just a little souvenir that I picked up. I'll tell you as soon as I've interviewed the Dowager. Hurry, and slip in while Jelly isn't looking."

They cast a quick glance over their shoulders toward the gymnasium instructor, who was arguing fat Irene McCullough into faster movements on the tennis court. Miss Jellings was insistent that "recreation" should be actively pursued out of doors. The two could easily have obtained permission to greet Patty's return inside; but it was the policy of the trio never to ask permission in minor matters. It wasted one's credit unnecessarily.

Priscilla and Conny turned upstairs lug ging the suit-case between them, while Patty approached the principal's study. Ten minutes later she joined her companions in Seven, Paradise Alley. They were sitting on the bed, their chins in their hands, studying the suit-case propped on a chair before them.

"Well?" they inquired in a breath.

"She says she's glad to see me back, and hopes I didn't eat too much wedding cake. If my lessons show any falling off—"

"*Who* owns it?"

"The man with the black eyebrows and the dimple in his chin who sang the funny songs third from the end on the right hand side."

"Jermyn Hilliard, Junior?" Priscilla asked breathlessly.

"Not really?" Conny laid her hand on her heart with an exaggerated sigh.

"Truly and honest!" Patty turned it over and pointed to the initials on the end. "J. H., Jr."

"It *is* his!" cried Priscilla.

"Where on earth did you get it, Patty?"

"Is it locked?"

"Yes," Patty nodded, "but my key will open it."

"What's in it?"

"Oh, a dress suit, and collars, and-and things."

"Where'd you get it?"

"Well," said Patty languidly, "it's a long story. I don't know that I have time before study hour —"

"Oh, tell us, please. I think you're beastly!"

"Well-the glee club was last Thursday night."

They nodded impatiently at this useless piece of information.

"And it was Friday morning that I left. As I was listening to the Dowager's parting remarks about being inconspicuous and reflecting credit on the school by my nice manners, Martin sent in word that Princess was lame and couldn't be driven. So instead of going to the station in the hearse, I went with Mam'selle in the trolley car. When we got in, it was *cram* full of men. The entire Yale Glee Club was going to the station! There were so many of them that they were sitting in each other's laps. The whole top layer rose, and said perfectly gravely and politely: 'Madame, take my seat.'

"Mam'selle was outraged. She said in French, which of course they all understood, that she thought American college boys had disgraceful manners; but I smiled a little —I couldn't help it, they were so funny. And then two of the bottom ones offered their seats, and we sat down. And you'll never believe it, but the third man from the end was sitting right next to me!"

"Not really?"

"Oh, Patty!"

"Is he as good-looking near to, as he was on the stage?"

"Better."

"Are those his real eyebrows or were they blacked?"

"They looked real but I couldn't examine them closely."

"Of course they're real!" said Conny indignantly.

"And what do you think?" Patty de manded. "They were going on my train. Did you ever hear of such a coincidence?"

"What did Mam'selle think of that?"

"She was as flustered as an old hen with one chicken. She put me in charge of the conductor with so many instructions, that I know he felt like a newly engaged nursemaid. The Glee Club men rode in the smoking-car, except Jermyn Hilliard, Junior, and he followed me right into the parlor car and sat down in the chair exactly opposite."

"Patty!" they cried in shocked chorus. "You surely didn't speak to him?"

"Of course not. I looked out of the window and pretended he wasn't there."

"Oh!" Conny murmured disappointedly.

"Then what happened?" Priscilla asked.

"Nothing at all. I got out at Coomsdale, and Uncle Tom met me with the automobile. The chauffeur took my suit-case from the porter and I didn't see it near to at all. We reached the house just at tea time, and I went straight in to tea without going upstairs. The butler took up my suit-case and the maid came and asked for the key so she could unpack. That house is simply running over with servants; I'm always scared to death for fear I'll do something that they won't think is proper.

"All the ushers and bridesmaids were there, and everything was very jolly, only I couldn't make out what they were talking about half the time, because they all knew each other and had a lot of jokes I couldn't understand."

Conny nodded feelingly.

"That's the way they acted at the seaside last summer. I think grown people have horrid manners."

"I did feel sort of young," Patty acknowledged. "One of the men brought me some tea and asked what I was studying in school. He was trying to obey Louise and amuse little cousin, but he was thinking all the time, what an awful bore it was talking to a girl with her hair braided."

"I told you to put it up," said Priscilla.

"Just wait!" said Patty portentously. "When I went upstairs to dress for dinner, the maid met me in the hall with her eyes popping out of her head.

"'Beg pardon, Miss Patty,' she said. 'But is that your suit-case?'

"'Yes,' I said, 'of course it's my suit-case. What's the matter with it?'

"She just waved her hand toward the table and didn't say a word. And there it was, wide open!"

Patty took a key from her pocket, unlocked the suit-case, and threw back the lid. A man's dress suit was neatly folded on the top, with a pipe, a box of cigarettes, some collars, and various other masculine trifles filling in the interstices.

"Oh!" they gasped in breathless chorus.

"They belong to him," Conny murmured fervently.

Patty nodded.

"And when I showed Uncle Tom that suit-case, he nearly died laughing. He telephoned to the station, but they didn't know anything about it, and I didn't know where the glee club was going to perform, so we couldn't telegraph Mr. Hilliard. Uncle Tom lives five miles from town, and there simply wasn't anything we could do that night."

"And just imagine his feelings when he started to dress for the concert, and found Patty's new pink evening gown spread out on top!" suggested Priscilla.

"Oh, Patty! Do you s'pose he opened it?" asked Conny.

"I'm afraid he did. The cases are exact twins, and the keys both seem to fit."

"I hope it looked all right?"

"Oh, yes, it looked beautiful. Everything was trimmed with pink ribbon. I always pack with an eye to the maid, when I visit Uncle Tom."

"But the dinner and the wedding? What did you do without your clothes?" asked Priscilla, in rueful remembrance of many trips to the dressmaker's.

"That was the best part of it!" Patty affirmed. "Miss Lord simply wouldn't let me get a respectable evening gown. She went with me herself, and told Miss Pringle how to make it-just like all my dancing dresses, nine inches off the floor, with elbow sleeves and a silly sash. I hated it anyway."

"You must remember you are a school girl," Conny quoted, "and until—"

"Just wait till I tell you!" Patty triumphed. "Louise brought me one of her dresses-one of her very best ball gowns, only she wasn't going to wear it any more, because she had all new clothes in her trousseau. It was white crêpe embroidered in gold spangles, and it had a train. It was long in front, too. I had to walk without lifting my feet. The maid came and dressed me; she did my hair up on top of my head with a gold fillet, and Aunt Emma loaned me a pearl necklace and some long gloves and I looked perfectly beautiful—I did, honestly-you wouldn't have known me. I looked *at least* twenty!

"The man who took me in to dinner never dreamed that I hadn't been out for years. And you know, he tried to flirt with me, he did, really. And he was getting awfully old. He must have been almost forty. I felt as though I were flirting with my grandfather. You know," Patty added, "it isn't so bad, being grown up. I believe you really do have sort of a good time-if you're pretty."

Six eyes sought the mirror for a reflective moment, before Patty resumed her chronicle.

"And Uncle Tom made me tell about the suit-case at the dinner table. Everybody laughed. It made a very exciting story. I told them about the whole school going to the Glee Club, and falling in love in a body with the third man from the end, and how we all cut his picture out of the program and pasted it in our watches. And then about my sitting across from him in the train and changing suit-cases. Mr. Harper-the man next to me-said it was the most romantic thing he'd ever heard in his life; that Louise's marriage was nothing to it."

"But about the suit-case," they prompted. "Didn't you do anything more?"

"Uncle Tom telephoned again in the morning, and the station agent said he'd got the party on the wire as had the young lady's case. And he was coming back here in two days, and I was to leave his suit-case with the baggage man at the station, and he would leave mine."

"But you didn't leave it."

"I came on the other road. I'm going to send it down."

"And what did you wear at the wedding?"

"Louise's clothes. It didn't matter a bit, my not matching the other bridesmaids, because I was maid of honor, and ought to dress differently anyway. I've been grown up for three days-and I just wish Miss Lord could have seen me with my hair on the top of my head talking to men!"

"Did you tell the Dowager?"

"Yes, I told her about getting the wrong suit-case; I didn't mention the fact that it belonged to the third man from the end."

"What did she say?"

"She said it was very careless of me to run off with a strange man's luggage; and she hoped he was a gentleman and would take it nicely. She telephoned to the baggage man that it was here, but she couldn't send Martin with it this afternoon because he had to go to the farm for some eggs."

Recreation was over, and the girls came trooping in to gather books and pads and pencils for the approaching study hour. Everyone who passed number Seven dropped in to hear the news. Each in turn received the story of the suit-case, and each in turn gasped anew at sight of the contents.

"Doesn't it smell tobaccoey and bay rummish?" said Rosalie Patton, sniffing.

"Oh, there's a button loose!" cried Florence Hissop, the careful housewife. "Where's some black silk, Patty?"

She threaded a needle and secured the button. Then she daringly tried on the coat. Eight others followed her example and thrilled at the touch. It was calculated to fit a far larger person than any present. Even Irene McCullough found it baggy.

"He had awfully broad shoulders," said Rosalie, stroking the satin lining.

They peered daintily at the other garments.

"Oh!" squealed Mae Mertelle. "He wears blue silk suspenders."

"And something else blue," chirped Edna Hartwell, peering over her shoulder. "They're pajamas!"

"And to think of such a thing happening to Patty!" sighed Mae Mertelle.

"Why not?" bristled Patty.

"You're so young and so-er —"

"Young! —Wait till you see me with my hair done up."

"I wonder what the end will be?" asked Rosalie.

"The end," said Mae unkindly, "will be that the baggage man will deliver the suit-case, and Jermyn Hilliard, Junior, will never know —"

A maid appeared at the door.

"If you please," she murmured, her amazed eyes on Irene who was still wearing the coat, "Mrs. Trent would like to have Miss Patty Wyatt come to the drawing-room, and I am to take the suit-case down. The gentleman is waiting."

"Oh, Patty!" a gasp went around the room.

"Do your hair up-quick!"

Priscilla caught Patty's twin braids and wound them around her head, while the others in a flutter of excitement, thrust in the coat and relocked the suit-case.

They crowded after her in a body and hung over the banisters at a perilous angle, straining their ears in the direction of the drawing-room. Nothing but a murmur of voices floated up, punctuated by an occasional deep bass laugh. When they heard the front door close, with one accord they invaded Harriet Gladden's room, which commanded the walk, and pressed their noses against the pane. A short, thick-set man of German build was waddling toward the gate and the trolley car. They gazed with wide, horrified eyes, and turned without a word to meet Patty as she trudged upstairs lugging her errant suit-case. A glance told her that they had seen, and dropping on the top step, she leaned her head against the railing and laughed.

"His name," she choked, "is John Hochstetter, Jr. He's a wholesale grocer, and was on his way to a grocers' convention, where he was to make a speech comparing American cheese with imported cheese. He didn't mind at all not having his dress-suit—never feels comfortable in it anyway, he says. He explained to the convention why he didn't have it on, and it made the funniest speech of the evening. There's the study bell."

Patty rose and turned toward Paradise Alley, but paused to throw back a further detail:

"He has a dear little daughter of his own just my age!"

Chapter V The Flannigan Honeymoon

The Murphy family, with a judicious eye to the buttered side of the bread, had adopted Saint Ursula as their patron saint. The family-consisting of Mr. and Mrs. Patrick Murphy, eleven little Murphys and "Gramma" Flannigan-occupied a five-room cottage close to the gates of St. Ursula's school. They subsisted on the vicarious charity of sixty-four girls, and the intermittent labor of Murphy *père*, who, in his sober intervals, was a sufficiently efficient stone-cutter and mason.

He had built the big entrance gates, and the long stone wall that enclosed the ten acres of "bounds." He had laid the foun dation of the new west wing-known as Paradise Alley-and had constructed all the chimneys and driveways and tennis courts on the place. The school was a monument to his long and leisurely career.

Mr. and Mrs. Murphy, with an unusual display of foresight, had christened their first baby after the school. Ursula Murphy may not be a euphuistic combination, but the child was amply repaid for carrying such a name, by receiving the cast-off clothes of generations of St. Ursula girls. There was danger, for a time, that the poor little thing would be buried beneath a mountain of wearing apparel; but her parents providentially discovered a second-hand clothes man, who relieved her of a part of the burden.

After Ursula, had come other little Murphys in regular succession; and it had grown to be one of the legendary privileges of the school to furnish the babies with names and baptismal presents. Mrs. Murphy was not entirely mercenary in her yearly request. She appreciated the artistic quality of the names that the girls provided. They had a distinction, that she herself, with her lack of literary training, would never have been able to give. The choosing of the names had come to be a matter involving politics almost as complicated as the election of the senior president. Different factions proposed different names; half-a-dozen tickets would be in the field, and the balloting was conducted with rousing speeches.

There was one hampering restriction. Every baby must have a patron saint. Upon this point, the Murphys stood firm. However, by a careful study of early Christian martyrs, the girls had managed to unearth a list of recondite saints with fairly unusual and picturesque names.

So far, the roll of the Murphy offspring read:

Ursula Marie, Geraldine Sabina, Muriel Veronica and Lionel Ambrose (twins), Aileen Clotilda, John Drew Dominick, Delphine Olivia, Patrick (he had been born in the summer vacation, and the long-suffering priest had insisted that the boy be named for his father), Sidney Orlando Boniface, Richard Harding Gabriel, Yolanda Genevieve. This completed the list, until one morning early in December, Patrick Senior presented himself at the kitchen door, with the news that another name —a boy's —would be seasonable.

The school immediately went into a committee of the whole. Several names had been put up, and the discussion was growing heated, when Patty Wyatt jumped to her feet with the proposal of "Cuthbert St. John." The suggestion was met with cheers; and Mae Van Arsdale indignantly left the room. The name was carried by unanimous vote.

Cuthbert St. John Murphy was christened the following Sunday, and received a gold-lined porridge spoon in a green plush box.

So delighted was the school at Patty's felicitous suggestion, that, by way of reward, they elected her chairman of the Christmas Carnival Committee. The Christmas Carnival was a charitable institution contemporaneous with the founding of the school. St. Ursula's scheme of education was broad; it involved growth in a wide variety of womanly virtues, and the greatest of these was charity. Not the modern, scientific, machine-made charity, but the comfortable, old-fashioned kind that leaves a pleasant glow of generosity in the heart of the giver. Every year at Christmastide a tree was decked, a supper laid, and the poor children of the neighborhood bidden to partake. The poor children were collected by the school girls, who drove about from house to house, in bob-sleighs or hay-wagons, according to the snow. The girls regarded it as the most diverting festival of the school year; and even the poor children, when they had overcome their first embarrassment, found it fairly diverting.

The original scheme had been for each girl to have an individual protégé, that she might call upon the family and come into personal relations with a humbler class. She was to learn the special needs of her child, and give something really useful, such as stockings or trousers or flannel petticoats.

It was an admirable scheme on paper, but in actual practice it fell down. St. Ursula's was situated in an affluent district given over to the estates of the idle rich, and the proletarian who clung to the skirts of these estates was amply provided with an opportunity to work. In the early days, when the school was small, there had been sufficient poor children to go round; but as St. Ursula's had grown, the poor seemed to have diminished, until now the school was confronted by an actual scarcity. But the Murphys, at least, they had always with them. They yearly offered thanks for this.

Patty accepted her chairmanship and appointed sub-committees to do the actual work. For herself and Conny and Priscilla she reserved the privilege of choosing the recipients of St. Ursula's bounty. This entailed several exhilarating afternoons out of bounds. A walk abroad is as inspiring to the inmates of a prison as a trip through Europe to those at large. They spent the better part of a week canvassing the neighborhood, only to reveal the embarrassing fact that there were nine possible children, aside from the Murphy brood, and that none of these nine were from homes that one could conscientiously term poor. The children's sober industrious parents could well supply their temperate Christmas demands.

"And there are only six Murphys the right age," Conny grumbled, as they turned homewards in the cold twilight of a wintry day, after an unprofitable two hours' tramp.

"That makes about one child to every five girls," Priscilla nodded dismally.

"Oh, this charity business makes me tired!" Patty burst out. "It's fun for the girls, and nothing else. The way we dole out stuff to perfectly nice people, is just plain insulting. If anybody poked a pink tarlatan stocking full of candy at me, and said it was because I'd been a good little girl, I'd throw it in their face."

In moments of intensity, Patty's English was not above reproach.

"Come on, Patty," Priscilla slipped a soothing hand through her arm, "we'll stop in at the Murphys' and count 'em over again. Maybe there's one we overlooked."

"The twins are only fifteen," said Conny hopefully. "I think they'll do."

"And Richard Harding's nearly four. He's old enough to enjoy a tree. The more Murphys we can get the better. They always love the things we give."

"I know they do!" Patty growled. "We're teaching the whole lot of them to be blooming beggars —I shall be sorry I ever used any slang, if we can't put the money to better use than this."

The funds for the carnival were yearly furnished by a tax on slang. St. Ursula demanded a fine of one cent for every instance of slang or bad grammar let fall in public. Of course, in the privacy of one's own room, in the bosom of one's chosen family, the rigor was relaxed. Your dearest friends did not report you-except in periods of estrangement. But your acquaintances and enemies and teachers did, and even, in moments of intense honorableness, you reported yourself. In any case, the slang fund grew. When the committee had opened the box this year, they found thirty-seven dollars and eighty-four cents.

Patty allowed herself, after some slight protest, to be drawn to the door of the Murphy domicile. She was not in an affable mood, and a call upon the Murphys required a great deal of conversation. They found the family hilariously assembled in an over-crowded kitchen. The entire dozen children babbled at once, shriller and shriller, in a vain endeavor to drown each other out. A cabbage stew, in progress on the stove, filled the room with an odorous steam. Shoved into a corner of the hearth, was poor old Gramma Flannigan, surrounded by noisy, pushing youngsters, who showed her gray hairs but scant consideration. The girls admired the new baby, while Yolanda and Richard Harding crawled over their laps with sticky hands. Mrs. Murphy, meanwhile, discanted in a rich brogue upon the merits of "Coothbert St. Jawn" as a name. She liked it, she declared, as well as any in the list. It sure ought to bring luck to a child to carry the name of two saints. She thanked the young ladies kindly.

Patty left Conny and Priscilla to carry off the social end of the call, while she squeezed herself onto the woodbox by Gramma Flannigan's chair. Mrs. Murphy's mother was a pathetic old body, with the winning speech and manners of Ireland a generation ago. Patty found her the most remunerative member of the household, so far as interest went. She always liked to get her started with stories of her girlhood, when she had been a lady's maid in Lord Stirling's castle in County Clare, and young Tammas Flannigan came and carried her off to America to help make his fortune. Tammas was now a bent old man with rheumatism, but in his keen blue eyes and Irish smile, Gramma still saw the lad who had courted her.

"How's your husband this winter?" Patty asked, knowing that she was taking the shortest road to the old woman's heart.

She shook her head with a tremulous smile.

"I'm not hearin' for four days. Tammas ain't livin' with us no more."

"It's a pity for you to be separated!" said Patty, with quick sympathy, not realizing on how sore a subject she was touching.

The flood gates of the old woman's garrulity broke down.

"With Ursuly an' Ger-r-aldine growin' oop an' havin' young min to wait on thim, 'twas needin' a parlor they was, an' they couldn't spare the room no longer for me'n Tammas. So they put me in the garret with the four gurrls, an' Tammas, he was sint oop the road to me son Tammas. Tammas's wife said as Tammas could sleep in the kitchen to pay for carryin' the wood an' watter, but she couldn't take us both because she takes boarders."

Patty cocked her head for a moment of silence, as she endeavored to pluck sense from this tangle of Tammases.

"It's too bad!" she comforted, laying a sympathetic hand on the old woman's knee.

Gramma Flannigan's eyes filled with the ready tears of old age.

"I'm not complainin', for it's the way o' the world. The owld must step off, an' make room for the young. But it's lonely I am without him! We've lived together for forty-seven years, an' we know each other's ways."

"But your son doesn't live very far away." Patty offered what solace she might. "You must see Thomas very often."

"That an' I don't! You might as well have a husband dead, as a mile an' a half away an' laid oop with rheumatism."

The clock pointed to a quarter of six, and the visitors rose. They had still to walk half a mile and dress before dinner.

The old woman clung to Patty's hand at parting. She seemed to find more comfort in the little stray sympathy that Patty had offered, than in all her exuberant brood of grandchildren.

"Isn't it dreadful to be old, and just sit around waiting to die?" Patty shuddered, as they faced the cold darkness outside.

"Dreadful!" Conny cordially agreed. "Hurry up! Or we'll be late for dinner, and this is chicken night."

They turned homeward at a jog trot that left little breath for speech; but Patty's mind was working as fast as her legs.

"I've got a perfectly splendid idea," she panted as she turned in at the gate and trotted up the driveway toward the big lighted house that spread wide wings to receive them.

"What?" they asked.

The quick insistent clang of the gong floated out to meet them, and on the instant, hurrying figures flitted past the windows-the summons to meals brought a readier response than the summons to study.

"I'll tell you after dinner. No time now," Patty returned as she peeled off her coat.

They were unlacing their blouses as they clattered up the back stairs, and pulling them over their heads in the upper hall.

"Go slow-please!" they implored of the down-going procession whose track they crossed. Dinner was the only meal which might be approached by the front stairs, which were carpeted instead of tinned.

Their evening frocks were fortunately in one piece, and they dove into them with little ceremony. The three presented themselves flushed of cheek and somewhat rumpled as to hair, but properly gowned and apologetic, just as grace was ended. To be late for grace only meant one demerit; the first course came higher, and the second higher still. Punishment increased by geometrical progression.

During the half hour's intermission before evening study, the three separated themselves from the dancers in the hall, and withdrew to a corner of the deserted schoolroom.

Patty perched herself on a desk, and loudly stated her feelings.

"I'm tired of having the Dowager get up at prayers, and make a speech about the beautiful Christmas spirit, and how sweet it is to make so many little children happy, when she knows perfectly well that it's just a lark for us. I'm chairman this year and I can do as I please. I've had enough of this fake charity; and I'm not going to have any Christmas tree!"

"No Christmas tree?" Conny echoed blankly.

"But what are you going to do with the thirty-seven dollars and eight-four cents?" asked Priscilla, the practical.

"Listen!" Patty settled to her argument. "There aren't any children around here who need a blessed thing, but Gramma and Granpa Flannigan do. That poor old woman, who is just as nice as she can be, is crowded in with all those horrid, yelling, sticky little Murphys; and Granpa Flannigan is poked into Tammas Junior's kitchen, running errands for Tammas Junior's wife, who is a per-fect-ly *terrible* woman. She throws kettles when she gets mad. Gramma worries all the time for fear he has rheumatism, and nobody to rub on liniment, or make him wear the right underclothes. They're exactly as fond of each other as any other husband and wife, and just because Ursula wants to have callers, I say it's a mean shame for them to be separated!"

"It is too bad," Conny agreed impartially. "But I don't see that we can help it."

"Why, yes! Instead of having a Christmas tree, we'll rent that empty little cottage down by the laurel walk, and mend the chimney-Patrick can do that for nothing-and put in new windows, and furnish it, and set them up in housekeeping."

"Do you think we can do it for thirty-seven dollars and eighty-four cents?" Priscilla asked.

"That's where the charity comes in! Every girl in school will go without her allowance for two weeks. Then we'll have more than a hundred dollars, and you can furnish a house perfectly beautifully for that. And it would be real charity to give up our allowances, because they are particularly useful at Christmas time."

"But will the girls want to give their allowances?"

"We'll fix it so they'll have to," said Patty. "We'll call a mass meeting and make a speech. Then everybody will file past and sign a paper. No one will dare refuse with the school looking on."

Patty's fire kindled an answering flame in the other two.

"It is a good idea!" Conny declared.

"And it would be a lark, fixing the house," said Priscilla. "Almost as much fun as getting married ourselves."

"Exactly," Patty nodded. "Those poor old things haven't had a chance to see each other alone for years. We'll give 'em a honeymoon all over again."

Patty was outwardly occupied with geometry the next hour, but her mind was busy hemming sheets and towels and tablecloths. It being Thursday evening, the hour between eight and nine was occupied with "manners." The girls took turns in coming gracefully downstairs, entering the drawing-room, announced by Claire du Bois in the rôle of footman, and shaking hands with their hostesses-Conny Wilder, as dowager mama, and towering above her, as débutante daugh ter, Irene McCullough, the biggest girl in the school. The gymnasium teacher who assigned the rôles, had a sense of humor. An appropriate remark was expected from each guest, the weather being barred.

"Mrs. Wilder!" Priscilla gushed, advancing with outstretched hand, "and dear little Irene! It doesn't seem possible that the child is actually grown. It was only yesterday that she was a mite of a thing toddling about—"

Priscilla was shoved on by Patty.

"Me dear Mrs. Wilder," she inquired in a brogue that would have put the Murphys to shame, "have ye heard the news that's goin' round? Mr. and Mrs. Tammas Flannigan have taken the Laurel Cottage for the season. They are thinkin' of startin' a salon. They will be at home ivery afternoon during recreation hour-and will serve limonade and gingerbread in summer, and soup and sandwiches in winter. Ye must take Irene to call on thim."

The moment "manners" was over, the three withdrew to the seclusion of Patty's and Conny's room in Paradise Alley, and closed the door against callers. Between nine and nine-thirty was the fashionable calling hour at St. Ursula's. The time was supposed to be occupied in getting ready for bed, but if one were clever about undressing in the dark, one might devote the thirty minutes to social purposes.

"Gone to sleep! Don't disturb us!" the placard read that they impaled upon the door, but the clatter of tongues inside belied the words.

"Isn't my idea fine about the lemonade and soup?" Patty demanded.

"The great thing about charity is not to make it charity. You must keep people self-supporting," Priscilla quoted from their last lesson in sociology.

"We'll fix little tables under the apple tree in summer and in the parlor in winter," Patty planned, "and all the school girls and automobiles will stop for lemonade. We'll charge the girls five cents a glass and the automobiles ten."

"And I say, let's make Patrick and Tam mas each contribute a dollar a week toward their support," Conny proposed. "They must eat up a dollar's worth of potatoes as they are living now."

They continued planning in whispers until long after "lights-out" had rung; and Priscilla, in a laudable desire to be inconspicuous, was obliged to crawl on hands and knees past Mademoiselle's open door, before she gained her own room at the end of the corridor.

The moment recreation sounded the next afternoon, they obtained permission to be out of bounds, and set off at a brisk trot. It was their business-like intention to have all the statistics complete, before submitting the matter to the assembled school.

"We'll first call on Patrick and Tammas and make 'em promise the dollar," said Patty.

Patrick readily promised his dollar-Patrick was always strong in promises-and the girls proceeded gaily to Tammas Junior's. They found Granpa on the back doorstep anxiously wiping his feet; he was a tremulous reed that bowed before every blast of the daughter-in-law's tongue. Tammas Junior, after being taken aside and told the project, thought he could manage two dollars a week. An expression of relief momentarily took the hunted look from his eyes. He was clearly glad to rescue his father from the despotic rule of his wife.

The girls turned away with their minds made up. It only remained to secure the cottage, coerce the school, and hem the sheets.

"You go and price furniture and wall paper," Patty issued her orders, "while I see about the rent. We'll meet at the soda-water fountain."

She found the real-estate man who owned the cottage established in an office over the bank; and by what she considered rare business ability, beat him down from nine dollars a month to seven. This stroke accomplished, she intimated her readiness for the lease.

"A lease will not be necessary," he said. "A month to month verbal agreement will do for me."

"I can't consider it without a lease," said Patty, firmly. "You might sell or something, and then we'd have to move out."

The gentleman amusedly filled in the form, and signed as party of the first part. He passed the pen to Patty and indicated the space reserved for the signature of the party of the second part.

"I must first consult my partners," she explained.

"Oh, I see! Have them sign here, and then bring the lease back."

"All of them?" she asked, dubiously scanning the somewhat cramped quarters. "I'm afraid there won't be room."

"How many partners have you?"

"Sixty-three."

He stared momentarily, then as his eye fell on the embroidered "St. U." on Patty's coat sleeve, he threw back his head and laughed.

"I beg your pardon!" he apologized, "but I was a bit staggered for a moment. I am not used to doing business on such a large scale. In order to be legal," he gravely explained, "the paper will have to be signed by all the parties to the contract. If there is not enough room, you might paste on an er—"

"Annex?" suggested Patty.

"Exactly," he agreed and with grave politeness bowed her out.

As the bell rang that indicated the end of study that evening, Patty and Conny and Priscilla jumped to their feet, and called a mass meeting of the school. The door was closed after the retreating Miss Jellings, and for half an hour the three made speeches separately and in unison. They were persuasive talkers and they carried the day. The allowance was voted with scarcely a dissenting voice, and the school filed past and signed the lease.

For two weeks St. Ursula's was a busy place-and also Laurel Cottage. Bounds were practically enlarged to include it. The girls worked in gangs during every recreation hour. The cellar was whitewashed by a committee of four, who went in blue, and came out speckled like a plover's egg. Tammas Junior had volunteered for this job, but it was one the girls could not relinquish. They did allow him to kalsomine the ceilings and hang the wall paper; but they painted the floors and lower reaches of woodwork themselves. The evening's hour of recreation no longer found them dancing, but sitting in a solid phalanx on the stairs hemming sheets and tablecloths. The house was to be furnished with a completeness that poor Mrs. Flannigan, in all her married life, had never known before.

When everything was finished, the day before the holidays, the school in a body wiped its feet on the door-mat and tiptoed through on a last visit of inspection. The cottage contained three rooms, with a cellar and woodshed besides. The wall paper and chintz hangings of the parlor were flaming pink peonies with a wealth of foliage—a touch of flamboyant for some tastes, but Granpa's and Gramma's eyes were failing, and they liked strong colors. Also, crafty questioning had elicited the fact that "pinies" were Gramma's favorite flower. The kitchen had turkey-red curtains with a cheerful strip of rag carpet and two comfortable easy chairs before the hearth. The cellar was generously stocked from the school farm-Miss Sallie's contribution-with potatoes and cabbages and carrots and onions, enough to make Irish stew for three months to come. The woodbin was filled, and even a five-gallon can of kerosene. Sixty-four pairs of eyes had scanned the rooms minutely to make sure that no essential was omitted.

Both the Murphy and Flannigan households had been agog for days over the proposed flitting of the pair. Even Mrs. Tammas had volunteered to wash the windows of the new cottage, and for a week she had scarcely been cross. The old man was already wondering at life. When the time arrived, Mrs. Murphy secretly packed Gramma's belongings and dressed her in her best, under the pretext that she was to be taken in a carriage to a Christmas party to have supper with her husband. The old woman was in a happy flutter at the prospect. Granpa was prepared for the journey by the same simple strategy.

Patty and Conny and Priscilla, as orig inators of the enterprise, had been appointed to install the old couple; but with tactful forbearance, they delegated the right to the son and daughter. They saw that the fires were burning, the lamps lighted, and the cat-there was even a cat-asleep on the hearth rug; then when the sound of carriage wheels in front told them that Martin had arrived with his passengers, they quietly slipped out the back way and jogged home to dinner through the snowy dusk.

They were met by a babel of questions.

"Was Gramma pleased with the parlor clock?"

"Did she know what to do with the chaffing-dish?"

"Were they disappointed at not having a feather bed?"

"Did they like the cat, or would they rather have had a parrot?" (The school had been torn asunder on this important point.)

At the dinner table that night-such of the school as was left-chattered only of Laurel Cottage. They were as excited over Gramma and Granpa's happiness, as over their own approaching holiday. All sixty-four were planning to drink tea, on the first day of their return, from Gramma's six cups.

Toward nine o'clock, Patty and Priscilla, by a special dispensation that allowed late hours in vacation, received permission to accompany Conny and ten other dear friends to the station for the western express. Driving back alone in the "hearse," still bubbling with the hilarity of Christmas farewells, they passed the Laurel Cottage.

"I believe they're still up!" said Priscilla. "Let's stop and wish 'em a Merry Christmas, just to make sure they like it."

Martin was readily induced to halt; his discipline also was relaxed in vacation. They approached the door, but hesitated at sight of the picture revealed by the lighted window. To interrupt with the boisterous greetings of the season, seemed like rudely breaking in upon the seclusion of lovers. Only a glance was needed to tell them that the house-warming was successful. Gramma and Granpa were sitting before the fire in their comfortable red-cushioned rocking- chairs; the lamp shed a glow on their radiant faces, as they held each other's hands and smiled into the future.

Patty and Priscilla tiptoed away and climbed back into the hearse, a touch sobered and thoughtful.

"You know," Patty pondered, "they are just as contented as if they lived in a palace with a million dollars and an automobile! It's funny, isn't it, what a little thing makes some people happy?"

Chapter VI The Silver Buckles

To be cooped up for three weeks with the two stupidest girls in the school—"

"Kid McCoy isn't so bad," said Conny consolingly.

"She's a horrid little tomboy."

"But you know she's entertaining, Patty."

"She never says a word that isn't slang, and *I* think she's the limit!"

"Well, anyway, Harriet Gladden—"

"Is perfectly dreadful and you know it. I would just as soon spend Christmas with a weeping angel on a tombstone."

"She is pretty mournful," Priscilla agreed. "I've spent three Christmases with her. But anyway, you'll have fun. You can be late for meals whenever you want, and Nora lets you make candy on the kitchen stove."

Patty sniffed disdainfully as she commenced the work of resettling her room, after the joyous upheaval of a Christmas packing. The other two assisted in silent sympathy. There was after all not much comfort to be offered. School in holiday time was a lonely substitute for home. Priscilla, whose father was a naval officer, and whose home was a peripatetic affair, had become inured to the experience; but this particular year, she was gaily setting out to visit cousins in New York-with three new dresses and two new hats! And Patty, whose home was a mere matter of two hours in a Pullman car, was to be left behind; for six-year old Thomas Wyatt had chosen this inopportune time to come down with scarlet fever. The case was of the lightest; Master Tommy was sitting up in bed and occupying himself with a box of lead soldiers. But the rest of the family were not so comfortable. Some were quarantined in, and the others out. Judge Wyatt had installed himself in a hotel and telegraphed the Dowager to keep Patty at St. Ursula's during the holidays. Poor Patty had been happily pack ing her trunk when the news arrived; and as she unpacked it, she distributed a few excusable tears through the bureau drawers.

Ordinarily, a number remained for the holidays,—girls whose homes were in the West or South, or whose parents were traveling abroad or getting divorces-but this year the assortment was unusually meager. Patty was left alone in "Paradise Alley." Margarite McCoy, of Texas, was stranded at the end of the South Corridor, and Harriet Gladden of Nowhere, had a suite of eighteen rooms at her disposal in "Lark Lane." These and four teachers made up the household.

Harriet Gladden had been five years straight at St. Ursula's—term time and vacations without a break. She came a lanky little girl of twelve, all legs and arms, and she was now a lanky big girl of seventeen, still all legs and arms. An invisible father, at intervals mentioned in the catalogue, mailed checks to Mrs. Trent; and beyond this made no sign. Poor Harriet was a mournful, silent, neglected child; entirely out of place in the effervescing life that went on around her.

She never had any birthday boxes from home, never any Christmas presents, except those that came from the school. While the other girls were clamoring for mail, Harriet stood in the background silent and unexpectant. Miss Sallie picked out her clothes, and Miss Sallie's standards were utilitarian rather than æsthetic. Harriet, with no exception, was the worst dressed girl in the school. Even her school uniform, which was an exact twin of sixty-three other uniforms, hung upon her with the grace of a meal-bag. Miss Sallie, with provident foresight, always ordered them a size too large in order to allow her to grow and Harriet invariably wore them out, before she had established a fit.

"What on earth becomes of Harriet Gladden during vacation?" Priscilla once wondered on the opening day.

"They keep her on ice through the summer," was Patty's opinion, "and she never gets entirely thawed out."

As a matter of fact this was, as nearly as possible, what they did do with her. Miss Sallie picked out a quiet, comfortable, healthy farmhouse, and installed Harriet in charge of the farmer's wife. By the end of three months she was so desperately lonely, that she looked forward with pleasurable excitement to the larger isolation of term time.

Patty, one day, had overheard two of the teachers discussing Harriet, and her reported version had been picturesque.

"Her father hasn't seen her for years and years. He just chucks her in here and pays the bills."

"I don't wonder he doesn't want her at home!" said Priscilla.

"There isn't any home. Her mother is divorced, and married again, and living in Paris. That was the reason Harriet couldn't go abroad with the school party last year. Her father was afraid that when she got to Paris, her mother would grab her-not that either of them really wants her, but they like to spite each other."

Priscilla and Conny sat up interestedly. Here was a tragic intrigue, such as you expect to meet only in novels, going on under their very noses.

"You girls who have had a happy home life, cannot imagine the loneliness of a childhood such as Harriet's," said Patty impressively.

"It's dreadful!" Conny cried. "Her father must be a perfect *Beast* not to take any notice of her."

"Harriet has her mother's eyes," Patty explained. "Her father can't bear to look at her, because she reminds him of the happy past that is dead forever."

"Did Miss Wadsworth say that?" they demanded in an interested chorus.

"Not in exactly those words," Patty confessed. "I just gathered the outline."

This story, with picturesque additions, lost no time in making the rounds of the school. Had Harriet chosen to play up to the romantic and melancholy rôle she was cast for, she might have attained popularity of a sort; but Harriet did not have the slightest trace of the histrionic in her make-up. She merely moped about, and continued to be heavy and uninteresting. Other more exciting matters demanded public attention; and Harriet and her blasted childhood were forgotten.

Patty stood on the veranda waving good-by to the last hearseful of Christmas travelers, then turned indoors to face an empty three weeks. As she was listlessly preparing to mount the stairs, Maggie waylaid her with the message:

"Mrs. Trent would like to speak to you in her private study, Miss Patty."

Patty turned back, wondering for just which of her latest activities she was to be called to account. A visit to the Dowager's private study usually meant that a storm was brewing. She found the four left-behind teachers cosily gathered about the tea table, and to her surprise, was received with four affable smiles.

"Sit down, Patty, and have some tea."

The Dowager motioned her to a chair, while she mingled an inch of tea with three inches of hot water. Miss Sallie furnished a fringed napkin, Miss Jellings presented buttered toast, and Miss Wadsworth, salted almonds. Patty blinked dazedly and ac cepted the offerings. To be waited on by four teachers was an entirely new experience. Her spirits rose considerably as she mentally framed the story for Priscilla's and Conny's delectation. When she had ceased to wonder why she was being thus honored, the reason appeared.

"I am sorry, Patty," said the Dowager, "that none of your special friends are to be here this year; but I am sure that you and Margarite and Harriet will get on very happily. Breakfast will be half an hour later than usual, and the rules about bounds will be somewhat relaxed-only of course we must always know where to find you. I shall try to plan a matinée party in the city, and Miss Sallie will take you to spend a day at the farm. The ice is strong enough now for you to skate, and Martin will get out the sleds for you to coast. You must be in the open air as much as possible; and I shall be very pleased if you and Margarite can interest Harriet in out-of-door sports. Speaking of Harriet —"

The Dowager hesitated momentarily, and Patty's acute understanding realized that at last they were getting at the kernel of the interview. The tea and toast had been merely wrapping.

She listened with a touch of suspicion, while the Dowager lowered her voice with an air of confidence.

"Speaking of Harriet, I should like to enlist your sympathy, Patty. She is very sweet and genuine. A girl that anyone might be proud to have for a friend. But through an accident, such as sometimes happens in a crowded, busy, selfish community, she has been overlooked and left behind. Harriet has never seemed to adjust herself so readily as most girls; and I fear that the poor child is often very lonely. It would be highly gratifying to me if you would make an effort to be friendly with her. I am sure that she will meet your advances half way."

Patty murmured a few polite phrases and retired to dress for dinner, stubbornly resolved to be as distant with Harriet as possible. Her friendship was not a commodity to be bought with tea and buttered toast.

The three girls had dinner alone at a little candle-lit table set in a corner of the dining-room, while the four teachers occupied a conveniently distant table in the opposite corner.

Patty commenced the meal by being as monosyllabic as possible; but it was not her natural attitude toward the world, and by the time the veal had arrived (it was Wednesday night) she was laughing whole-heartedly at Kid's ingenuous conversation. Miss McCoy's vocabulary was rich in the vernacular of the plains, and in vacation she let herself go. During term time she was forced to curb her discourse, owing to the penny tax on slang. Otherwise, her entire allowance would have gone to swell the public coffers.

It was a relief to let dinner-table conversation flow where it listed; usually, with a teacher in attendance and the route marked out, there was a cramped formality about the meal. French conversation was supposed to occupy the first three courses five nights in the week, and every girl must contribute at least two remarks. It cannot be said that on French nights the dining-room was garrulous. Saturday night was devoted to a discussion (in English) of current events, gleaned from a study of the editorials in the morning paper. Nobody at St. Ursula's had much time for editorials, and even on an English Saturday conversation languished. But the school made up for it on Sunday. This day, being *festa*, they could talk about anything they chose; and sixty-four magpies chattering their utmost, would have been silence in comparison to St. Ursula's at dinner time on Sunday.

* * * * *

The four days preceding Christmas passed with unexpected swiftness. A snow-storm marked the first, followed by three days of glistening sunshine. Martin got out the bobs, and the girls piled in and rode to the wood-lot for evergreens. There were many errands in the village, and the novelty of not always having a teacher at one's heels, proved in itself diverting.

Patty found the two companions which circumstances had forced upon her unexpectedly companionable. They skated and coasted and had snow fights; and Harriet, to Patty's wide-eyed astonishment, assumed a very ap preciable animation. On Christmas Eve they had been out with Martin delivering Christmas baskets to old time protégés of the school; and on the way home, through pure overflowing animal spirits, for a mile or more they had "caught on" the back of the bob, and then tumbled out and run and caught on again, until they finally dove head foremost into the big piled-up drift by the porte-cochère. They shook the snow from their clothes, like puppies from a pond, and laughing and excited trooped indoors. Harriet's cheeks were red from contact with the snow, her usually prim hair was a tangled mass about her face, her big dark eyes had lost their mournful look. They were merry, mischievous, girlish eyes. She was not merely pretty, but beautiful, in a wild, unusual gypsyish way that compelled attention.

"I say," Patty whispered to Kid McCoy as they divested themselves of rubbers and leggins in the lower hall. "Look at Harriet! Isn't she pretty?"

"Golly!" murmured the Kid. "If she knew enough to play up to her looks, she'd be the ravingest beauty in all the school."

"Let's make her!" said Patty.

At the top of the stairs they met Osaki with a hammer and chisel.

"I open two box," he observed. "One Mees Margarite McCoy. One Mees Patty Wyatt."

"Hooray!" cried the Kid, starting at a gallop for her room in the South Wing.

A Christmas box to Kid McCoy meant a lavish wealth of new possessions out of all proportion to her desserts. She owned a bachelor guardian who was subject to fits of such erratic generosity that the Dowager had regularly to remind him that Margarite was but a school girl with simple tastes. Fortunately he always forgot this warning before the next Christmas-or else he knew Kid too well to believe it-and the boxes continued to come.

Patty had also started without ceremony for Paradise Alley, when she became aware of deserted Harriet, slowly trailing down the dim length of Lark Lane. She ran back and grasped her by an elbow.

"Come on, Harry! And help me open my box."

Harriet's face flushed with sudden pleasure; it was the first time, in the five and a half years of her school career, that she had ever achieved the dignity of a nickname. She accompanied Patty with some degree of eagerness. The next best thing to receiving a Christmas box of your own, is to be present at the reception of a friend's.

It was a big square wooden box, packed to the brim with smaller boxes and parcels tied with ribbon and holly, and tucked into every crevice funny surprises. You could picture, just from looking at it, the kind of home that it came from, filled with jokes and nonsense and love.

"It's the first Christmas I've ever spent away from home," said Patty, with the suggestion of a quiver in her voice.

But her momentary soberness did not last; the business of exploration was too absorbing to allow any divided emotion. Harriet sat on the edge of the bed and watched in silence, while Patty gaily strewed the floor with tissue paper and scarlet ribbon. She unpacked a wide assortment of gloves and books and trinkets, each with a message of love. Even the cook had baked a Christmas cake with a fancy top. And little Tommy, in wobbly uphill printing, had labeled an elephant filled with candy, "for dere cister from tom."

Patty laughed happily as she plumped a chocolate into her mouth, and dropped the elephant into Harriet's lap.

"Aren't they dears to go to such a lot of trouble? I tell you, it pays to stay away sometimes, they think such a lot more of you! This is from Mother," she added, as she pried off the cover of a big dressmaker's box, and lifted out a filmy dancing frock of pink crêpe.

"Isn't it perfectly sweet?" she demanded, "and I didn't need it a bit! Don't you love to get things you don't need?"

"I never do," said Harriet.

Patty was already deep in another parcel.

"From Daddy, with all the love in the world," she read. "Dear old Dad! What on earth do you s'pose it is? I hope Mother suggested something. He's a perfect idiot about choosing presents, unless-Oh!" she squealed. "Pink silk stockings and slippers to match; and look at those perfectly lovely buckles!"

She offered for Harriet's inspection a pink satin slipper adorned with the daintiest of silver buckles, and with heels dizzily suggestive of France.

"Isn't my father a lamb?" Patty gaily kissed her hand toward a dignified, judicial-looking portrait on the bureau. "Mother suggested the slippers, of course, but the buckles and French heels were his own idea. She likes me sensible, and he likes me frivolous."

She was deep in the absorbing business of holding the pink frock before the glass to make sure that the color was becoming, when she was suddenly arrested by the sound of a sob, and she turned to see Harriet throw herself across the bed and clutch the pillow in a storm of weeping. Patty stared with wide-open eyes; she herself did not indulge in such emotional demonstrations, and she could not imagine any possible cause. She moved the pink satin slippers out of reach of Harriet's thrashing feet, gathered up the fallen elephant and scattered chocolates, and sat down to wait until the cataclysm should pass.

"What's the matter?" she mildly inquired, when Harriet's sobs gave place to choking gasps.

"My father never sent me any s-silver b-buckles."

"He's way off in Mexico," said Patty, awkwardly groping for consolation.

"He never sends me anything! He doesn't even know me. He wouldn't recognize me if he met me on the street."

"Oh, yes, he would," Patty assured her with doubtful comfort. "You haven't changed a bit in four years."

"And he wouldn't like me if he did know me. I'm not pretty, and my clothes are never nice, and —" Harriet was off again.

Patty regarded her for a moment of thoughtful silence, then she decided on a new tack. She stretched out a hand and shook her vigorously.

"For goodness' sake, stop crying! That's what's the matter with your father. No man can stand having tears dripped down his neck all the time."

Harriet arrested her sobs to stare.

"If you could see the way you look when you cry! Sort of streaked. Come here!" She took her by the shoulder and faced her before the mirror. "Did you ever see such a fright? And I was just thinking, before you began, about how pretty you looked. I was, honestly. You could be as pretty as any of the rest of us, if you'd only make up your mind —"

"No, I couldn't! I'm just as ugly as I can be. Nobody likes me and —"

"It's your own fault!" said Patty sharply. "If you were fat, like Irene McCullough, or if you didn't have any chin like Evalina Smith, there might be some reason, but there isn't anything on earth the matter with you, except that you're so *damp!* You cry all the time, and it gets tiresome to be forever sympathizing. I'm telling you the truth because I'm beginning to like you. There's never any use bothering to tell people the truth when you don't like them. The reason Conny and Pris and I get on so well together, is because we always tell each other the exact truth about our faults. Then we have a chance to correct them-that's what makes us so nice," she added modestly.

Harriet sat with her mouth open, too surprised to cry.

"And your clothes are awful," pursued Patty interestedly. "You ought not to let Miss Sallie pick 'em out. Miss Sallie's nice; I like her a lot, but she doesn't know any more than a rabbit about clothes; you can tell that by the way she dresses herself. And then, too, you'd be a lot nicer if you wouldn't be so stiff. If you'd just laugh the way the rest of us do —"

"How can I laugh when I don't think things are funny? The jokes the girls make are awfully silly —"

Speech was no longer possible, for Kid McCoy came stampeding down the corridor with as much racket as a cavalcade of horses. She was decked in a fur scarf and a necklace set with pearls, she wore a muff on her head, drum-major fashion; a lace handkerchief and a carved ivory fan protruded from the pocket of her blouse and a pink chiffon scarf floated from her shoulders; her wrist was adorned with an Oriental bracelet and she was lugging in her arms a silver-mounted Mexican saddle, of a type that might be suited to the plains of Texas, but never to the respectable country lanes adjacent to St. Ursula's.

"Bully for Guardie!" she shouted as she descended upon them. "He's a daisy; he's a ducky; he's a lamb. Did you ever see such a perfectly corking saddle?"

She plumped it over a chair, transformed the pink chiffon scarf into a bridle, and proceeded to mount and canter off.

"Get up! Whoa! Hi, there! Clear the road."

Harriet jumped aside to avoid being bumped, while Patty snatched her pink frock from the path of the runaway. They were shrieking with laughter, even Harriet, the tearful.

"Now you see!" said Patty, suddenly interrupting her mirth. "It's perfectly easy to laugh if you just let yourself go. Kid isn't really funny. She's just as silly as she can be."

Kid brought her horse to a stand.

"Well I like that!"

"Excuse me for telling the truth," said Patty politely, "I'm just using you for an illustration-Heavens! There's the bell!"

She commenced unlacing her blouse with one hand, while she pushed her guests to the door with the other.

"Hurry and dress, and come back to button me up. It would be a very delicate attention for us to be on time to-night. We've been late for every meal since vacation began."

* * * * *

The girls spent Christmas morning coasting. They were on time for luncheon-and with appetites!

The meal was half over when Osaki ap peared with a telegram, which he handed to the Dowager. She read it with agitated surprise and passed it to Miss Sallie, who raised her eyebrows and handed it to Miss Wadsworth, who was thrown into a very visible flutter.

"What on earth can it be?" Kid wondered.

"Lordy's eloped, and they've got to hunt for a new Latin teacher," was Patty's interpretation.

As the three girls left the table, the Dowager waylaid Harriet.

"Step into my study a moment. A telegram has just come—"

Patty and Kid climbed the stairs in wide-eyed wonder.

"It can't be bad news, for Miss Sallie was smiling—" meditated Patty. "And I can't think of any good news that can be happening to Harriet."

Ten minutes later there was the sound of footsteps on the stairs, and Harriet burst into Patty's room wild with excitement.

"He's coming!"

"Who?"

"My father."

"When?"

"Right now-this afternoon-He's been in New York on business, and is coming to see me for Christmas."

"I'm so glad!" said Patty heartily. "Now, you see the reason he hasn't come before is because he has been away off in Mexico."

Harriet shook her head, with a sudden drop in her animation.

"I suppose he thinks he ought."

"Nonsense!"

"It's so. He doesn't care for me-really. He likes girls to be jolly and pretty and clever like you."

"Well, then—*be* jolly and pretty and clever like me."

Harriet's eyes sought the mirror, and filled with tears.

"You're a perfect idiot!" said Patty, despairingly.

"I'm an awful fright in my green dress," said Harriet.

"Yes," Patty grudgingly conceded. "You are."

"The skirt is too short, and the waist is too long."

"And the sleeves are sort of queer," said Patty.

Faced by these dispiriting facts, she felt her enthusiasm ebbing.

"What time is he coming?" she asked.

"Four o'clock."

"That gives us two hours," Patty rallied her forces. "One can do an awful lot in two hours. If you were only nearer my size, you could wear my new pink dress-but I'm afraid—" She regarded Harriet's long legs dubiously. "I'll tell you!" she added, in a rush of generosity. "We'll take out the tucks and let down the hem."

"Oh, Patty!" Harriet was tearfully afraid of spoiling the gown. But when Patty's zeal in any cause was roused, all other considerations were swept aside. The new frock was fetched from the closet, and the ripping began.

"And you can wear Kid's new pearl neck lace and pink scarf, and my silk stockings and slippers-if you can get 'em on-and I think Conny left a lace petticoat that came back from the laundry too late to pack-and-Here's Kid now!"

Miss McCoy's sympathies were enlisted and in fifteen minutes the task of transforming a remonstrating, excited, and occasionally tearful Harriet into the school beauty, was going gaily forward. Kid McCoy was supposed to be an irreclaimable tomboy, but in this crucial moment the eternal feminine came triumphantly to the fore. She sat herself down, with Patty's manicure scissors, and for three-quarters of an hour painstakingly ripped out tucks.

Patty meanwhile addressed her attention to Harriet's hair.

"Don't strain it back so tight," she ordered. "It looks as though you'd done it with a monkey-wrench. Here! Give me the comb."

Patty meanwhile addressed her attention to Harriet's hair.

She pushed Harriet into a chair, tied a towel about her neck, and accomplished the coifing by force.

"How's that?" she demanded of Kid.

"Bully!" Kid mumbled, her mouth full of pins.

Harriet's hair was rippled loosely about her face, and tied with a pink ribbon bow. The ribbon belonged to Conny Wilder, and had heretofore figured as a belt; but individual property rights were forced to bow before the cause.

The slippers and stockings did prove too small, and Patty frenziedly ransacked the bureaus of a dozen of her absent friends in the vain hope of unearthing pink footwear. In the end, she had reluctantly to permit Harriet's appearing in her own simple cotton hose and patent leather pumps.

"But after all," Patty reassured her, "it's better for you to wear black. Your feet would be sort of conspicuous in pink." She was still in her truthful mood. "I'll tell you!" she cried, "you can wear my silver buckles." And she commenced cruelly wrenching them from their pink chiffon setting.

"Patty! *Don't!*" Harriet gasped at the sacrilege.

"They're just the last touch that your costume needs." Patty ruthlessly carried on the work of destruction. "When your father sees those buckles, he'll think you're *beautiful!*"

For a feverish hour they worked. They clothed her triumphantly in all the grandeur that they could command. The entire corridor had contributed its quota, even to the lace-edged handkerchief with a hand-embroidered "H" that had been left behind in Hester Pringle's top drawer. The two turned her critically before the mirror, the pride of creation in their eyes. As Kid had truly presaged, she was the ravingest beauty in all the school.

Irish Maggie appeared in the door.

"Mr. Gladden is in the drawin'-room, Miss Harriet." She stopped and stared. "Sure, ye're that beautiful I didn't know ye!"

Harriet went with a laugh-and a fighting light in her eyes.

Patty and Kid restlessly set themselves to reducing the chaos that this sudden butterfly flight had caused in Paradise Alley-it is always dreary work setting things to rights, after the climax of an event has been reached.

It was an hour later that the sudden quick patter of feet sounded in the hall, and Harriet ran in-danced in-her eyes were shining; she was a picture of youth and happiness and bubbling spirits.

"Well?" cried Patty and Kid in a breath.

She stretched out her wrist and displayed a gold-linked bracelet set with a tiny watch.

"Look!" she cried, "he brought me that for Christmas. And I'm going to have all the dresses I want, and Miss Sallie isn't going to pick them out ever again. And he's going to stay for dinner to-night, and eat at the little table with us. And he's going to take us into town next Saturday for luncheon and the matinée, and the Dowager says we may go!"

"Gee!" observed the Kid. "It paid for all the trouble we took."

"And what do you think?" Harriet caught her breath in a little gasp. "*He likes me!*"

"I knew those silver buckles would fetch him!" said Patty.

Chapter VII "Uncle Bobby"

While St. Ursula's was still dallying with a belated morning-after-Christmas breakfast, the mail arrived, bringing among other matters, a letter for Patty from her mother. It contained cheering news as to Tommy's scarlet fever, and the expressed hope that school was not too lonely during the holidays; it ended with the statement that Mr. Robert Pendleton was going to be in the city on business, and had promised to run out to St. Ursula's to see her little daughter.

The last item Patty read aloud to Harriet Gladden and Kid McCoy (christened Margarite). The three "left-behinds" were occupying a table together in a secluded corner of the dining-room.

"Who's Mr. Robert Pendleton?" inquired Kid, looking up from her own letter.

"He used to be my father's private secretary when I was a little girl. I always called him 'Uncle Bobby.'"

Kid returned to her mail. She took no interest in the race of uncles, either real or fictitious. But Patty, being in a reminiscent mood, continued the conversation with Harriet, who had no mail to deflect her.

"Then he went away and commenced practising for himself. It's been ages since I've seen him; but he was really awfully nice. He used to spend his entire time-when he wasn't writing Father's speeches-in getting me out of scrapes. I had a goat named Billy-Boy—"

"Is he married?" asked Harriet.

"N-no, I don't think so. I believe he had a disappointment in his youth, that broke his heart."

"What fun!" cried Kid, reëmerging. "Is it still broken?"

"I suppose so," said Patty.

"How old is he?"

"I don't know, I'm sure. He must be *quite* old by now." (Her tone suggested that he was tottering on the brink of the grave.) "It has been seven years since I've seen him, and he was through college then."

Kid dismissed the subject. Old men, even with broken hearts, contained no interest for her.

That afternoon, as the three girls were gathered in Patty's room enjoying an indigestible four o'clock tea of milk and bread and butter (furnished by the school) and fruit cake and candy and olives and stuffed prunes, the expressman arrived with a belated consignment of Christmas gifts, among them a long narrow parcel addressed to Patty. She tore off the wrapping, to find a note and a white pasteboard box. She read the note aloud while the others looked over her shoulder. Patty always generously shared experiences with anyone who might be near.

> "*My Dear Patty,* —
>
> "Have you forgotten 'Uncle Bobby' who used to stand between you and many well-de served spankings? I trust that you have grown into a very good girl now that you are old enough to go away to school!
>
> "I am coming to see for myself on Thursday afternoon. In the meantime, please accept the accompanying Christmas remembrance, with the hope that you are having a happy holiday, in spite of having to spend it away from home.
>
> "Your old playfellow,
>
> "Robert Pendleton."

"What do you s'pose it is?" asked Patty, as she addressed herself to unknotting the gold cord on the box.

"I hope it's either flowers or candy," Harriet returned. "Miss Sallie says it isn't proper to—"

"Looks to me like American Beauty roses," suggested Kid McCoy.

Patty beamed.

"Isn't it a lark to be getting flowers from a *man?* I feel awfully grown up!"

She lifted the cover, removed a mass of tissue paper, and revealed a blue-eyed, smiling doll.

The three girls stared for a bewildered moment, then Patty slid to the floor, and buried her head in her arms against the bed and laughed.

"It's got real hair!" said Harriet, gently lifting the doll from its bed of tissue paper, and entering upon a detailed inspection. "Its clothes come off, and it opens and shuts its eyes."

"Whoop!" shouted Kid McCoy, as she snatched a shoe-horn from the bureau and commenced an Indian war dance.

Patty checked her hysterics sufficiently to rescue her new treasure from the danger of being scalped. As she squeezed the doll in her arms, safe from harm's way, it opened its lips and emitted a grateful, *"Ma-ma!"*

They laughed afresh. They laid on the floor and rolled in an ecstasy of mirth until they were weak and gasping. Could Uncle Bobby have witnessed the joy his gift brought to three marooned St. Ursulites, he would have indeed been gratified. They continued to laugh all that day and the following morning. By afternoon Patty had just recovered her self-control sufficiently to carry off with decent gravity Uncle Bobby's promised visit.

As a usual thing, callers were discouraged at St. Ursula's. They must come from away, accredited with letters from the parents, and then must pass an alarming assemblage of chaperones. Miss Sallie remained in the drawing-room during the first half of the call (which could last an hour), but was then supposed to withdraw. But Miss Sallie was a social soul, and she frequently neglected to withdraw. The poor girl would sit silent in the corner, a smile upon her lips, mutiny in her heart, while Miss Sallie entertained the caller.

But rules were somewhat relaxed in the holidays. On the day of Uncle Bobby's visit, by a fortuitous circumstance, Miss Sallie was five miles away, superintending a new incubator house at the school farm. The Dowager and Miss Wadsworth and Miss Jellings were scheduled for a reception in the village, and the other teachers were all away for the holidays. Patty was told to receive him herself, and to remember her manners, and let him do a little of the talking.

This left her beautifully free to carry out the outrageous scheme that she had concocted over night. Harriet and Kid lent their delighted assistance, and the three spent the morning planning for her entrance in character. They successfully looted the "Baby Ward" where the fifteen little girls of the school occupied fifteen little white cots set in fifteen alcoves. A white, stiffly starched sailor suit was discovered, with a flaring blue linen collar, and a kilted skirt, that was shockingly short. Kid McCoy gleefully unearthed a pair of blue and white socks that exactly matched the dress, but they proved very much too small.

"They wouldn't look well anyway," said Patty, philosophically, "I've got an awful scratch on one knee."

Gymnasium slippers with spring heels reduced her five feet by an inch. She spent the early afternoon persuading her hair to hang in a row of curls, with a spanking blue bow over her left ear. When she was finished, she made as sweet a little girl as one would ever find romping in the park on a sunny morning.

"What will you do if he kisses you?" inquired Kid McCoy.

"I'll try not to laugh," said Patty.

She occupied the fifteen minutes of waiting in a dress rehearsal. By the time Maggie arrived with the tidings that the visitor was below, she had her part letter-perfect. Kid and Harriet followed as far as the first landing, where they remained dangling over the banisters, while Patty shouldered her doll and descended to the drawing-room.

She sidled bashfully into the door, dropped a courtesy, and extended a timid hand to the tall young gentleman who rose and advanced to meet her.

"How do you do, Uncle Wobert?" she lisped.

"Well, well! Is this little Patty?"

He took her by the chin and turned up her face for a closer inspection-Mr. Pendleton was, mercifully, somewhat near-sighted. She smiled back sweetly, with wide, innocent, baby eyes.

"You're getting to be a great big girl!" he pronounced with fatherly approval. "You reach almost to my shoulder."

She settled herself far back in a deep leather chair, and sat primly upright, her feet sticking straight out in front, while she clasped the doll in her arms.

"Sank you very much, Uncle Bobby, for my perfectly beautiful doll!" Patty imprinted a kiss upon the smiling bisque lips.

Uncle Bobby watched with gratified approval. He liked this early manifestation of the motherly instinct.

"And what are you going to name her?" he inquired.

"I can't make up my mind." She raised anxious eyes to his.

"How would Patty Junior do?"

She repudiated the suggestion; and they finally determined upon Alice, after "Alice in Wonderland." This point happily disposed of, they settled themselves for conversation. He told her about a Christmas pantomime he had seen in London, with little girls and boys for actors.

Patty listened, deeply interested.

"I'll send you the fairy book that has the story of the play," he promised, "with colored pictures; and then you can read it for yourself. You know how to read, of course?" he added.

"Oh, yes!" said Patty, reproachfully. "I've known how to read a *long* time. I can read anyfing-if it has big print."

"Well! You are coming on!" said Uncle Bobby.

They fell to reminiscing, and the conversation turned to Billy-Boy.

"Do you remember the time he chewed up his rope and came to church?" Patty dimpled at the recollection.

"Jove! I'll never forget it!"

"And usually Faver found an excuse for not going, but that Sunday Mover *made* him, and when he saw Billy-Boy marching up the aisle, with a sort of dignified smile on his face —"

Uncle Bobby threw back his head and laughed.

"I thought the Judge would have a stroke of apoplexy!" he declared.

"But the funniest thing," said Patty, "was to see you and Father trying to get him out! You pushed and Father pulled, and first Billy balked and then he butted."

She suddenly realized that she had neglected to lisp, but Uncle Bobby was too taken up with the story to be conscious of any lapse. Patty inconspicuously reassumed her character.

"And Faver scolded me because the rope broke-and it wasn't my fault at all!" she added with a pathetic quiver of the lips. "And the next day he had Billy-Boy shot."

At the remembrance Patty drooped her head over the doll in her arms. Uncle Bobby hastily offered comfort.

"Never mind, Patty! Maybe you'll have another goat some day."

She shook her head, with the suggestion of a sob.

"No, I never will! They don't let us keep goats here. And I loved Billy-Boy. I'm *awfully* lonely without him."

"There, there, Patty! You're too big a girl to cry." Uncle Bobby patted her curls, with kindly solicitude. "How would you like to go to the circus with me some day next week, and see all the animals?"

Patty cheered up.

"Will there be ele-phunts?" she asked.

"There'll be several," he promised. "And lions and tigers and camels."

"Oh, goody!" she clapped her hands and smiled through her tears. "I'd love to go. Sank you very, *very* much."

Half an hour later Patty rejoined her friends in Paradise Alley. She executed a few steps of the sailor's hornpipe with the doll as partner, then plumped herself onto the middle of the bed and laughingly regarded her two companions through over-hanging curls.

"Tell us what he said," Kid implored. "We nearly pulled our necks out by the roots stretching over the banisters, but we couldn't hear a word."

"Did he kiss you?" asked Harriet.

"N-no." There was a touch of regret in her tone. "But he patted me on the head. He has a very sweet way with children. You'd think he'd had a course in kindergarten training."

"What did you talk about?" insisted Kid, eagerly.

Patty outlined the conversation.

"And he's going to take me to the circus next Wednesday," she ended, "to see the elephunts!"

"The Dowager will never let you go," objected Harriet.

"Oh, yes, she will!" said Patty. "It's perfectly proper to go to the circus with your uncle — 'specially in vacation. We've got it all planned. I'm to go into town with Waddy. I heard her say she had an appointment at the dentist's —and he'll be at the station with a hansom —"

"More likely a baby carriage," Kid put in quickly.

"Miss Wadsworth will never take you into town in *those* clothes," Harriet objected.

Patty hugged her knees and rocked back and forth, while her dimples came and went.

"I think," she said, "that the next time I'll give him an entirely different kind of a sensation."

And she did.

Anticipatory of the coming event, she sent her suit to the tailor's and had him lengthen the hem of the skirt two inches. She spent an entire morning retrimming her hat along more mature lines, and she purchased a veil-with spots! She also spent twenty-five cents for hairpins, and did up her hair on the top of her head. She wore Kid McCoy's Christmas furs and Harriet's bracelet watch; and, as she set off with a somewhat bewildered Miss Wadsworth, they assured her that she looked *old*.

They reached the city a trifle late for Miss Wadsworth's appointment. Patty spied Mr. Pendleton across the waiting-room.

"There's Uncle Robert!" she said; and to her intense satisfaction, Miss Wadsworth left her to accost him alone.

She sauntered over in a very blasé fashion and held out her hand. The spots in the veil seemed to dazzle him; for a moment he did not recognize her.

"Mr. Pendleton! How do you do?" Patty smiled cordially. "It's really awfully good of you to devote so much time to my entertainment. And so original of you to think of a circus! I haven't attended a circus for years. It's really refreshing after such a dose of Shakespeare and Ibsen as the theaters have been offering this winter."

Mr. Pendleton offered a limp hand and hailed a hansom without comment. He leaned back in the corner and continued to stare for three silent minutes; then he threw back his head and laughed.

"Good Lord, Patty! Do you mean to tell me that you've grown up?"

Patty laughed too.

"Well, Uncle Bobby, what do you think about it?"

* * * * *

Dinner was half over that night before the two travelers returned. Patty dropped into her seat and unfolded her napkin, with the weary air of a society woman of many engagements.

"What happened?" the other two clam ored. "Tell us about it! Was the circus nice?"

Patty nodded.

"The circus was charming-and so were the elephants-and so was Uncle Bobby. We had tea afterwards; and he gave me a bunch of violets and a box of candy, instead of the fairy book. He said he wouldn't be called 'Uncle Bobby' by anyone as old as me-that I'd got to drop the 'Uncle' —It's funny, you know, but he really seems younger than he did seven years ago."

Patty dimpled and cast a wary eye toward the faculty table across the room.

"He says he has business quite often in this neighborhood."

Chapter VIII The Society of Associated Sirens

Conny had gone home to recuperate from a severe attack of pink-eye. Priscilla had gone to Porto Rico to spend two weeks with her father and the Atlantic Fleet. Patty, lonely and abandoned, was thrown upon the school for society; and Patty at large, was very likely to get into trouble.

On the Saturday following the double departure, she, with Rosalie Patton and Mae Van Arsdale, made a trip into the city in charge of Miss Wadsworth, to accomplish some spring shopping. Patty and Rosalie each needed new hats-besides such minor matters as gloves and shoes and petticoats —and Mae was to have a fitting for her new tailor suit. These duties performed, the afternoon was to be given over to relaxation; at least to such relaxation as a Shakespearean tragedy affords.

But when they presented themselves at the theater, they were faced by the announcement that the star had met with an automobile accident on his way to the performance, and that he was too damaged to appear; money would be refunded at the box office. The girls still clamored for their matinée, and Miss Wadsworth hurriedly cast about for a fitting substitute for Hamlet.

Miss Wadsworth was middle-aged and vacillating and easily-led and ladylike and shockable. She herself knew that she had no strength of character; and she conscientiously strove to overcome this cardinal defect in a chaperon, by stubbornly opposing whatever her charges elected to do.

To-day they voted for a French farce with John Drew as hero. Miss Wadsworth said "no" with all the firmness she could assume, and herself picked out a drama entitled "The Wizard of the Nile," under the impression that it would assist their knowledge of ancient Egypt.

But the Wizard turned out to be a recent and spurious imitation of the original historical wizard. She was ultra-modern English, with a French flavor. The time was to-morrow, and the scene the terrace of Shepherd's Hotel. She wore long, clinging robes of chiffon and gold cut in the style of Cleopatra along Parisian lines. Her rose-tinted ears were enhanced by drooping earrings, and her eyes were cunningly lengthened at the corners, in a fetching Egyptian slant. She was very beautiful and very merciless; she broke every masculine heart in Cairo. As a climax to her shocking career of wickedness, she *smoked cigarettes!*

Poor bewildered Miss Wadsworth sat through the four acts, worried, breathless, horrified-fascinated; but the three girls were simply fascinated. They thrilled over the scenery and music and costumes all the way back in the train. Cairo, to their dazzled eyes, opened up realms of adventure, undreamed of in the proper bounds of St. Ursula's. The Mecca of all travel had become Shepherd's Hotel.

That night, long after "Lights-out" had rung, when Patty's mind was becoming an agreeable jumble of sphinxes and pyramids and English officers, she was suddenly startled wide awake by feeling two hands rise from the darkness and clutch her shoulders on the right and left. She sat upright with a very audible gasp, and demanded in unguardedly loud tones, "Who's that?"

The two hands instantly covered her mouth.

"Sh-h! Keep quiet! Haven't you any sense?"

"Mademoiselle's door is wide open, and Lordy's visiting her."

Rosalie perched on the right of the bed, and Mae Mertelle on the left.

"What do you want?" asked Patty, crossly.

"We've got a perfectly splendid idea," whispered Rosalie.

"A secret society," echoed Mae Mertelle.

"Let me alone!" growled Patty. "I want to go to sleep."

She laid down again in the narrow space left by her visitors. They paid no attention to her inhospitality, but drawing their bath robes closer about them, settled down to talk. Patty, being comfortably inside and warm, while they shivered outside, was finally induced to lend a drowsy ear.

"I've thought of a new society," said Mae Mertelle. She did not propose to share the honor of creation with Rosalie. "And it's going to be *really* secret this time. I'm not going to let in the whole school. Only us three. And this society hasn't just a few silly secrets; it has an *aim*."

"We're going to call it the Society of Associated Sirens," Rosalie eagerly broke in.

"That *what?*" demanded Patty.

Rosalie rolled off the sonorous syllables a second time.

"The Sho-shiety of Ash-sho-she-ated Shi-rens," Patty mumbled sleepily. "It's too hard to say."

"Oh, but we won't call it that in public. The name's a secret. We'll call it the S. A. S."

"What's it for?"

"You'll promise not to tell?" Mae asked guardedly.

"No, of course I won't tell."

"Not even Pris and Conny when they get back?"

"We'll make them members," said Patty.

"Well-perhaps-but this is the kind of society that's better small. And we three are the only ones who really ought to be members, because we saw the play. But anyhow; you must promise not to tell unless Rosalie and I give you permission. Do you promise that?"

"Oh, yes! I promise. What's it for?"

"We're going to become sirens," Mae whispered impressively. "We're going to be beautiful and fascinating and ruthless —"

"Like Cleopatra," said Rosalie.

"And avenge ourselves on Man," added Mae.

"Avenge ourselves-what for?" inquired Patty, somewhat dazed.

"Why-for-for breaking our hearts and destroying our faith in —"

"My heart hasn't been broken."

"Not yet," said Mae with a touch of impatience, "because you don't know any men, but you will know them some day, and then your heart will be broken. You ought to have your weapons ready."

"In time of peace prepare for war," quoted Rosalie.

"Do-you think it's quite ladylike to be a siren?" asked Patty dubiously.

"It's *perfectly* ladylike!" said Mae. "Nobody but a lady could possibly be one. Did you ever hear of a washerwoman who was a siren?"

"N-no," Patty confessed. "I don't believe I have."

"And look at Cleopatra," put in Rosalie. "I'm sure she was a lady."

"All right!" Patty agreed. "What are we going to do?"

"We're going to become beautiful and fascinating, with a fatal charm that ensnares every man who approaches."

"Do you think we can?" There was some doubt in Patty's tone.

"Mae's got a book," put in Rosalie eagerly, "about 'Beauty and Grace.' You soak your face in oatmeal and almond-oil and honey, and let your hair hang in the sun, and whiten your nose with lemon juice, and wear gloves at night, and —"

"You really ought to have a bath of asses' milk," interrupted Mae. "Cleopatra had; but I'm afraid it will be impossible to get."

"And you ought to learn to sing," added Rosalie, "and have some one song like the 'Lorelei!' that you always hum when you're about to ensnare a victim."

The project was foreign to Patty's ordinary train of thought, but it did have an element of novelty and allurement. Neither Mae nor Rosalie were the partners she would naturally have chosen in any enterprise, but circumstances had thrown them together that day, and Patty was an obliging soul. Also, her natural common sense was wandering; she was still under the spell of the Egyptian sorceress.

They discussed the new society for several minutes more, until they heard the murmur of Miss Lord's voice, bidding Mademoiselle goodnight.

"There's Lordy!" Patty whispered warily. "I think you'd better to go to bed. We can plan the rest in the morning."

"Yes, let's," said Rosalie, with a shiver. "I'm freezing!"

"But we must first take the vow," insisted Mae Mertelle. "We ought really to do it at midnight-but maybe half-past ten will do as well. I've got it all planned. You two say it after me."

They joined hands and whispered in turn:

"I most solemnly promise to keep secret the name and object of this society; and if I break this oath, may I become freckled and bald and squint-eyed and pigeon-toed, now and forever more."

The three members of the S. A. S. devoted their leisure during the next few days to a careful study of the work on Beauty; and painstakingly set about putting its precepts into practice. Some of these seemed perplexingly at variance. The hair, for example, was to be exposed to air and sunlight, but the face was not. They cleverly circumvented this difficulty however. The week's allowance went for chamois-skin. During every recreation hour, they retired to an airy knoll in the lower pasture, and sat in a patient row, with hair streaming in the wind, and faces protected by homemade masks.

One afternoon, a little Junior A, wandering far afield in a game of hide-and-seek, came upon them unawares; and returned to the safe confines of the playground with frightened shrieks. Dark rumors began to float about the school as to the aim and scope of the new society. Suggestions ranged all the way from Indian squaws to Druid priestesses.

They almost met with disaster while acquiring the ingredients of the oatmeal poultice. The oatmeal and lemon were compar atively easy; the cook supplied them without much fuss. But she stuck at the honey. There were jars and jars of strained honey in the storeroom; but the windows were barred, and the key was in the bottom of Nora's pocket. Confronted by the immediate necessity of becoming beautiful, they could not placidly sit down for five days, and wait for the weekly shopping trip to the village. Besides, with a teacher in attendance, there would be no possible chance of making the purchase. Honey was a contraband article, in the same class with candy and jam and pickles.

They discussed the feasibility of filing through the iron gratings, or of chloroforming Nora and stealing the key, but in the end Patty accomplished the matter by the use of a little simple blarney. She dropped into the kitchen one afternoon with the plaintive admission that she was hungry. Nora hastened to supply a glass of milk and a piece of bread and butter, while Patty perched on a corner of the carving-table and settled herself for conversation. The girls were not supposed to visit the kitchen, but the law was never rigidly enforced. Nora was a social soul and she welcomed callers. Patty praised the apple dumplings of last night's dessert; progressed from that to a discussion of the engaging young plumber who at the moment claimed all of Nora's thoughts; then, by a natural transition, she passed to honey. Before she left, she had obtained Nora's promise to substitute it for marmalade the next morning at breakfast.

The members of the S. A. S. brought pin-trays to the meal, and unobtrusively transferred a supply from their plates to their laps.

But even so, disaster still threatened. Patty had the misfortune to collide with Evalina Smith in the upper hall, and she dropped her pin-tray, honey-side down, in the middle of the rug. At the same instant, Miss Lord bore down upon her from the end of the corridor. Patty was a young person of resource; the emergency of the moment rarely found her napping. She plumped down on her knees in the midst of the puddle, and with widespread skirts, commenced frantically searching for an imaginary stick-pin.

"Is it necessary for you to block up the entire hall?" was Miss Lord's only comment as she passed.

The rug was happily reversible, and by the simple process of turning it over, Patty satisfactorily cleaned up the mess. The other two girls were generous, and shared their supply: so in the end she obtained her honey.

For three wakeful nights they stuck to the poultice-though perhaps it would be more accurate to say that the poultice stuck to them. In spite of many washings in hot water, their faces became noticeably scaly.

Miss Sallie, who represented St. Ursula's board of health, met Patty Wyatt in the hall one morning. She took her by the chin and turned her to the light. Patty squirmed embarrassedly.

"My dear child! What is the matter with your face?"

"I —I don't know-exactly. It seems sort of-of-dandruffy."

"I should think it did! What have you been eating?"

"Only what I get at meals," said Patty, relievedly telling the truth.

"There's something the matter with your blood," diagnosed Miss Sallie. "What you need is a tonic. I shall prescribe boneset tea for you."

"Oh, Miss Sallie!" Patty earnestly remonstrated. "I don't need it, *really*. I'm sure I'll be all right." She had tried boneset tea before; it was the bitterest brew that was ever concocted.

When Miss Sallie met Mae Van Arsdale suffering from the same complaint, and later still, Rosalie Patton, she commenced to be perturbed. The apple trees under her care at the farm had been afflicted that spring with San José scale, but she had hardly expected the disease to spread to the school girls. That afternoon she superintended an infusion of boneset, of gigantic proportions, and at bedtime a reluctant school formed in line and filed past Miss Sallie, who, ladle in hand, presided over the punch bowl. Each received a flowing cupful and drank it with what grace she might, until Patty's turn came. She disposed of hers in a blue china umbrella holder which stood in the hall behind Miss Sallie's back. The remainder of the line successfully followed her lead.

Miss Sallie watched her little charges closely for the next few days; and sure enough, the scales disappeared. (The Associated Sirens had discarded poultices.) She was more than ever convinced of the efficacy of boneset.

Shortly after the founding of the society, Mae Mertelle returned from a week-end visit to her home. (Her mother was ill and she had been sent for. Someone in Mae's family was conveniently ill a great deal of the time.) She brought with her three bracelets of linked scales representing a serpent swallowing his tail. S. A. S. in tiny letters was engraved between the emerald eyes.

"They are perfectly sweet!" said Patty, with grateful appreciation. "But why a snake?"

"It isn't a snake; it's a serpent," Mae explained. "To represent Cleopatra. She was the Serpent of the Nile. We'll be Serpents of the Hudson."

With the appearance of the bracelets, curiosity in the S. A. S. increased, but unlike the other secret societies which had appeared from time to time, its *raison d'être* remained a mystery. The school really commenced to believe that the society had a secret. Miss Lord, who had the reputation of being curious, stopped Patty one day as she was leaving the Virgil class, and admired the new bracelet.

"And what may be the meaning of S. A. S.?" she inquired.

"It's a secret society," said Patty.

"Ah, a secret society!" Miss Lord smiled. "Then I suppose the name is a deep mystery." She lowered her voice, as she said it, to sepulchral depths.

There was something peculiarly irritating about Miss Lord's manner; it always suggested that she was amused by the vagaries of her little pupils. She did not possess Miss Sallie's happy faculty of meeting them on a level. Miss Lord peered down from above (through lorgnettes).

"Of course the name is a secret," said Patty. "If that got out, it would give the whole thing away."

"And what is the object of this famous society? Or is that too a secret?"

"Why, yes, that is, I mustn't tell you exactly."

Patty smiled up at Miss Lord with the innocent, seraphic gaze that always warned those who knew her best that is was wisest to let her alone.

"It's a sort of branch of the Sunshine Society," she added confidentially. "We're to-well-to smile on people, you know, and make them like us."

"I see!" said Miss Lord, with an air of friendly understanding. "Then S. A. S. stands for 'Sunshine and Smiles?' "

"Oh, please! You mustn't say it out loud," Patty lowered her voice and threw an anxious glance over her shoulder.

"I wouldn't tell anybody for worlds," Miss Lord promised solemnly.

"Thank you," said Patty. "It would be dreadful if it got out."

"It is a very sweet, womanly society," Miss Lord added approvingly. "But you ought not to keep it all to yourselves. Can't you let me be an honorary member of the S. A. S.?"

"Certainly, Miss Lord!" said Patty sweetly. "If you care to belong, we should *love* to have you."

"Lordy wants to be a Siren!" she announced to her two fellow members when she met them shortly in the gymnasium. The account of the interview was received with hilarity. Miss Lord was anything but the accepted type of siren.

"I thought a few smiles might relieve the gloom of Latin class," Patty explained. "It amuses Lordy to think she's helping the children in their play; and it doesn't hurt the children."

For a time the S. A. S. flourished with the natural health of youth, but as the novelty wore off, the business of becoming beautiful grew onerous. Mae and Rosalie continued to study the beauty book with dogged perseverance,—the subject lay along the line of their natural ambitions-but Patty felt other matters calling. Spring field sports had commenced, and the nearness of the annual match with Highland-Hall, crowded out her interest in cold cream and almond meal. She and Mae were not naturally *simpatica*, and in spite of Mae's insistence, Patty became an apathetic siren.

One Saturday just after the spring recess, Patty received permission to lunch in town with "Uncle Bobby." He was an uncle by courtesy only, but Patty had failed to inform the Dowager that the title was not his by natural right. She knew well what the result would be. It is quite proper to have luncheon with an uncle; and quite improper with even the oldest and baldest of family friends.

When the "hearse" returned from the station at dusk with Mademoiselle and the city contingent, Rosalie Patton was waiting the arrival on the porte-cochère. She separated Patty from the group and whispered in her ear.

"The most awful thing has happened!"

"What?" Patty demanded.

"The S. A. S. All is discovered!"

"Not really!" cried Patty, aghast.

"Yes! Come in here."

Rosalie drew her into the empty cloak-room and shut the door.

"You mean-they've found out the name-and everything?" Patty demanded breathlessly.

"Not quite everything, but they would have if it hadn't been for Lordy. She saved us for once."

"Lordy saved us!" There was incredulity mixed with Patty's horror. "What do you mean?"

"Well, yesterday, Mae went shopping in the village with Miss Wadsworth-and you know what kind of a chaperone Waddy makes." Patty nodded impatiently. "*Anybody* could fool her. And Mae, right under her very nose, commenced a flirtation with the *Soda-Water Clerk*."

"Oh!" said Patty hotly. "How perfectly horrid!"

"She didn't care anything about it, really. She was just trying to put the principles of the S. A. S. into practice."

"She might at least have picked out somebody decent!"

"Well, he is quite decent. He's engaged to the girl at the underwear counter in Bloodgood's, and he didn't want to be flirted with a bit. But you know how persistent Mae Mertelle is, when she makes up her mind. The poor young man just couldn't help himself. He was so embarrassed that he didn't know what he was doing. He gave Hester Pringle half chocolate and half sarsaparilla, and she says it was a *perfectly awful* combination. It made her feel so sick that she couldn't eat any dinner. And all this time Waddy just sat and smiled into space and saw nothing; but all the girls saw, —and *so did the drugstore man!*"

"Oh!" said Patty breathlessly.

"And this morning Miss Sallie went to the drugstore to get some potash for Harriet Gladden's sore throat, and he told her all about it."

"What did Miss Sallie do?" Patty asked faintly.

"Do! She came back with blood in her eye, and told the Dowager, and they called up Mae Mertelle and then —" Rosalie closed her eyes and shuddered.

"Well," said Patty impatiently. "What happened?"

"The Dowager was *perfectly outraged!* She told Mae that she had disgraced the school and that she would be expelled. And she wrote a telegram to Mae's father to come and take her away. And she asked Mae if she had anything to say for herself, and Mae said it wasn't her fault. That you and I were to blame just as much as she, because we were all in a society together, but that she couldn't tell about it because she'd sworn."

"Beast!" said Patty.

"So then they sent for me and commenced asking questions about the S. A. S. I tried not to tell, but you know the way the Dowager looks when she's angry. Even a sphinx would break down and tell everything it knew, and I never did pretend to be a sphinx."

"All right," said Patty, bracing herself for the shock. "What did they say when they heard?"

"They didn't hear! I was just on the point of breaking my vows and telling all, when who should pop in but Lordy. And she was *perfectly splendid!* She said she knew all about the S. A. S. That it was a very admirable institution, and that she was a member herself! She said it was a branch of the Sunshine Society, and that Mae had never meant to flirt with the young man. She had just meant to smile and be kind to everybody she came in contact with, and he had taken advantage. And Mae said, yes, that was the way of it, and she shoved off all the blame on that poor innocent soda-water clerk."

"Just like her," Patty nodded.

"And now Mae is *perfectly furious* with him for getting her into trouble. She says that he's a horrid little thing with a turn-up nose, and that she'll never drink another glass of soda-water as long as she stays in St. Ursula's."

"And they're going to let her stay?"

"Yes. The Dowager tore up the telegram. But she gave Mae ten demerits, and made her go without dessert for a week, and learn Thanatopsis by heart. And she can't *ever* go shopping in the village any more. When she needs new hair ribbons or stockings or anything, she must send for them by some of the other girls."

"And what's the Dowager going to do to us?"

"Nothing at all-and if it hadn't been for Lordy, we'd all three have been expelled."

"And I've always detested Lordy," said Patty contritely. "Isn't it dreadful? You simply can't keep enemies. Just as you think people are perfectly horrid, and begin to enjoy hating them, they all of a sudden turn out nice."

"I hate Mae Mertelle," said Rosalie.

"So do I!" Patty agreed cordially.

"I'm going to leave her old society."

"I'm already out." Patty glanced toward the mirror. "And I'm not freckled and I'm not squint-eyed."

"What do you mean?" Rosalie stared; she had for the moment forgotten the dread nature of the oath.

"I've told Uncle Bobby."

"Oh, Patty! How could you?"

"I—I—that is—" Patty appeared momentarily confused. "You see," she confessed, "I thought myself that it would be sort of interesting to practice on somebody, so I—I—just tried—"

"And did he —"

Patty shook her head.

"It was awfully uphill work. He never helped a bit. And then he noticed my bracelet and wanted to know what S. A. S. meant. And before I knew it, I was telling him!"

"What did he say?"

"First he roared; then he got awfully sober, and he gave me a long lecture-it was really very impressive-sort of like Sunday School, you know. And he took the bracelet away from me and put it in his pocket. He told me he'd send me something nicer."

"What do you s'pose it will be?" asked Rosalie interestedly.

"I hope it won't be a doll!"

Two days later the morning mail brought a small parcel for Miss Patty Wyatt. She opened it under her desk in geometry class. Buried in jeweler's cotton she found a gold linked bracelet that fastened with a padlock in the shape of a heart. On the back of one of Uncle Bobby's cards was written: —

"This is your heart. Keep it locked until the chap turns up who has the key."

Patty deflected Rosalie as she was turning into French and privately exhibited the bracelet with pride.

Rosalie regarded it with sentimental interest.

"What has he done with the key?" she wondered.

"I s'pose," said Patty, "he's got it in his pocket."

"How awfully romantic!"

"It sounds sort of romantic," Patty agreed with the suggestion of a sigh. "But it isn't really. He's thirty years old, and beginning to be bald."

Chapter IX The Reformation of Kid McCoy

Miss Mccoy, of Texas, had been subjected to the softening influences of St. Ursula's School for three years, without any perceptible result. She was the toughest little tomboy that was ever received-and retained-in a respectable-boarding-school.

"Margarite" was the name her parents had chosen, when the itinerant bishop made his quarterly visit to the mining-camp where she happened to be born. It was the name still used by her teachers, and on the written reports that were mailed monthly to her Texas guardian. But "Kid" was the more appropriate name that the cowboys on the ranch had given her; and "Kid" she remained at St. Ursula's, in spite of the distressed expostulation of the ladies in charge.

Kid's childhood had been picturesque to a degree rarely found outside the pages of a Nick Carter novel. She had possessed an adventurous father, who drifted from mining-camp to mining-camp, making fortunes and losing them. She had cut her teeth on a poker chip, and drunk her milk from a champagne glass. Her father had died-quite opportunely-while his latest fortune was at its height, and had left his little daughter to the guardianship of an English friend who lived in Texas. The next three turbulent years of her life were spent on a cattle range with "Guardie," and the ensuing three in the quiet confines of St. Ursula's.

The guardian had brought her himself, and after an earnest conference with the Dowager, had left her behind to be molded by the culture of the East. But so far, the culture of the East had left her untouched. If any molding had taken place, it was Kid herself who shaped the clay.

Her spicy reminiscences of mining-camps and cattle ranches made all permissible works of fiction tame. She had given the French dancing master, who was teaching them a polite version of a Spanish waltz, an exposition of the real thing, as practised by the Mexican cow-punchers on her guardian's ranch. It was a performance that left him sympathetically breathless. The English riding master, who came weekly in the spring and autumn, to teach the girls a correct trot, had received a lesson in bareback riding that caused the dazed query:

"Was the young lady trained in a circus?"

The Kid was noisy and slangy and romping and boisterous; her way was beset with reproofs and demerits and minor punishments, but she had never yet been guilty of any actual felony. For three years, however, St. Ursula's had been holding its breath waiting for the crash. Miss McCoy, from her very nature, was bound to give them a sensation sometime.

When at last it came, it was of an entirely unexpected order.

Rosalie Patton was the Kid's latest room-mate —- she wore her room-mates out as fast as she did her shoes. Rosalie was a lovable little soul, the essence of everything feminine. The Dowager had put the two together, in the hope that Rosalie's gentle example might calm the Kid's tempestuous mood. But so far, the Kid was in her usual spirits, while Rosalie was looking worn.

Then the change came.

Rosalie burst into Patty Wyatt's room one evening in a state of wide-eyed amazement.

"What do you think?" she cried. "Kid McCoy says she's going to be a lady!"

"A what?" Patty emerged from the bath towel with which she had been polishing her face.

"A *lady*. She's sitting down now, running pale blue baby ribbon through the embroidery in her night gown."

"What's happened to her?" was Patty's question.

"She's been reading a book that Mae Mertelle brought back."

Rosalie settled herself, Turk fashion, on the window seat, disposed the folds of her pink kimono in graceful billows about her knees, and allowed two braids of curly yellow hair to hang picturesquely over her shoulders. She was ready for bed and could extend her call until the last stroke of the "Lights-out" bell.

"What kind of a book?" asked Patty with a slightly perfunctory note in her voice.

Rosalie was apt to burst into one's room with a startling announcement and then, having engaged everybody's attention, settle down to an endless, meandering recital sprinkled with anti-climaxes.

"It's about a sweet young English girl whose father owned a tea estate in Asia-or maybe Africa. But anyway, where it was hot, and there were a lot of natives and snakes and centipedes. Her mother died and she was sent back home to boarding-school when she was a tiny little thing. Her father was quite bad. He drank and swore and smoked. The only thing that kept him from being awfully bad, was the thought of his sweet little golden-haired daughter in England."

"Well, what of it?" Patty inquired, politely suppressing a yawn. Rosalie had a way of trailing off into golden-haired sentiment if one didn't haul her up sharp.

"Just wait! I'm coming to it. When she was seventeen she went back to India to take care of her father, but almost right off he got a sunstroke and died. And in his death-bed he entrusted Rosamond-that was her name-to his best friend to finish bringing up. So when Rosamond went to live with her guardian, and took charge of his bungalow and made it beautiful and homelike and comfortable-she wouldn't let him drink or smoke or swear any more. And as he looked back over the past —"

"He was eaten with remorse at the thought of the wasted years," Patty glibly supplied, "and wished that he had lived so as to be more worthy of the sweet, womanly influence that had come into his wicked life."

"You've read it!" said Rosalie.

"Not that I know of," said Patty.

"Anyway," said Rosalie, with an air of challenge, "they fell in love and were married —"

"And her father and mother, looking down from heaven, smiled a blessing on the dear little daughter who had brought so much happiness to a lonely heart?"

"Um-yes," agreed Rosalie, doubtfully.

There was no amount of sentiment that she would not swallow, but she knew from mortifying experience that Patty was not equally voracious.

"It's a very touching story," Patty commented, "but where does Kid McCoy come in?"

"Why, don't you see?" Rosalie's violet eyes were big with interest. "It's exactly Kid's own story! I realized it the minute I saw the book, and I had the *awfulest* time making her read it. She made fun of it at first, but after she'd really got into it, she appreciated the resemblance. She says now it was the Hand of Fate."

"Kid's story? What *are* you talking about?" Patty was commencing to be interested.

"Kid has a wicked English guardian just like the Rosamond in the book. Anyway, he's English, and she thinks probably he's wicked. Most ranchmen are. He lives all alone with only cow-punchers for companions, and he needs a sweet womanly influence in his home. So Kid's decided to be a lady, and go back and marry Guardie, and make him happy for the rest of his life."

Patty laid herself on the bed and rolled in glee. Rosalie rose and regarded her with a touch of asperity.

"I don't see anything so funny —I think it's very romantic."

"Kid exerting a sweet womanly influence!" Patty gurgled. "She can't even pretend she's a lady for an hour. If you think she can *stay* one —"

"Love," pronounced Rosalie, "has accomplished greater wonders than that-you wait and see."

And the school did see. Kid McCoy's reformation became the sensation of the year. The teachers attributed the felicitous change in her deportment to the good influence of Rosalie, and though they were extremely relieved, they did not expect it to last. But week followed week, and it did last.

Kid McCoy no longer answered to "Kid." She requested her friends to call her "Margarite." She dropped slang and learned to embroider; she sat through European Travel and Art History nights with clasped hands and a sweetly pensive air, where she used to drive her neighbors wild by a solid hour of squirming. Voluntarily, she set herself to practising scales. The reason she confided to Rosalie, and Rosalie to the rest of the school.

They needed the softening influence of music on the ranch. One-eyed Joe played the accordion, and that was all the music they had. The school saw visions of the transformed Margarite, dressed in white, sitting before the piano in the twilight singing softly the "Rosary," while Guardie watched her with folded arms; and the cowboys, with bowie knives sheathed in their boots, and lariats peacefully coiled over their shoulders, gathered by the open window.

Lenten services that year, instead of being forcibly endured by a rebellious Kid, were attended by a sweetly reverent Margarite. The entire school felt an electric thrill at sight of Miss McCoy walking up the aisle with downcast eyes, and hands demurely clasping her prayer book. Usually she looked as much in place in the stained-glass atmosphere of Trinity Chapel as an unbroken broncho colt.

This amazing reform continued for seven weeks. The school was almost beginning to forget that there was ever a time when Kid McCoy was not a lady.

Then one day a letter came from Guardie with the news that he was coming East to visit his little girl. Subdued excitement prevailed in the South Corridor. Rosalie and Margarite and an assemblage of neighbors held earnest conferences as to what she should wear and how she should behave. They finally decided upon white muslin and blue ribbons. They pondered a long time over whether or not she should kiss him, but Rosalie decided in the negative.

"When he sees you," she explained, "the realization will sweep over him that you are no longer a child. You have grown to womanhood in the past three years. And he will feel unaccountably shy in your presence."

"Um," said Margarite, with a slightly doubtful note. "I hope so."

It was on a Sunday that Guardie arrived. The school-in a body-flattened its nose against the window watching his approach. They had rather hoped for a flannel shirt and boots and spurs, and, in any case, for a sombrero. But the horrible truth must be told. He wore a frock coat of the most unimpeachable cut, with a silk hat and a stick, and a white gardenia in his buttonhole. To look at him, one would swear that he had never seen a pistol or a lariat. He was born to pass the plate in church.

But the worst is still to tell.

He had planned a surprise for his little ward. When she should come back to the ranch, it would be to a real home. A sweet, womanly influence would have transformed it into a fitting abode for a young girl. Guardie was not alone. He was accompanied by his bride—a tall, fair, beautiful woman with a low voice and gracious manners. She sang for the girls after dinner, and as sixty-four pairs of eyes studied the beautiful presence, sixty-four—no, sixty-three—of her auditors decided to grow up to be exactly like her. Margarite did the honors in a state of dazed incomprehension. Her make-believe world of seven weeks had crumbled in an hour, and she had not had time to readjust herself. Never-she realized it perfectly-could she have competed in femininity with Guardie's wife. It wasn't in her, not even if she had commenced to practise from the cradle.

They went back to the city in the evening, and before the entire school, Guardie patted her on the head and told her to be a good little kiddie and mind her teachers. His wife, with a protecting arm about her shoulders, kissed her forehead and called her "dear little daughter."

After evensong on Sundays, came two hours of freedom. The teachers gathered in the Dowager's study for coffee and conversation, and the girls presumably wrote letters home. But that night, the South Corridor followed no such peaceful occupation. Margarite McCoy experienced a reversion to type. In her own picturesque language, she "shot up the town."

The echoes of the orgie at last reached the kaffee klatsch below. Miss Lord came to investigate-and she came on her tiptoes.

Miss McCoy, arrayed in a sometime picture hat cocked over one ear, a short gymnasium skirt, scarlet stockings and a scarlet sash, was mounted upon a table, giving an imitation of a clog dance in a mining-camp, while her audience played rag-time on combs and clapped.

"Margarite! Get down!" someone suddenly warned in frightened tones above the uproar.

"You needn't call me Margarite. I'm Kid McCoy of Cripple Creek."

Her eye caught sight of Miss Lord tower ing above the heads crowded in the doorway and she quite suddenly climbed down. For once, Miss Lord was without words. She stared for a space of three minutes; finally, she managed to articulate:

"Sunday evening in a Church school!"

The audience dispersed, and Miss Lord and Miss McCoy remained alone. Rosalie fled to the farthermost reaches of Paradise Alley and discussed possible punishments with Patty and Conny for a trembling hour. "Lights-out" had rung before she summoned courage to steal back to the darkened South Corridor. The sound of smothered sobbing came from Margarite's bed. Rosalie sank down on her knees and put her arm around her room-mate. The sobbing ceased while Margarite rigidly held her breath.

"Kid," she comforted, "don't mind Lordie-she's a horrid, snooping old thing! What did she say?"

"I'm not to leave bounds for a month, have to learn five psalms by heart and take f-fifty demerits."

"Fifty! It's a perfect shame! You'll never work them off. She had no *right* to make a fuss when you'd been good so long."

"I don't care!" said Kid, fiercely, as she struggled to free herself from Rosalie's embrace. "She'll never have a chance again to call me her sweet little daughter."

The perimeters of similar polygons are as their homologous sides."

Patty dreamily assured herself of this important truth for the twentieth time, as she sat by the open schoolroom window, her eyes on the billowing whiteness of the cherry tree which had burst into blossom overnight.

It was particularly necessary that she should finish her lessons with dispatch, because it was Saturday, and she was going to the city with Mademoiselle's party to spend an hour in the dentist's chair. But the weather was not conducive to concentrated effort. After an hour of half-hearted study, she closed her geometry, and started upstairs to dress, leaving the stay-at-homes to another hour of work.

She started upstairs; but she did not get very far on the way. As she passed the open door that led to the back porch, she stepped outside to examine the cherry tree at close range; then she strolled the length of the pergola to see how the wistaria was coming on; from there, it was just a step to the lane, with its double row of pink-tipped apple trees. Before she knew it, Patty found herself sitting on the stone wall at the end of the lower pasture. Behind her lay the confines of St. Ursula's. Before her the World.

She sat on the top of the wall, and dangled her feet out of bounds. The very most scandalous crime one could commit at St. Ursula's was to go out of bounds without permission. Patty sat and gazed at the forbidden land. She knew that she had no time to waste if she were to catch the hearse and the train and the dentist's chair. But still she sat and dreamed. Finally, far across the fields on the highroad, she spied the hearse bowling merrily to the station. Then it occurred to her that she had forgotten to report to Mademoiselle that she was going, and that Mademoiselle, accordingly, would not be missing her. At the school, of course, they would think that she had gone, and likewise would not be missing her. Without any premeditated iniquity, she was free!

She sat a few moments longer to let the feeling penetrate. Then she slid over the wall and started —a joyous young mutineer, seeking adventure. Following the cheery course of the brook, she dipped into a tangled ravine and stretch of woodland, raced down a hillside and across a marshy meadow, leaping gaily from hummock to hummock-occasionally missing and going in. She laughed aloud at these misadventures, and waved her arms and romped with the wind. In addition to the delicious sense of feeling free, was added the delicious sense of feeling bad. The combination was intoxicating.

And so, always following the stream, she came at last to another wood-not a wild wood like the first, but a tame, domesticated wood. The dead limbs were cut away, and the ground was neatly brushed up under the trees. The brook flowed sedately between fern-bordered banks, under rustic bridges, and widened occasionally into pools carpeted with lily pads. Mossy paths set with stepping-stones led off into mysterious depths that the eye could not penetrate: the leaves were just out enough to half hide and to tantalize. The grass was starred with crocuses. It looked like an enchanted wood in a fairy tale.

This second wood, however, was bordered by a solid stone wall, and on top of the wall, by four strands of barbed wire. Signs appeared at intervals-three were visible from where Patty stood-stating that these were private grounds, and that trespassers would be prosecuted to the full extent of the law.

Patty knew well to whom it belonged; she had often passed the front gates which faced on the other road. The estate was celebrated in the neighborhood, in the United States, for the matter of that. It comprised 500 acres and belonged to a famous-or infamous-multi-millionaire. His name was Silas Weatherby, and he was the originator of a great many Wicked Corporations. He had beautiful conservatories full of tropical plants, a sunken Italian garden, an art collection and picture gallery. He was a crusty old codger always engaged in half-a-dozen lawsuits. He hated the newspapers, and the newspapers hated him. He was in particularly bad repute at St. Ursula's, because, in response to a politely couched note from the principal, asking that the art class might view his Botticelli and the botany class his orchids, he had ungraciously replied that he couldn't have a lot of school girls running over his place-if he let them come one year, he would have to let them come another, and he didn't wish to establish a precedent.

Patty looked at the "No Trespassing" signs and the barbed wire, and she looked at the wood beyond. They couldn't do anything if they did catch her, she reasoned, except turn her out. People weren't jailed nowadays for taking a peaceable walk in other people's woods. Besides, the millionaire person was attending a directors' meeting in Chicago. This bit of neighborhood gos sip she had gleaned that morning in her weekly perusal of the daily press-Saturday night at dinner they were supposed to talk on current topics, so Saturday morning they glanced at the headlines and an editorial. Since the family were not at home, why not drop in and inspect the Italian garden? The servants were doubtless more polite than the master.

She selected a portion of the wall where the wire seemed slack, and wriggled under, stomach-wise, tearing only a small hole in the shoulder of her blouse. She played with the enchanted wood half an hour or so; then following a path, she quite suddenly left the wood behind, and popped out into a garden-not a flower garden, but a kitchen garden on an heroic scale. Neat plots of sprouting vegetables were bordered by currant bushes, and the whole was surrounded by a high brick wall, against which pear trees were trained in the English fashion.

A gardener was engaged, with his back toward Patty, in setting out baby onions. She studied him dubiously, divided between a prompting to run, and a social instinct of friendliness. He was an extremely picturesque gardener, dressed in knickerbockers and leather gaiters, with a touch of red in his waistcoat, and a cardigan jacket and a cap on the side of his head. He did not look very affable; but he did look rheumatic-even if he chased her, she was sure that she could run faster than he. So she settled herself on his wheelbarrow and continued to watch him, while she pondered an opening remark.

He glanced up suddenly and caught sight of her. The surprise nearly tipped him over.

"Good morning!" said Patty pleasantly.

"Ugh!" grunted the man. "What are you doing there?"

"Watching you plant onions."

This struck Patty as a self-evident truth, but she was perfectly willing to state it.

He grunted again as he straightened his back and took a step toward her.

"Where'd you come from?" he demanded gruffly.

"Over there." Patty waved her hand largely to westward.

"Humph!" he remarked. "You belong to that school-Saint Something or Other?"

She acknowledged it. Saint Ursula's monogram was emblazoned large upon her sleeve.

"Do they know you're out?"

"No," she returned candidly, "I don't believe they do. I am quite sure of it in fact. They think I've gone to the dentist's with Mam'selle, and she thinks I'm at school. So it leaves me entirely at leisure. I thought I'd come over and see what Mr. Weatherby's Italian garden looks like. I'm interested in Italian gardens."

"Well I'll be —!" He commenced, and came a trifle nearer and stared again. "Did you happen to see any 'No Trespassing' signs as you came through?"

"Mercy, yes! The whole place is peppered with 'em."

"They don't seem to have impressed you much."

"Oh, I never pay any attention to 'No Trespassing' signs," said Patty easily. "You'd never get anywhere in this world if you let *them* bother you."

The man unexpectedly chuckled.

"I don't believe you would!" he agreed. "I've never let them bother me," he added meditatively.

"Can't I help you plant your onions?" Patty asked politely. It struck her that this might be the quickest route to the Italian garden.

"Why, yes, thank you!"

He accepted her offer with unexpected cordiality, and gravely explained the mode of work. The onions were very tiny, and they must be set right-side up with great care; because it is very difficult for an embryonic onion to turn itself over after it has once got started in the wrong direction.

Patty grasped the business very readily, and followed along in the next row three feet behind him. It turned out sociable work; by the end of fifteen minutes they were quite old friends. The talk ranged far-over philosophy and life and morals. He had a very decided opinion on every subject-she put him down as Scotch-he seemed a well-informed old fellow though, and he read the papers. Patty had also read the paper that morning. She discoursed at some length upon whether or not corporations should be subject to state control. She stoutly agreed with her editor that they should. He maintained that they were like any other private property, and that it was nobody's damned business how they managed themselves.

"A penny, please," said Patty, holding out her hand.

"A penny?—what for?"

"That 'damn.' Every time you use slang or bad grammar you have to drop a penny in the charity box. 'Damn' is much worse than slang; it's swearing. I ought to charge you five cents, but since this is the first offense, I'll let you off with one."

He handed over his penny, and Patty gravely pocketed it.

"What sort of things do you learn in that school?" he inquired with a show of curiosity.

She obligingly furnished a sample:

"The perimeters of similar polygons are as their homologous sides."

"You will find that useful," he commented with the suggestion of a twinkle in his eye.

"Very," she agreed—"on examination day."

After half an hour, onion-planting grew to be wearying work; but Patty was bound to be game, and stick to her job as long as he did. Finally, however, the last onion was in, and the gardener rose and viewed the neat rows with some satisfaction.

"That will do for to-day," he declared; "we've earned a rest."

They sat down, Patty on the wheelbarrow, the man on an upturned tub.

"How do you like working for Mr. Weatherby?" she inquired. "Is he as bad as the papers make out?"

The gardener chuckled slightly as he lighted his pipe.

"Well," he said judiciously, "he's always been very decent to me, but I don't know as his enemies have any cause to love him."

"I think he's horrid!" said Patty.

"Why?" asked the man with a slight air of challenge. He was quite willing to run his master down himself, but he would not permit an outsider to do it.

"He's so terribly stingy with his old conservatories. The Dowager—I mean Mrs. Trent, the principal, you know-wrote and asked him to let the botany class see his orchids, and he was just as rude as he could be!"

"I'm sure he didn't mean it," the man apologized.

"Oh, yes, he did!" maintained Patty. "He said he couldn't have a lot of school girls running through and breaking down his vines-as if we would do such a thing! We have perfectly beautiful manners. We learn 'em every Thursday night."

"Maybe he was a little rude," he agreed. "But you see, he hasn't had your advantages, Miss. He didn't learn his manners in a young ladies' boarding-school."

"He didn't learn them anywhere," Patty shrugged.

The gardener took a long pull at his pipe and studied the horizon with narrowed eyes.

"It isn't quite fair to judge him the way you would other people," he said slowly. "He's had a good deal of trouble in his life; and now he's old, and I dare say pretty lonely sometimes. All the world's against him-when people are decent, he knows it's because they're after something. Your teacher, now, is polite when she wants to see his conservatories, but I'll bet she believes he's an old thief!"

"Isn't he?" asked Patty.
The man grinned slightly.
"He has his moments of honesty like the rest of us."
"Perhaps," Patty grudgingly conceded, "he may not be so bad when you know him. It's often the way. Now, there was Lordy, our Latin teacher. I used to despise her; and then-in the hour of trial-she came up to the scratch, and was *per-fect-ly bully!*"
He held out his hand.
"A penny."
Patty handed him back his own.
"She kept me from getting expelled-she did, really. I've never been able to hate her since. And you know, I miss it dreadfully. It's sort of fun having an enemy."
"I've had a good many," he nodded, "and I've always managed to enjoy them."
"And probably they're really quite nice?" she suggested.
"Oh, yes," he agreed, "the worst criminals are often very pleasant people when you see their right side."
"Yes, that's true," said Patty. "It's mainly chance that makes people bad —I know it is in my own case. This morning for instance, I got up with every intention of learning my geometry and going to the dentist's—and yet-here I am! And so," she pointed a moral, "you always ought to be kind to criminals and remember that under different circumstances you might have been in jail yourself."
"That thought," he acknowledged, "has often occurred to me. I—we-that is," he resumed after a moment of amused meditation, "Mr. Weatherby believes in giving a man a chance. If you have any convict friends, who are looking for a job, this is the place to send them. We used to have a cattle thief taking care of the cows, and a murderer in charge of the orchids."
"What fun!" cried Patty. "Have you got him now? I should love to see a murderer."
"He left some time ago. The place was too slow for him."
"How long have you been working for Mr. Weatherby?" she asked.
"A good many years-and I've worked hard!" he added, with a slight air of challenge.
"I hope he appreciates you?"
"Yes, I think on the whole that he does."
He knocked the ashes from his pipe and rose.
"And now," he suggested, "should you like me to show you the Italian garden?"
"Oh, yes," said Patty, "if you think Mr. Weatherby wouldn't mind."
"I'm head gardener. I do what I please."
"If you're head gardener, what makes you plant onions?"
"It's tiresome work-good for my character."
"Oh!" Patty laughed.
"And then you see, when I have a tendency to overwork the men under me, I stop and think how my own back ached."
"You're much too nice a man to work for him!" she pronounced approvingly.
"Thank ye, Miss," he touched his hat with a grin.
The Italian garden was a fascinating spot, with marble steps and fountains and clipped yew trees.
"Oh, I wish Conny could see it!" Patty cried.
"And who is she?"
"Conny's my room-mate. She's awfully interested in gardens this year, because she's going to get the botany prize for analyzing the most plants-at least, I think she's going to get it. It's between her and Keren Hersey; all the rest of the class have dropped out. Mae Van Arsdale is working against Conny, to spite me, because I wouldn't stay in an old secret society that she started. She gets orchids from the city and gives them to Keren."
"H'm," he frowned over this tangle of intrigue. "Is it entirely fair for the rest to help?"

"Oh, yes!" said Patty. "They have to do the analyzing, but their friends can collect and paste. Every time anybody goes for a walk, she comes back with her blouse stuffed full of specimens for either Conny or Keren. The nice girls are for Conny. Keren's an awful dig. She wears eye-glasses and thinks she knows everything."

"I'm for Miss Conny myself," he declared. "Is there any way in which I could help?"

Patty glanced about tentatively.

"You have quite a number of plants," she suggested, "that Conny hasn't got in her book."

"You shall take back as many as you can carry," he promised. "We'll pay a visit to the orchid house."

They left the garden behind, and turned toward the glass roofs of the conservatories. Patty was so entertained, that she had entirely forgotten the passage of time, until she came face to face with a clock in the gable of the carriage house; then she suddenly realized that St. Ursula's luncheon had been served three quarters of an hour before-and that she was in a starving condition.

"Oh, goodness gracious! I forgot all about luncheon!"

"Is it a very grave crime to forget about luncheon?"

"Well," said Patty, with a sigh, "I sort of miss it."

"I might furnish you with enough to sustain life for a short time," he suggested.

"Oh, could you?" she asked relievedly.

She was accustomed to having a table spread three times a day, and she cared little who furnished it.

"Just some milk," she said modestly, "and some bread and butter and-er-cookies. Then, you see, I won't have to go back till four o'clock when they come from the station, and maybe I can slip in without being missed."

"You just wait in the pavilion, and I'll see what the gardener's cottage can supply us."

He was back in fifteen minutes, chuckling as he lugged a big hamper.

"We'll have a picnic," he proposed.

"Oh, let's!" said Patty joyously. She did not mind eating with him in the least, for he had washed his hands, and appeared quite clean.

She helped him unpack the hamper and set the table in the little pavilion beside the fountain. He had lettuce sandwiches, a pat of cottage cheese, a jug of milk, orange marmalade, sugar cookies, and gingerbread hot from the oven.

"What a perfectly bully spread!" she cried.

He held out his hand.

"Another penny!"

Patty peered into an empty pocket.

"You'll have to charge it. I've used up all my ready money."

The spring sun was warm, the fountain was splashing, the wind was sprinkling the pavilion floor with white magnolia petals. Patty helped herself to marmalade with a happy sigh of contentment.

"The most fun in the world is to run away from the things you ought to do," she pronounced.

He acknowledged this immoral truth with a laugh.

"I suppose you ought to be working?" she asked.

"There are one or two little matters that might be the better for my attention."

"And aren't you glad you're not doing them?"

"Bully glad!"

She held out her hand.

"Give it back."

The cent returned to her pocket, and the meal progressed gaily. Patty was in an elated frame of mind, and Patty's elation was catching. Escaping from bounds, tres passing on a private estate, planting onions, and picnicking in the Italian garden with the head gardener-she had never had such a dizzying whirl of adventures. The head gardener also seemed to enjoy the sensation of offering sanctuary to a runaway school girl. Their appreciation of the lark was mutual.

As Patty, with painstaking honesty, was dividing the last of the gingerbread into two exact halves, she was startled by the sound of a footstep on the gravel path behind; and there walked into their party a groom —a crimson-faced, gaping young man who stood mechanically bobbing his head. Patty stared back a touch apprehensively. She hoped that she hadn't got her friend into trouble. It was very possibly against the rules for gardeners to entertain runaway school girls in the Italian garden. The groom continued to stare and to duck his head, and her companion rose and faced him.

"Well?" he inquired with a note of sharpness. "What do you want?"

"Beg pardon, sir, but this telegram come, and Richard says it might be important, sir, and he says for me to find you, sir."

He received the telegram, ran his eyes over it, scribbled an answer on the back with a gold pencil which he extracted from his pocket, and dismissed the man with a curt nod. The envelope had fluttered to the table and lay there face up. Patty inadvertently glanced at the address, and as the truth flashed across her, she hid her head against the back of the stone seat in a gale of laughter. Her companion looked momentarily sheepish, then he too laughed.

"You have enjoyed the privilege of telling me exactly how rude you think I am. Not even the reporters always allow themselves that pleasure."

"Oh, but that was before I knew you! I think now that you have perfectly beautiful manners."

He bowed his thanks.

"I shall endeavor to have better in the future. It will be my pleasure to put my greenhouses at the disposal of the young ladies of St. Ursula's some afternoon soon."

"Really?" she smiled. "That's awfully nice of you!"

They repacked the hamper and divided the crumbs among the goldfish in the fountain.

"And now," he inquired, "which will you visit first-the picture gallery or the orchids?"

Patty emerged from the orchid house at four o'clock, her arms filled with an unprecedented collection for Conny's book. The big yellow four-in-hand coach was standing outside the stable being washed. She examined it interestedly.

"Should you like to have me drive you home on that?"

"Oh, I'd love it!" Patty dimpled. "But I'm afraid it wouldn't be wise," she added on second thought. "No, I am sure it wouldn't be wise," she firmly turned her back. Her eyes fell on the road, and an apprehensive light sprang to her face.

"There's the hearse!"

"The hearse?"

"Yes, the school wagonette. I think I'd better be going."

He accompanied her back, through the vegetable garden and the enchanted wood, and held her flowers while she crawled under the fence, tearing a hole in the other shoulder of her blouse.

They shook hands through the barbed wire.

"I've enjoyed both the onions and the orchids," said Patty politely, "and particularly the gingerbread. And if I ever have any convict friends in need of employment, I may send them to you?"

"Do so," he urged. "I will find them a job here."

She started off, then turned to wave good-by to him.

"I've had a perfectly bully time!"

"A penny!" he called.

Patty laughed and ran.

Chapter XI The Lemon Pie and the Monkey-Wrench

Evalina Smith was a morbid young person who loved to dabble in the supernatural. Her taste in literature was for Edgar A. Poe. In religion she inclined toward spiritualism. Her favorite amusement was to gather a few shuddering friends about her, turn out the gas, and tell ghost stories. She had an extensive repertoire of ghoulish incidents, that were not fiction but the actual experience of people she knew. She had even had one or two spiritual adventures herself; and she would set forth the details with wide eyes and lowered voice, while her auditors held one another's hands and shivered. The circle in which Evalina moved had not much sense of humor.

One Saturday evening St. Ursula's School was in an unusually social mood. Evalina was holding a ghost party in her room in the East Wing; Nancy Lee had invited her ten dearest friends to a birthday spread in Center; the European History class was celebrating the completion of the Thirty-Years War by a molasses-candy pull in the kitchen; and Kid McCoy was conducting a potato race down the length of the South Corridor-the entrance fee a postage stamp, the prize sealed up in a large bandbox and warranted to be worth a quarter.

Patty, who was popular, had been invited to all four of the functions. She had declined Nancy's spread, because Mae Van Arsdale, her particular enemy, was invited; but had accepted the other invitations, and was busily spending the evening as an itinerant guest.

She carried her potato, insecurely balanced on a teaspoon, over one table and under another, through a hoop suspended from the ceiling, and deposited it in the wastebasket at the end of the corridor, in exactly two minutes and forty-seven seconds. (Kid McCoy had a stop-watch.) This was far ahead of anyone else's record, and Patty lingered hopefully a few minutes in the neighborhood of the bandbox; but a fresh inrush of entries postponed the bestowal of the prize, so she left the judges to settle the question at their leisure, and drifted on to Evalina's room.

She found it dark, except for the fitful blue flare of alcohol and salt burning in a fudge pan. The guests were squatting about on sofa cushions, looking decidedly spotty in the unbecoming light. Patty silently dropped down on a vacant cushion, and lent polite attention to Evalina, who at the moment held the floor.

"Well, you know, I had a very remarkable experience myself last summer. Happening to visit a spiritualist camp, I attended a materializing séance."

"What's that?" asked Rosalie Patton.

"A séance in which spirits appear to mediums in the material form they occupied dur ing life," Evalina condescendingly explained. Rosalie was merely an invited guest. She did not belong to the inner cult.

"Oh!" said Rosalie, vaguely enlightened.

"I didn't really expect anything to happen," Evalina continued, "and I was just thinking how foolish I was to have wasted that dollar, when the medium shut her eyes and commenced to tremble. She said she saw the spirit of a beautiful young girl who had passed over five years before. The girl was dressed in white and her clothes were dripping wet, and she carried in her hand a monkey-wrench."

"A monkey-wrench!" cried Patty. "What on earth —"

"I don't know any more than you do," said Evalina impatiently. "I'm just telling what happened. The Medium couldn't get her full name, but she said her first name commenced with 'S.' And instantly, it came over me that it was my Cousin Susan who fell into a well and was drowned. I hadn't thought of her for years, but the description answered perfectly. And I asked the me dium, and after a little, she said yes, it was Susan, and that she had come to send me a warning."

Evalina allowed an impressive pause to follow, while her auditors leaned forward in strained attention.

"A warning!" breathed Florence Hissop.

"Yes. She told me never to eat lemon pie."

Patty choked with sudden laughter. Evalina cast her a look and went on.

"The medium shivered again and came out of the trance, and she couldn't remember a thing she had said! When I told her about the monkey-wrench and the lemon pie, she was just as much puzzled as I was. She said that the messages that came from the spirit world were often inexplicable; though they might seem to deal with trivial things, yet in reality they contained a deep and hidden truth. Probably some day I would have an enemy who would try to poison me with lemon pie, and I must never, on *any* account, taste it again."

"And haven't you?" Patty asked.

"Never," said Evalina sadly.

Patty composed her features into an expression of scientific inquiry.

"Do you think the medium told the truth?"

"I've never had any cause to doubt it."

"Then you really believe in ghosts?"

"In spirits?" Evalina amended gently. "Many strange things happen that cannot be explained in any other manner."

"What would you do if her spirit should appear to you? Would you be scared?"

"Certainly not!" said Evalina, with dignity. "I was very fond of Cousin Susan. I have no cause to fear her spirit."

The smell of boiling molasses penetrated from below; Patty excused herself and turned toward the kitchen. The spiritual heights on which Evalina dwelt, she found a trifle too rare for ordinary breathing.

The candy was on the point of being poured into pans.

"Here, Patty!" Priscilla ordered, "you haven't done any work. Run down to the storeroom and get some butter to keep our hands from sticking."

Patty obligingly accompanied the cook to the cellar, with not a thought in the world beyond butter. On a shelf in the storeroom stood to-morrow's dessert —a row of fifteen lemon pies, with neatly decorated tops of white meringue. As Patty looked at them, she was suddenly assailed by a wicked temptation; she struggled with it for a moment of sanity, but in the end she fell. While Nora's head was bent over the butter tub, Patty opened the window and deftly plumped a pie through the iron grating onto the ledge without. By the time Nora raised her head, the window was shut again, and Patty was innocently translating the label on a bottle of olive oil.

As they pulled their candy in a secluded corner of the kitchen, Patty hilariously confided her plan to Conny and Priscilla. Conny was always game for whatever mischief was afoot, but Priscilla sometimes needed urging. She was-most inconveniently-beginning to develop a moral nature, and the other two, who as yet were comfortably un-moral, occasionally found her difficult to coerce.

Priscilla finally lent a grudging consent, while Conny enthusiastically volunteered to acquire a monkey-wrench. Being captain of sports, she could manage the matter better than Patty. On a flying visit to the stables, ostensibly to consult with Martin as to a re-marking of the tennis courts, she singled out from his tool bench the monkey-wrench of her choice, casually covered it with her sweater, and safely bore it away. She and Patty conveyed their booty by devious secret ways to Paradise Alley. A great many alarms were given on the passage, a great deal of muffled giggling ensued, but finally the monkey-wrench and the pie-slightly damaged as to its meringue top, but still distinctly recognizable as lemon-were safely cached under Patty's bed to await their part in the night's adventure.

"Lights-out" as usual, rang at nine-thirty, but it rang to deaf ears. A spirit of restless festivity was abroad. The little girls in the "Baby Ward" larked about the halls in a pillow fight, until they were sternly ordered to bed by the Dowager herself. It was close to ten o'clock when the candy-pullers washed their sticky hands and turned upstairs.

Patty found a delegation of potato racers waiting with the news that she had won the prize. An interested crowd gathered to watch her open the box; it contained a tin funeral wreath that had been displayed that winter in the window of the village undertaker-Kid had bought it cheap, owing to fly specks that would not rub off. The wreath was hoisted on the end of a shinny stick and marched through the corridor to the tune of "John Brown's Body," while Mademoiselle ineffectually wrung her hands and begged for quiet.

"*Mes chères enfantes* —it is ten o'clock. *Soyez tranquilles.* Patty —*Mon Dieu* —How you are bad! Margarite McCoy, you do not listen to me? *Nous verrons!* Go to your room, dis in-stant! You do not belong in my hall. Children! I implore. Go to bed-all —*tout de suite!*"

The procession cheered and marched on, until Miss Lord descended from the East and commanded silence. Miss Lord when incensed was effectual. The peace of conquest settled for a time over Paradise Alley, and she returned to her own camp. But a fresh hub-bub broke out, when it was discovered that someone had sprinkled granulated sugar, in liberal quantities, through every bed in the Alley. Patty and Conny would have been suspected, had their own sheets not yielded a plentiful harvest. It was another half hour before the beds were remade, and the school finally composed to sleep.

When the teacher on duty had made her last rounds, and everything was quiet, Patty turned back the covers of her bed and cautiously stepped to the floor. She was still fully clothed, except that she had changed her shoes for softer soled bedroom slippers, better fitted for nocturnal adventures. Priscilla and Conny joined her. Fortunately a full moon shone high in the sky, and they needed no artificial light. Aided by her two assistants, Patty draped the sheets of her bed about her into two voluminous wings, and fastened them securely with safety pins. A pillow slip was pulled over her head and the corners tied into ears. They hesitated a moment with scissors suspended.

"Hurry up and cut a nose," Patty whispered. "I'm smothering!"

"It seems sort of too bad to spoil a perfectly good pillow slip," said Priscilla, with a slight access of conscience.

"I'll drop some money in the missionary box," Patty promised.

The nose and eyes were cut; a grinning mouth and devilishly curved eyebrows were added with burnt cork. The pillow slip was tied firmly about her neck to allow no chance of slipping, the ears waved lopsidedly; she was the most amazing specter that ever left a respectable grave.

These preparations had occupied some time. It was already ten minutes of twelve.

"I'll wait till the stroke of midnight," said Patty. "Then I'll flutter into Evalina's room, and wave my wings, and whisper, 'Come!' The monkey-wrench and the pie, I'll leave on the foot of her bed, so she'll know she wasn't dreaming."

"What if she screams?" asked Priscilla.

"She won't scream. She loves ghosts-especially Cousin Susan. She said to-night she'd be glad to meet her."

"But what if she does scream?" persisted Priscilla.

"Oh, that's easy! I'll dash back and pop into bed. Before anybody wakes, I'll be sound asleep."

They made a reconnoitering excursion into the empty corridors to make sure that all was quiet. Only regular breathing issued from open doors. Evalina fortunately lived in a single, but unfortunately, it was at the extreme end of the East Wing in the opposite corner of the building from Patty's own domicile. Conny and Priscilla, in bedroom slippers and kimonos, tiptoed after Patty as she took her flight down the length of the Alley. She sailed back and forth and waved her wings in the moonlight that streamed through the skylight in the central hall. The two spectators clung together and shiv ered delightedly. In spite of having been behind the scenes and assisted at the make-up, they received a distinct sensation-what it would be to one suddenly wakened from sleep, to a believer in ghosts, they were a bit apprehensive to consider. At the entrance to the East Wing, they handed Patty her pie and monkey-wrench, and retreated to their own neighborhood. In case of an uproar, they did not wish to be discovered too far from home.

Patty flitted on down the corridor, past yawning doors, into Evalina's room, where she took up a central position in a patch of moonlight. A few sepulchral "Comes!" brought no response. Evalina was a sound sleeper.

Evalina sat up and clutched the bedclothes about her neck

Patty shook the foot of the bed. The sleeper stirred slightly but slept on. This was annoying. The ghost had no mind to make noise enough to disturb the neighbors. She laid the pie and the monkey-wrench on the counterpane, and shook the bed again, with the insistence of an earthquake. As she was endeavoring to resume her proper ties, Evalina sat up and clutched the bed clothes about her neck with a frenzied jerk. Patty just had time to save the pie-the monkey-wrench went to the floor with a crash; and the crash, to Patty's startled senses, was echoed and intensified from far down the hall. She had no chance to wave her wings or murmur, "Come." Evalina did not wait for her cue. She opened her mouth as wide as it would open, and emitted shriek after shriek of such ear-splitting intensity, that Patty, for a moment, was too aghast to move. Then, still hugging the pie in her arms, she turned and ran.

To her consternation the cries were answered ahead. The whole house seemed to be awake and shrieking. She could hear doors banging and frightened voices demanding the cause of the tumult. She was making a quick dash for her own room, trusting to the confusion and darkness to make good her escape, when Miss Lord, gaily attired in a flowered bath-robe, appeared at the end of the corridor. Patty was headed straight for her arms. With a gasp of terror, she turned back toward the shrieking Evalina.

She realized by now that she was in a trap.

A narrow passage led from the East Wing to the servants' quarters. She dived into this. If she could reach the back stairs it would mean safety. She pushed the door open a crack, and to her horror, was confronted by a worse uproar. The servants' quarters were in a state of panic. She saw Maggie dashing past, wrapped in a pink striped blanket, while above the general confusion rose Norah's rich brogue:

"Help! Murther! I seen a bur-r-gu-lar!"

She shut the door and shrank back into the passage. Behind her Evalina was still hysterically wailing:

"I saw a ghost! I saw a ghost!"

Before her the cry of "Burglars!" was growing louder.

Utterly bewildered at this double demonstration, Patty flattened herself against the wall in the friendly darkness of the passage, while she soulfully thanked Heaven that the proposed electric lights had not yet been installed. A dozen voices were calling for matches, but no one seemed to find any. She pantingly tugged at the pillowcase fastened about her neck; but Conny had tied it firmly with a white hair ribbon, and the knot was behind. In any case, even if she could remove her masquerade, she was lost if they found her; for she was still wearing the white dress of the evening, and not even Patty's imagination could compass an excuse for that at twelve o'clock at night.

The search was growing nearer; she caught the glimmer of a light ahead. At any moment they might open the door of the passage. The linen closet was the only refuge at hand-and that was very temporary. She felt for the door handle and slipped inside. If she could find a pile of sheets, she might dive to the bottom and hope to escape notice, being mostly sheet herself. But it was Saturday, and all the linen had gone down. A long, slippery, inclined chute connected the room with the laundry in the basement two floors below. Steps were already audible in the passage. She heard Miss Lord's voice say:

"Bring a light! We'll search the linen closet."

Patty did not hesitate. In imagination she could already feel the pressure of Miss Lord's grasp upon her shoulder. A broken neck was preferable.

Still hugging the lemon pie-in all her excitement she had clasped it firmly-she climbed into the chute, stretched her feet out straight in front, and pushed off. For two breathless seconds she dashed through space, then her feet hit the trap door at the bottom, and she shot into the laundry.

One instant earlier, the door from the kitchen stairs had cautiously opened, and a man had darted into the laundry. He had just had time to cast a glance of boundless relief about the empty, moonlit room, when Patty and the pie catapulted against him. They went down together in a whirl of waving wings. Patty being on top picked her self up first. She still clutched her pie-at least what was left of it; the white meringue was spread over the man's hair and face; but the lemon part was still intact. The man sat up dazedly, rubbed the meringue from his eyes, cast one look at his assailant, and staggered to his feet. He flattened himself against the wall with arms thrown wide for support.

"Holy gee!" he choked. "What in hell uv I got into?"

Patty excused his language, as he did not appear to know that he was addressing a lady. He seemed to be laboring under the impression that she was the devil.

Her pillow slip by now was very much askew; one ear pointed northward, the other southeast, and she could only see out of one eye. It was very hot inside and she was gasping for breath. For a palpitating moment they merely stared and panted. Then Patty's mind began to work.

"I suppose," she suggested, "you are the burglar they are screaming about?"

The man leaned back limply and stared, his wide, frightened eyes shining through a fringe of meringue.

"I," said Patty, completing the introduction, "am the ghost."

He muttered something under his breath. She could not make out whether he was praying or swearing.

"Don't be afraid," she added kindly. "I won't hurt you."

"Is it a bloomin' insane asylum?"

"Just a girl's school."

"Gosh!" he observed.

"Hush!" said Patty. "They're coming this way now!"

The sound of running feet became audible in the kitchen above, while bass voices were added to the shrill soprano that had sounded the former tocsin. The men had arrived from the stables. The burglar and the ghost regarded each other for a moment of suspended breathing; their mutual danger drew them together. Patty hesitated an instant, while she studied his face as it showed through the interstices of the meringue. He had honest blue eyes and yellow curls. She suddenly stretched out a hand and grasped him by an elbow.

"Quick! They'll be here in a minute. I know a place to hide. Come with me."

She pushed him unresisting down a passage and into a storeroom, boarded off from the main cellar, where the scenery of the dramatic society was kept.

"Get down on your hands and knees and follow me," she ordered, as she stooped low and dived behind a pile of canvas.

The man crawled after. They emerged at the farther end into a small recess behind some canvas trees. Patty sat on a stump and offered a wooden rock to her companion.

"They'll never think of looking here," she whispered. "Martin's too fat to crawl through."

A small barred window let in some faint moonlight and they had an opportunity to study each other more at leisure. The man did not yet seem comfortable in Patty's presence; he was occupying the farthest possible corner of his rock. Presently he rubbed his coat sleeve over his head and looked long and earnestly at the meringue. He was evidently at a loss to identify the substance; in the rush of events he had taken no note of the pie.

Patty brought her one eye to bear down upon him.

"I'm simply melting!" she whispered. "Do you think you could untie that knot?"

She bent her head and presented the back of her neck.

The man by now was partially reassured as to the humanness of his companion, and he obediently worked at the knot but with hands that trembled. At last it came loose, and Patty with a sigh of relief emerged into the open. Her hair was somewhat tousled and her face was streaked with burnt cork, but her blue eyes were as honest as his own. The sight reassured him.

"Gee!" he muttered in a wave of relief.

"Keep still!" Patty warned.

The hunt was growing nearer. There was the sound of tramping feet in the laundry and they could hear the men talking.

"A ghost and a burglar!" said Martin, in fine scorn. "That's a likely combination, ain't it now?"

They made an obligatory and superficial search through the coal cellar. Martin jocularly inquiring:

"Did ye look in the furnace, Mike? Here Osaki, me lad, ye're small. Take a crawl oop the poipes and see if the ghost ain't hidin' there."

They opened the door of the property-room and glanced inside. The burglar ducked his head and held his breath, while Patty struggled with an ill-timed desire to giggle. Martin was in a facetious mood. He whistled in the manner of calling a dog.

"Here, Ghostie! Here, Burgie! Come here, old fellow!"

They banged the door shut and their footsteps receded. Patty was rocking back and forth in a species of hysterics, stuffing the corner of the sheet into her mouth to keep from laughing audibly. The burglar's teeth were chattering.

"Lord!" he breathed. "It may be funny for you, Miss. But it means the penitentiary for me."

Patty interrupted her hysterics and regarded him with disgust.

"It would mean expulsion for me, or at least something awfully unpleasant. But that's no reason for going all to pieces. You're a nice sort of a burglar! Brace up and be a sport!"

He mopped his brow and removed another portion of icing.

"You must be an awful amateur to break into a house like this," she said contemptuously. "Don't you know the silver's plated?"

"I didn't know nuthin' about it," he said sullenly. "I see the window open over the shed roof and I clum up. I was hungry and was lookin' for somethin' to eat. I ain't had nothin' since yesterday mornin'."

Patty reached to the floor beside her.

"Have some pie."

The man ducked aside as it was poked at him.

"W-what's that?" he gasped.

He was as nervous as a mouse in a cage.

"Lemon pie. It looks a little messy but it's all right. The only thing the matter with it is that it has lost its meringue top. That's mostly on your head. The rest of it is spread over me and the laundry floor and Evalina Smith's bed and the clothes chute."

"Oh!" he murmured in evident relief, as he rubbed his hand over his hair for the fourth time. "I was wonderin' what the blame stuff was."

"But the lemon's all here," she urged. "You'd better eat it. It's quite nourishing, I believe."

He accepted the pie and fell to eating it with an eagerness that carried out the truth of his assertion as to yesterday's breakfast.

Patty watched him, her natural curiosity struggling with her acquired politeness. The curiosity triumphed.

"Do you mind telling me how you came to be a burglar? You make such a remarkably bad one, that I should think you would have chosen almost any other profession."

He told his story between bites. To one more experienced in police records, it might have sounded a trifle fishy, but he had an honest face and blue eyes, and it never entered her head to doubt him. The burglar commenced it sullenly; no one had ever believed him yet and he wasn't expecting her to. He would like to have invented something a little more plausible, but he lacked the imagination to tell a convincing lie. So, as usual, he lamely told the truth.

Patty listened with strained attention. His tale was somewhat muffled by lemon pie, and his vocabulary did not always coincide with her own, but she managed to get the gist of it.

By rights he was a gardener. In the last place where he worked he used to sleep in the attic, because the gentleman he was away a lot, and the lady she was afraid not to have a man in the house. And a gas-fitter, that he had always thought was his friend, give him some beer one night and got him drunk, and took away the key of the back door. And while he (the gardener) was sound asleep on the children's sand pile under the apple tree in the back yard, the gas-fitter entered the house and stole an overcoat and a silver coffee-pot and a box of cigars and a bottle of whisky and two umbrellas. And they proved it on him (the gardener) and he was sent up for two years. And when he come out, no one wouldn't give him no work.

"An' ye can't make me believe," he added bitterly, "that that beer wasn't doped!"

"Oh, but it was terrible of you to get drunk!" said Patty, shocked.

"'Twas an accident," he insisted.

"If you are *sure* that you'll never do it again," she said, "I'll get you a job. But you must promise, on your word of honor as a gentleman. You know I couldn't recommend a drunkard."

The man grinned feebly.

"I guess ye'll not be findin' anybody that will be wantin' a jailbird."

"Oh, yes, I will! I know exactly the man. He's a friend of mine, and he likes jailbirds. He realizes that it's only luck that made him a millionaire instead of a convict. He always gives a man a chance to start again. He used to have a murderer in charge of his greenhouses, and a cattle thief to milk the cows. I'm sure he'll like you. Come with me, and I'll write you a letter of introduction."

Patty gathered her sheets about her and prepared to crawl out.

"What are ye doin'?" he demanded quickly. "Y' aren't goin' to hand me over?"

"Is it likely?" She regarded him with scorn. "How could I hand you over, without handing myself over at the same time?"

The logic of this appealed to him, and he followed meekly on hands and knees. She approached the laundry door and listened warily; the search had withdrawn to other quarters. She led the way along a passage and up a flight of stairs and slipped into the deserted kindergarten room.

"We're safe here," she whispered. "They've already searched it."

She cast about for writing materials. No ink was to be found, but she discovered a red crayon pencil, and tore a sheet of paper from a copy book. "Honesty is the best policy," was inscribed in flowing characters at the top.

She hesitated with her crayon poised.

"If I get you a nice job in charge of onions and orchids and things, will you promise never again to drink any beer?"

"Sure," he agreed, but without much enthusiasm.

There was a light of uneasiness in his eye. Nothing in his past experience tallied with to-night's adventure; and he suspected an ambush.

"Because," said Patty, "it would be awfully embarrassing for me if you did get drunk. I should never dare recommend another burglar."

She wrote her note on the window ledge, by moonlight, and read it aloud:

"*Dear Mr. Weatherby*, —

"Do you remember the conversation we had the day I ran away and dropped into your onion garden? You said you thought criminals were often quite as good as the rest of us, and that you would find a job for any convict friend I might present. This is to introduce a burglar of my acquaintance who would like to secure a position as gardener. He was trained to be a gardener and much prefers it to burglaring, but finds it difficult to find a place because he has been in prison. He is faithful, honest and industrious, and promises to be sober. I shall appreciate any favor you may show him.

"Sincerely yours,

"Patty Wyatt."

"P. S. —Please excuse this red crayon. I am writing at midnight, by moonlight in the kindergarten room, and the ink's all locked up. The burglar will explain the circumstances, which are too complicated to write.

"Yours ever,

"P. W."

She enclosed her note in a large manila envelope that had contained weaving mats, and addressed it to Silas Weatherby, Esq. The man received it gingerly. He seemed to think that it might go off.

"What's the matter?" said Patty. "Are you afraid of it?"

"Ye're sure," he asked suspiciously, "that Silas Weatherby ain't a cop?"

"He's a railroad president."

"Oh!" The burglar looked relieved.

Patty unlocked the window, then paused for a final moral lecture.

"I am giving you a chance to begin again. If you are game, and present this letter, you'll get a job. If you're a coward, and don't dare present it, you can keep on being a burglar for the rest of your life for all I care-and a mighty poor one you'll make!"

She opened the window and waved her hand invitingly toward the outside world.

"Good-by, Miss," he said.

"Good-by," said Patty cordially. "And good luck!"

He paused, half in, half out, for a last reassurance.

"Ye're sure it's on the straight, Miss? Y' ain't pitchin' me no curve?"

"It's on the straight." She pledged her word. "I ain't pitchin' you no curve."

Patty crept upstairs the back way, and by a wide detour avoided the excited crowd still gathered in the East Wing. A fresh hub -bub had arisen, for Evalina Smith had found a monkey-wrench on the floor of her room. It was shown to the scoffing Martin as visible proof that the burglar had been there.

"An it's me own wrench!" he cried in wide-eyed amazement. "Now, what do ye think of his nerve?"

Patty hurriedly undressed and tumbled into a kimono. Sleepily rubbing her eyes, she joined the assemblage in the hall.

"What's happened?" she asked, blinking at the lights. "Has there been a fire?"

A chorus of laughter greeted the question.

"It's a burglar!" said Conny, exhibiting the wrench.

"Oh, *why* didn't you wake me?" Patty wailed. "I've wanted all my life to see a burglar."

* * * * *

Two weeks later, a groom arrived on horseback with a polite note for the Dowager.

Mr. Weatherby presented his compliments to Mrs. Trent, and desired the pleasure of showing the young ladies of the Senior class through his art gallery on Friday next at four o'clock.

The Dowager was at a loss to account for this gratuitous courtesy on the part of her hitherto unneighborly neighbor. After a moment of deliberation, she decided to meet him half way; and the groom rode back with an equally polite acceptance.

On Friday next, as the school hearse turned in at the gates of Weatherby Hall, the owner stood on the portico waiting to welcome his guests. If there were a shade more *empressement* in his greeting to Patty than to her companions, the Dowager did not notice it.

He made an exceptionally attentive host. In person he conducted them through the gallery and pointed out the famous Botticelli. Tea was served at little tables set on the western terrace. Each girl found a gardenia at her plate and a silver bonbonnière with the St. Ursula monogram on the cover. After tea their host suggested a visit to the Italian garden. As they strolled through the paths, Patty found herself walking beside him and the Dowager. His conversation was addressed to Mrs. Trent, but an occasional amused glance was directed toward Patty. They turned a corner behind a marble pavilion, and came upon a fountain and a gardener man, intent upon a border of maiden-hair ferns.

"I have a very remarkable new Swedish gardener," Mr. Weatherby casually remarked to the Dowager. "The man is a genius at making plants grow. He came highly recommended. Oscar!" he called. "Bring the ladies some of those tulips."

The man dropped his watering-can, and approached, hat in hand. He was a golden-haired, blue-eyed young chap with an honest smile. He presented his flowers, first to the elder lady and then to Patty. As he caught her interested gaze, a light of comprehension suddenly leaped to his eyes. Her costume and make-up to-day were so very dissimilar to those which she had assumed on the occasion of their first meeting, that recognition on his part had not been instantaneous.

Patty fell back a step to receive her flowers and the others strolled on.

"I have to thank ye, Miss," he said gratefully, "for the finest job I ever had. It's all right!"

"You know now," Patty laughed, "that I didn't pitch you no curves?"

Chapter XII The Gypsy Trail

Heels together. Hips firm, one, two, three, four-Irene McCullough! *Will* you keep your shoulders back and your stomach in? How many times must I tell you to stand straight? That's better! We'll start again. One, two, three, four."

The exercise droned on. Some twenty of the week's delinquents were working off demerits. It was uncongenial work for a sunny Saturday. The twenty pairs of eyes gazed beyond Miss Jellings' head-across ropes and rings and parallel bars-toward the green tree tops and the blue sky; and twenty girls, for that brief hour, regretted their past badnesses.

Miss Jellings herself seemed to be a bit on edge. She snapped out her orders with a curtness that brought a jerkily quick response from forty waving Indian clubs. As she stood straight and slim in her gymnasium suit, her cheeks flushed with exercise, she looked quite as young as any of her pupils. But if she appeared young, she also appeared determined. No instructor in the school, not even Miss Lord in Latin, kept stricter discipline.

"One, two, three, four-Patty Wyatt! Keep your eyes to the front. It isn't necessary for you to watch the clock. I shall dismiss the class when I am ready. Over your heads. One, two, three, four." Finally, when nerves were almost at the breaking point, came the grateful order, "Attention! Right about face. March. Clubs in racks. Double quick. Halt. Break ranks."

With a relieved whoop, the class dispersed.

"Thank heaven, there's only one more week of it!" Patty breathed, as they regained their own quarters in Paradise Alley.

"Good-by to Gym forever!" Conny waved a slipper over her head. "Hooray!"

"Isn't Jelly awful?" Patty demanded, still smarting from the recent insult. "She never used to be so bad. What on earth has got into her?"

"She is pretty snappy," Priscilla agreed. "But I like her just the same. She's so-so sort of *spirited*, you know-like a skittish horse."

"Urn," growled Patty. "I'd like to see a good, big, husky man get the upper hand of Jelly once, and *just make her toe the mark!*"

"You two will have to hurry," Priscilla warned, "if you want to get into your costumes up here. Martin starts in half an hour."

"We'll be ready!" Patty was already plunging her face into an inky mixture in the wash bowl.

The fancy-dress lawn fête, which St. Ursula's School held on the last Friday in every May, had occurred the evening before; and this afternoon the girls were redonning their costumes to make a trip to the village photographer's. The complicated costumes, that required time and space for their proper adjustment, were to be assumed at the school and driven down in the hearse. Those more simple of arrangement were to go in the trolley car, and be donned in the cramped quarters of the gallery dressing-room.

Patty and Conny, whose make-up was a very delicate matter, were dressing at the school. They had gone as Gypsies-not comic opera Gypsies, but real Gypsies, dirty and ragged and patched. (They had daily dusted the room with their costumes for a week before the fête.) Patty wore one brown stocking and one black, with a conspicuous hole in the right calf. Conny's toes protruded from one shoe, and the sole of the other flapped. Their hair was unkempt and the stain on their faces streaked. They were the last word in realism.

They scrambled into their dresses to-day with little ceremony, and hitched them together anyhow. Conny caught up a tambourine and Patty a worn-out pack of cards, and they clattered down the tin-covered back stairs. In the lower hall they came face to face with Miss Jellings, clothed in cool muslin, and in a more affable frame of mind. Patty never held her grudges long; she had already forgotten her momentary indignation at not being allowed to look at the clock.

"You cross-a my hand with silver? I tell-a your fortune."

She danced up to the gymnasium teacher with a flutter of scarlet petticoats, and poked out a dirty hand.

"Nice-a fortune," Conny added with a persuasive rattle of the tambourine. "Tall, dark-a young man."

"You impudent little ragamuffins!" Miss Jellings took them each by the shoulder and turned them for inspection. "What have you done to your faces?"

"Washed 'em in black coffee."

Miss Jellings shook her head and laughed.

"You're a disgrace to the school!" she pronounced. "Don't let any policeman see you, or he'll arrest you for vagabonds."

"Patty! Conny! —Hurry up. The hearse is starting."

Priscilla appeared in the doorway and waved her gridiron frantically. Priscilla, late about finding a costume, at the last moment had blasphemously gone as St. Laurence, draped in a sheet, with the kitchen broiler under her arm.

"We're coming! Tell him to wait." Patty dashed out.

"Don't you want a coat?" Conny shrieked after her.

"No-come on-we don't need coats."

The two raced down the drive after the wagonette-Martin never waited for laggards; he let them run and catch up. They sprang onto the rear step; and half-a-dozen outstretched hands hauled them in, head first.

They found the photographer's waiting-room a scene of the maddest confusion. When sixty excited people occupy the normal space of twelve, the effect is not restful.

"Did anyone bring a button-hook?"

"Lend me some powder."

"That's *my* safety-pin!"

"Where'd you put the burnt cork?"

"Is my hair a perfect sight?"

"Fasten me up-please!"

"Does my petticoat show?"

Everybody babbled at once, and nobody listened.

"I say, let's get out of this —I'm simply roasting!"

St. Laurence seized the Gypsies by the shoulder and shoved them into the vacant gallery. They squeezed themselves, with a sigh of relief, onto a shaky flight of six narrow stairs before the breezes of an open window.

"I know exactly what ails Jelly!" Patty spoke with the air of carrying on a conversation.

"What?" asked the others, with interest.

"She's had a quarrel with that Laurence Gilroy man who is manager at the electric light place. Don't you remember how he used to be hanging about all the time? And now he never comes at all? He was out every day in the Christmas vacation. They used to go walking together-and without any chaperone, too! You would think the Dowager would have made an awful fuss, but she didn't seem to. Anyway, you should have seen the way Miss Jellings treated that man-it was *per-fect-ly dreadful!* The way she jumps on Irene McCullough is *nothing* to the way she jumped on him."

"*He* doesn't have to work off demerits. He's a fool to stand it," said Conny simply.

"He doesn't stand it any more."

"How do you know?"

"Well, I —sort of heard. I was in the library alcove one day in the Christmas vacation, reading the 'Murders in the Rue Morgue,' when Jelly and Mr. Gilroy walked in. They didn't see me, and I didn't pay any attention to them at first —I'd just got to the place where the detective says, 'Is that the mark of a *human* hand?' —but pretty soon they got to scrapping so that I couldn't help but hear, and I felt sort of embarrassed about interrupting."

"What did they say?" asked Conny, impatiently brushing aside her apologies.

"I didn't grasp it entirely. He was trying to explain about something, and she wouldn't listen to a word he said-she was *perfectly horrid.* You know, —the way she is when she says, 'I understand it perfectly. I don't care to hear any excuse. You may take ten demerits, and report on Saturday for extra gymnasium.'—Well, they kept that up for fifteen minutes, both of 'em getting stiffer and stiffer. Then he took his hat and went. And you know, I don't believe he ever came back—*I've* never seen him. And now, she's sorry. She's been as cross as a bear ever since."

"And she can be awfully nice," said Priscilla.

"Yes, she *can*," said Patty. "But she's too cocky. I'd just like to see that man come back, and show her her place!"

The masqueraders trooped in and the serious business of the day commenced. The school posed as a whole, then an infinity of smaller groups disentangled themselves and posed separately, while those who were not in the picture stood behind the camera and made the others laugh.

"Young ladies!" the exasperated photographer implored. "Will you kindly be quiet for just two seconds? You have made me spoil three plates. And will that monk on the end stop giggling? Now! All ready. Please keep your eyes on the stove-pipe hole, and hold your positions while I count three. One, two, three-thank you very much!"

He removed his plate with a flourish, and dove into the dark room.

It was Patty's and Conny's turn to be taken alone, but St. Ursula and her Eleven Thousand Virgins were clamoring for precedence on the ground of superior numbers, and they made such a turmoil that the two Gypsies politely stood aside.

Keren Hersey, as St. Ursula, and eleven little Junior A's—each playing the manifold part of a Thousand Virgins-made up the group. It was to be a symbolical picture, Keren explained.

When the Gypsies' turn came a second time, Patty had the misfortune to catch her dress on a nail and tear a three-cornered rent in the front. It was too large a hole for even a Gypsy to carry off with propriety; she retired to the dressing-room and fastened the edges together with white basting thread.

Finally, last of all, they presented themselves in their dirt and tatters. The photographer was an artist, and he received them with appreciative delight. The others had been patently masqueraders, but these were the real thing. He photographed them dancing, and wandering on a lonely moor with threatening canvas clouds behind them. He was about to take them in a forest, with a camp fire, and a boiling kettle slung from three sticks-when Conny suddenly became aware of a brooding quiet that had settled on the place.

"Where is everybody?"

She returned from a hasty excursion into the waiting-room, divided between consternation and laughter.

"Patty! The hearse has gone!—And the street-car people are waiting on the corner by Marsh and Elkins's."

"Oh, the beasts! They knew we were in here." Patty dropped her three sticks and rose precipitately. "Sorry!" she called to the photographer, who was busily dusting off the kettle. "We've got to run for it."

"And we haven't any coats!" wailed Conny. "Miss Wadsworth won't take us in the car in these clothes."

"She'll have to," said Patty simply. "She can't leave us on the corner."

They clattered downstairs, but wavered an instant in the friendly darkness of the doorway; there was no time, however, for maidenly hesitations, and taking their courage in both hands, they plunged into the Saturday afternoon crowd that thronged Main Street.

"Oh, Mama! Quick! Look at the Gypsies," a little boy squealed as the two pushed past.

"Heavens!" Conny whispered. "I feel like a circus parade."

"Hurry!" Patty panted, taking her by the hand and beginning to run. "The car's stopped and they're getting in-Wait! Wait!" She frenziedly waved the tambourine above her head.

An express wagon at the crossing blocked their progress. The last of the Eleven Thousand Virgins climbed aboard, without once glancing over her shoulder; and the car, unheeding, clanged away, and became a yellow spot in the distance. The two Gypsies stood on the corner and stared at one another in blank interrogation.

"I haven't a cent-have you?"

"Not one."

"How are we going to get home?"

"I haven't an idea."

Patty felt her elbow jostled. She turned to find young John Drew Dominick Murphy, a protégé of the school, and an intimate acquaintance of her own, regarding her with impish delight.

"Hey, youse! Give us a song and dance."

"At least our friends don't recognize us," said Conny, drawing what comfort she could from her incognito.

Quite a crowd had gathered by now, and it was rapidly growing larger. Pedestrians had to make a detour into the street in order to get past.

"It wouldn't take us long," said Patty, a spark of mischief breaking through the blankness of her face, "to earn money enough for a carriage-you thump the tambourine and I'll dance the sailor's hornpipe."

"Patty! Behave yourself." Conny for once brought a dampening supply of common sense to bear on her companion. "We're going to graduate in another week. For goodness' sake, *don't* let's get expelled first."

She grasped her by the elbow and shoved her insistently down a side street. John Drew Murphy and his friends followed for several blocks, but having gazed their fill, and perceiving that the Gypsies had no entertainment to offer, they gradually dropped away.

"Well, what shall we do?" asked Conny when they had finally shaken off the last of the small boys.

"I s'pose we could walk."

"Walk!" Conny exhibited her flapping sole. "You don't expect me to walk three miles in that shoe?"

"Very well," said Patty. "What *shall* we do?"

"We might go back to the photographer's and borrow some car-fare."

"No! I'm not going to parade myself the length of Main Street again with *that* hole in my stocking."

"Very well," Conny shrugged. "Think of something."

"I suppose we could go to the livery stable and—"

"It's on the other side of town—I can't flap all that distance. Every time I take a step, I have to lift my foot ten inches high."

"Very well." It was Patty's turn to shrug. "Perhaps you can think of something better?"

"I think the simplest way would be to take a car, and ask the conductor to charge it to us."

"Yes-and explain for the benefit of all the passengers that we belong at St. Ursula's School? It would be all over town by night, and the Dowager would be furious."

"Very well-what shall we do?"

They were standing at the moment before a comfortable frame house with three children romping on the veranda. The children left off their play to come to the top of the steps and stare.

"Come on!" Patty urged. "We'll sing the 'Gypsy Trail.'" (This was the latest song that had swept the school.) "I'll play an accompaniment on the tambourine, and you can flap your sole. Maybe they'll give us ten cents. It would be a beautiful lark to earn our car-fare home—I'm *sure* it's worth ten cents to hear me sing."

Conny glanced up and down the deserted street. No policeman was in sight. She grudgingly allowed herself to be drawn up the walk, and the music began. The children applauded loudly; and the two were just congratulating themselves on a very credible performance, when the door opened and a woman appeared—a first cousin to Miss Lord.

"Stop that noise immediately! There's somebody sick inside."

The tone also was reminiscent of Latin. They turned and ran as fast as Conny's flapping sole would take her. When they had put three good blocks between themselves and the Latin woman, they dropped down on a friendly stepping-stone, and leaned against each other's shoulders and laughed.

A man rounded the corner of the house before them, pushing a mowing machine.

"Here, you!" he ordered. "Move on."

They got up, meekly, and moved on several blocks further. They were going in exactly the opposite direction from St. Ursula's school, but they couldn't seem to hit on anything else to do, so they kept on moving mechanically. They had arrived in the outskirts of the village by now, and they presently found themselves face to face with a tall chimney and a group of low buildings set in a wide enclosure-the water-works and electric plant.

A light of hope dawned in Patty's eyes.

"I'll tell you! We'll go and ask Mr. Gilroy to take us home in his automobile."

"Do you know him?" Conny asked dubiously. She had received so many affronts that she was growing timid.

"Yes! I know him *intimately*. He was under foot every minute during the Christmas vacation. We had a snow fight one day. Come on! He'll love to run us out. It will give him an excuse to make up with Jelly."

They passed up a narrow tarred walk toward the brick building labeled "Office." Four clerks and a typewriter girl in the outer office interrupted their work to laugh as the two apparitions appeared in the door. The young man nearest them whirled his chair around in order to get a better view.

"Hello, girls!" he said with cheerful familiarity. "Where'd you spring from?"

The typewriter, meanwhile, was making audible comments upon the discrepancies in Patty's hosiery.

Patty's face flushed darkly under the coffee.

"We have called to see Mr. Gilroy," she said with dignity.

"This is Mr. Gilroy's busy day," the young man grinned. "Wouldn't you rather talk to me?"

Patty drew herself up haughtily.

"Please tell Mr. Gilroy—*at once*—that we are waiting to speak to him."

"Certainly! I *beg* your pardon." The young man sprang to his feet with an air of elaborate politeness. "Will you kindly give me your cards?"

"I don't happen to have a card with me to-day. Just say that two ladies wish to speak with him."

"Ah, yes. One moment, please-Won't you be seated?"

He offered his own chair to Patty, and bringing forward another, presented it to Conny with a Chesterfieldian bow. The clerks tittered delightedly at this bit of comedy acting, but the Gypsies did not condescend to think it funny. They accepted the chairs with a frigid, "Thank you," and sat stiffly upright staring at the wastebasket in their most distant society manner. While the deferential young man was conveying the message to the private office of his chief, public comment advanced from Patty's stockings to Conny's shoes. He returned presently, and with unruffled politeness invited them please to step this way. He ushered them in with a bow.

Mr. Gilroy was writing, and it was a second before he glanced up. His eyes widened with astonishment-the clerk had delivered the message verbatim. He leaned back in his chair and studied the ladies from head to foot, then emitted a curt:

"Well?"

There was not a trace of recognition in his glance.

Patty's only intention had been to announce their identity, and invite him to deliver them at St. Ursula's door, but Patty was incapable of approaching any matter by the direct route when a labyrinth was also available. She drew a deep breath, and to Conny's consternation, plunged into the labyrinth.

"You Mr. Laurence K. Gilroy?" she dropped a curtsy. "I come find-a you."

"So I see," said Mr. Laurence K. Gilroy, dryly. "And now that you've found me, what do you want?"

"I want tell-a your fortune," Patty glibly dropped into the lingo she and Conny had practised on the school the night before. "You cross-a my hand with silver —I tell-a your fortune."

This was no situation of Conny's choosing, but she was always staunchly game.

"Nice-a fortune," she backed Patty up. "Tall young lady. Ver' beautiful."

"Well, of all the nerve!"

Mr. Gilroy leaned back in his chair and regarded them severely, but with a gleam of amusement flickering through.

"Where did you get my name?" he demanded.

Patty waved her hand airily toward the open window and the distant horizon-as it showed between the coal sheds and the dynamo building.

"Gypsy peoples, dey learn signs," she explained lucidly. "Sky, wind, clouds-all talk-but you no understand. I get message for you-Mr. Laurence K. Gilroy-and we come from long-a way off to tell-a your fortune." With a pathetic little gesture, she indicated their damaged foot gear. "Ver' tired. We travel far."

Mr. Gilroy put his hand in his pocket and produced two silver half dollars.

"Here's your money. Now be honest! What sort of a bunco game is this? And where in thunder did you get my name?"

They pocketed the money, dropped two more curtsies, and evaded inconvenient questions.

"We tell-a your fortune," said Conny, with business-like directness. She brought out the pack of cards, plumped herself cross-legged on the floor, and dealt them out in a wide circle. Patty seized the gentleman's hand in her two coffee-stained little paws, and turned it palm up for inspection. He made an embarrassed effort to draw away, but she clung with the tenacious grip of a monkey.

"I see a lady!" she announced with promptitude.

"Tall young lady-brown eyes, yellow hair, ver' beautiful," Conny echoed from the floor, as she leaned forward and intently studied the queen of hearts.

"But she make-a you lot of trouble," Patty added, frowning over a blister on his hand. "I see li'l' quarrel."

Mr. Gilroy's eyes narrowed. In spite of himself, he commenced to be interested.

"You like-a her very much," pronounced Conny from below.

"But you never see her any more," chimed in Patty. "One-two-three-four months, you no see her, no spik with her." She looked up into his startled eyes. *"But you think about her every day!"*

He made a quick movement of withdrawal, and Patty hastily added a further detail.

"Dat tall young lady, she ver' unhappy too. She no laugh no more like she used."

He arrested the movement and waited with a touch of anxious curiosity to hear what was coming next.

"She feel ver' bad-ver' cross, ver' unhappy. She thinks always 'bout that li'l' quarrel. Four months she sit and wait-but you never come back."

Mr. Gilroy rose abruptly and strode to the window.

His unexpected visitors had dropped from the sky at the psychological moment. For two straight hours that afternoon he had been sitting at his desk grappling with the problem, which they, in their broken English, were so ably handling. Should he swallow a great deal of pride, and make another plea for justice? St. Ursula's vacation was at hand; in a few days more she would be gone-and very possibly she would never come back. The world at large was full of men, and Miss Jellings had a taking way.

Conny continued serenely to study her cards.

"One-More-Chance!" She spoke with the authority of a Grecian sibyl. "You try again, you win. No try, you lose."

Patty leaned over Conny's shoulder, eager to supply a salutary bit of advice.

"Dat tall young lady too much —" she hesitated a moment for fitting expression —"too much head in air. Too *bossy*. You make-a her mind? Understand?"

Conny, gazing at the round-faced, chubby Jack of Diamonds, had received a new idea.

"I see 'nother man," she murmured. "Red hair and-and —*fat*. Not too good-looking but —"

"*Very dangerous!*" interpolated Patty. "You have no time to waste. He comes soon."

Now, they had fabricated this detail out of nothing in the world but pure fancy and the Jack of Diamonds, but as it happened, they had touched an open wound. It was an exact description of a certain rich young man in the neighboring city, who loaded Miss Jellings with favors, and whom Mr. Gilroy detested from the bottom of his soul. All that afternoon, mixed in with his promptings and hesitations and travail of spirit, had loomed large, the fair, plump features of his fancied rival. Mr. Gilroy was a common-sense young business man, as free as most from superstition; but when a man's in love he is open to omens.

He stared fixedly about the familiar office and out at the coal sheds and dynamo, to make sure that he was still on solid earth. His gaze came back to his visitors from the sky in absolute, anxious, pleading bewilderment.

They were studying the cards again in a frowning endeavor to wrest a few further items from their overtaxed imaginations. Patty felt that she had already given him fifty cents' worth, and was wondering how to bring the interview to a graceful end. She realized that they had carried the farce too impertinently far, ever to be able to announce their identity and suggest a ride home. The only course now, was to preserve their incognito, make good their escape, and get back as best they could-at least they had a dollar to aid in the journey!

She glanced up, mentally framing a peroration.

"I see good-a fortune," she commenced, "if—"

Her glance passed him to the open window, and her heart missed a beat. Mrs. Trent and Miss Sarah Trent, come to complain about the new electric lights, were serenely descending from their carriage, not twenty feet away.

Patty's hand clutched Conny's shoulder in a spasmodic grasp.

"Sallie and the Dowager!" she hissed in her ear. "Follow me!"

With a sweep of her hand, Patty scrambled the cards together and rose. There would be no chance to escape by the door; the Dowager's voice was already audible in the outer office.

"Goo' by!" said Patty, springing to the window. "Gypsies call. We must go."

She scrambled over the sill and dropped eight feet to the ground. Conny followed. They were both able pupils of Miss Jellings.

Mr. Laurence K. Gilroy, open-mouthed, stood staring at the spot where they had been. The next instant, he was bowing courteously to the principals of St. Ursula's, and striving hard to concentrate a dazed mind upon the short-circuit in the West Wing.

Patty and Conny left the car-and a number of interested passengers-at the corner before they reached the school. Circumnavigating the wall, until they were opposite the stables, they approached the house modestly by the back way. They had the good fortune to encounter no one more dangerous than the cook (who gave them some gingerbread) and they ultimately reached their home in Paradise Alley none the worse for the adventure-and ninety cents to the good.

* * * * *

When the long, light evenings came, St. Ursula's no longer filled in the interim between dinner and evening study with indoor dancing, but romped about on the lawn outside. To-night, being Saturday, there was no evening study to call them in, and everybody was abroad. The school year was almost over, the long vacation was at hand-the girls were as full of bubbling spirits as sixty-four young lambs. Games of blindman's-buff, and pussy-wants-a-corner, and cross-tag were all in progress at once. A band of singers on the gymnasium steps was drowning out a smaller band on the porte-cochère; half-a-dozen hoop-rollers were trotting around the oval, and scattered groups of strollers, meeting in the narrow paths, were hailing each other with cheerful calls.

Patty and Conny and Priscilla, washed and dressed and chastened, were wandering arm in arm through the summer twilight, talking—a trifle soberly-of the long-looked-forward-to future that was now so oppressively close upon them.

"You know," Patty spoke with a sort of frightened gulp—"in another week we'll be *grown-up!*"

They stopped and silently looked back toward the gay crowd romping on the lawn, toward the big brooding house, that through four tempestuous, hilarious, care-free years had sheltered them so kindly. Grown-upness seemed a barren state. They longed to stretch out their hands and clutch the childhood that they had squandered with so little thought.

"Oh, it's horrible!" Conny breathed with sudden fierceness. *"I want to stay young!"*

In this unsocial mood, they refused an offered game of hare-and-hounds, and evading the singers on the gymnasium steps-the song was the "Gypsy Trail"—they sauntered on down the pergola to the lane, sprinkled with fallen apple blossoms. At the end of the lane, they came suddenly upon two other solitary strollers, and stopped short with a gasp of unbelieving wonder.

"It's Jelly!" Conny whispered.

"And Mr. Gilroy," Patty echoed.

"Shall we run?" asked Conny, in a panic.

"No," said Patty, "pretend not to notice him at all."

The three advanced with eyes discreetly bent upon the ground, but Miss Jellings greeted them gaily as she passed. There was an intangible, excited, happy thrill about her manner-something *electric*, Patty said.

"Hello, you bad little Gypsies!"

It was a peculiarly infelicitous salutation, but she was smilingly unconscious of any slip.

"Gypsies?"

Mr. Gilroy repeated the word, and his benumbed faculties began to work. He stopped and scanned the trio closely. They were clothed in dainty muslin, three as sweet young girls as one would ever meet. But Patty and Conny, even in the failing light, were still noticeably brunette-it takes boiling water to get out coffee stain.

"Oh!"

He drew a deep breath of enlightenment, while many emotions struggled for supremacy in his face. Conny dropped her gaze embarrassedly to the ground; Patty threw back her head and faced him. He and she eyed each other for a silent instant. In that glance, each asked the other not to tell-and each mutely promised.

The breeze brought the chorus of the "Gypsy Trail"; and as they sauntered on, Miss Jellings fell softly to humming the words in tune with the distant singers:

"And the Gypsy blood to the Gypsy blood
Ever the wide world over.
Ever the wide world over, lass,
Ever the trail held true
Over the world and under the world
And back at the last to you.
Follow the Romany patteran —"

The words died away in the shadows.

Conny and Patty and Priscilla stood hand in hand and looked after them.

"The school has lost Jelly!" Patty said, "and I'm afraid that we're to blame, Con, dear."

"I'm glad of it!" Conny spoke with feeling. "She's much too nice to spend her whole life telling Irene McCullough to stand up straight and keep her stomach held in."

"Anyway," Patty added, "he has no right to be angry, because-without us-he never would have dared."

They kept on across the meadow till they came to the pasture bars, where they leaned in a row with their heads tipped back, scanning the darkening sky. Miss Jellings's mood was somehow catching; the little contretemps had stirred them strangely. They felt the thrill of the untried future, with Romance waiting around the corner.

"You know," Conny broke silence after a long pause—"I think, after all, maybe it will be sort of interesting."

"What?" asked Priscilla.

She stretched out her arm in a wide gesture that comprised the night.

"Oh, everything!"

Priscilla nodded understandingly, and presently added with an air of challenge:

"I've changed my mind. I don't believe I'll go to college."

"Not go to college!" Patty echoed blankly. "Why not?"

"I think—I'll get married instead."

"Oh!" Patty laughed softly. "*I* am going to do both!"

When Patty Went to College

Chapter I Peters the Susceptible

Paper-weights," observed Patty, sucking an injured thumb, "were evidently not made for driving in tacks. I wish I had a hammer."

This remark called forth no response, and Patty peered down from the top of the step-ladder at her room-mate, who was sitting on the floor dragging sofa-pillows and curtains from a dry-goods box.

"Priscilla," she begged, "you aren't doing anything useful. Go down and ask Peters for a hammer."

Priscilla rose reluctantly. "I dare say fifty girls have already been after a hammer."

"Oh, he has a private one in his back pocket. Borrow that. And, Pris," —Patty called after her over the transom, —"just tell him to send up a man to take that closet door off its hinges."

Patty, in the interval, sat down on the top step and surveyed the chaos beneath her. An Oriental rush chair, very much out at the elbows, several miscellaneous chairs, two desks, a divan, a table, and two dry-goods boxes radiated from the center of the room. The floor, as it showed through the interstices, was covered with a grass-green carpet, while the curtains and hangings were of a not very subdued crimson.

"One would scarcely," Patty remarked to the furniture in general, "call it a symphony in color."

A knock sounded on the door.

"Come in," she called.

A girl in a blue linen sailor-suit reaching to her ankles, and with a braid of hair hanging down her back, appeared in the doorway. Patty examined her in silence. The girl's eyes traveled around the room in some surprise, and finally reached the top of the ladder.

"I—I'm a freshman," she began.

"My dear," murmured Patty, in a deprecatory tone, "I should have taken you for a senior; but"—with a wave of her hand toward the nearest dry-goods box—"come in and sit down. I need your advice. Now, there are shades of green," she went on, as if continuing a conversation, "which are not so bad with red; but I ask you frankly if *that* shade of green would go with anything?"

The freshman looked at Patty, and looked at the carpet, and smiled dubiously. "No," she admitted; "I don't believe it would."

"I knew you would say that!" exclaimed Patty, in a tone of relief. "Now what would you advise us to do with the carpet?"

The freshman looked blank. "I—I don't know, unless you take it up," she stammered.

"The very thing!" said Patty. "I wonder we hadn't thought of it before."

Priscilla reappeared at this point with the announcement, "Peters is the most suspicious man I ever knew!" But she stopped uncertainly as she caught sight of the freshman.

"Priscilla," said Patty, severely, "I *hope* you didn't divulge the fact that we are hanging the walls with tapestry"—this with a wave of her hand toward the printed cotton cloth dangling from the molding.

"I tried not to," said Priscilla, guiltily, "but he read 'tapestry' in my eyes. He had no sooner looked at me than he said, 'See here, miss; you know it's against the rules to hang curtains on the walls, and you mustn't put nails in the plastering, and I don't believe you need a hammer anyway.'"

"Disgusting creature!" said Patty.

"But," continued Priscilla, hastily, "I stopped and borrowed Georgie Merriles's hammer on my way back. Oh, I forgot," she added; "he says we can't take the closet door off its hinges-that as soon as we get ours off five hundred other young ladies will be wanting theirs off, and that it would take half a dozen men all summer to put them back again."

A portentous frown was gathering on Patty's brow, and the freshman, wishing to avert a possible domestic tragedy, inquired timidly, "Who is Peters?"

"Peters," said Priscilla, "is a short, bow-legged gentleman with a red Vandyke beard, whose technical title is janitor, but who is really dictator. Every one is afraid of him-even Prexy."

"I'm not," said Patty; "and," she added firmly, "that door is coming down whether he says so or not, so I suppose we shall have to do it ourselves." Her eyes wandered back to the carpet and her face brightened. "Oh, Pris, we've got a beautiful new scheme. My friend here says she doesn't like the carpet at all, and suggests that we take it up, get some black paint, and put it on the floor ourselves. I agree," she added, "that a Flemish oak floor covered with rugs would be a great improvement."

Priscilla glanced uncertainly from the freshman to the floor. "Do you think they'd let us do it?"

"It would never do to ask them," said Patty.

The freshman rose uneasily. "I came," she said hesitatingly, "to find out-that is, I understand that the girls rent their old books, and I thought, if you wouldn't mind—"

"Mind!" said Patty, reassuringly. "We'd rent our souls for fifty cents a semester."

"It-it was a Latin dictionary I wanted," said the freshman, "and the girls next door said perhaps you had one."

"A beautiful one," said Patty.

"No," interrupted Priscilla; "hers is lost from O to R, and it's all torn; but mine,"—she dived down into one of the boxes and hauled out a chunky volume without any covers,—"while it is not so beautiful as it was once, it is still as useful."

"Mine's annotated," said Patty, "and illustrated. I'll show you what a superior book it is," and she began descending the ladder; but Priscilla charged upon her and she retreated to the top again. "Why," she wailed to the terrified freshman, "did you not say you wanted a dictionary before she came back? Let me give you some advice at the beginning of your college career," she added warningly. "Never choose a room-mate bigger than yourself. They're dangerous."

The freshman was backing precipitously toward the door, when it opened and revealed an attractive-looking girl with fluffy reddish hair.

"Pris, you wretch, you walked off with my hammer!"

"Oh, Georgie, we need it worse than you do! Come in and help tack."

"Hello, Georgie," called Patty, from the ladder. "Isn't this room going to be beautiful when it's finished?"

Georgie looked about. "You are more sanguine than I should be," she laughed.

"You can't tell yet," Patty returned. "We're going to cover the wall-paper with this red stuff, and paint the floor black, and have dark furniture, and red hangings, and soft lights. It will look just like the Oriental Room in the Waldorf."

"How in the world," Georgie demanded, "do you ever make them let you do all these things? I stuck in three innocent little thumb-tacks to-day, and Peters descended upon me bristling with wrath, and said he'd report me if I didn't pull them out."

"We never ask," explained Patty. "It's the only way."

"You've got enough to do if you expect to get settled by Monday," Georgie remarked.

"*C'est vrai*," agreed Patty, descending the ladder with a sudden access of energy; "and you've got to stay and help us. We have to get all this furniture moved into the bedrooms and the carpet up before we even *begin* to paint." She regarded the freshman tentatively. "Are you awfully busy?"

"Not very. My room-mate hasn't come yet, so I can't settle."

"That's nice; then you can help us move furniture."

"Patty!" said Priscilla, "I think you are too bad."

"I should really love to stay and help, if you'll let me."

"Certainly," said Patty, obligingly. "I forgot to ask your name," she continued, "and I don't suppose you like to be called 'Freshman'; it's not specific enough."

"My name is Genevieve Ainslee Randolph."

"Genevieve Ains-dear me! I can't remember anything like that. Do you mind if I call you Lady Clara Vere de Vere for short?"

The freshman looked doubtful, and Patty proceeded: "Lady Clara, allow me to present my room-mate Miss Priscilla Pond-no relation to the extract. She's athletic and wins hundred-yard dashes and hurdle races, and gets her name in the paper to a really gratifying extent. And my dear friend Miss Georgie Merriles, one of the oldest families in Dakota. Miss Merriles is very talented-sings in the glee club, plays on the comb—"

"And," interrupted Georgie, "let me present Miss Patty Wyatt, who—"

"Has no specialty," said Patty, modestly, "but is merely good and beautiful and bright."

A knock sounded on the door, which opened without waiting for a response. "Miss Theodora Bartlet," continued Patty, "commonly known as the Twin, Miss Vere de Vere."

The Twin looked dazed, murmured, "Miss Vere de Vere," and dropped down on a dry-goods box.

"The term 'Twin,'" explained Patty, "is used in a merely allegorical sense. There is really only one of her. The title was conferred in her freshman year, and the reason has been lost in the dim dawn of antiquity."

The freshman looked at the Twin and opened her mouth, but shut it again without saying anything.

"My favorite maxim," said Patty, "has always been, 'Silence is golden.' I observe that we are kindred spirits."

"Patty," said Priscilla, "do stop bothering that poor child and get to work."

"Bothering?" said Patty. "I am not bothering her; we are just getting acquainted. However, I dare say it is not the time for hollow civilities. Do you want to borrow anything?" she added, turning to the Twin, "or did you just drop in to pay a social call?"

"Just a social call; but I think I'll come in again when there's no furniture to move."

"You don't happen to be going into town this afternoon?"

"Yes," said the Twin. "But," she added guardedly, "if it's a curtain-pole, I refuse to bring it out. I offered to bring one out for Lucille Carter last night, because she was in a hurry to give a house-warming, and I speared the conductor with it getting into the car; and while I was apologizing to him I knocked Mrs. Prexy's hat off with the other end."

"We have all the curtain-poles we need," said Patty. "It's just some paint-five cans of black paint, and three brushes at the ten-cent store, and thank you very much. Good-by. Now," she continued, "the first thing is to get that door down, and I will wrest a screw-driver from the unwilling Peters while you remove tacks from the carpet."

"He won't give you one," said Priscilla.

"You'll see," said Patty.

Five minutes later she returned waving above her head an unmistakable screw-driver. "*Voilà, mes amies!* Peters's own private screw-driver, for which I am to be personally responsible."

"How did you get it?" inquired Priscilla, suspiciously.

"You act," said Patty, "as if you thought I knocked him down in some dark corner and robbed him. I merely asked him for it politely, and he asked me what I wanted to do with it. I told him I wanted to take out screws, and the reason impressed him so that he handed it over without a word. Peters," she added, "is a dear; only he's like every other man-you have to use diplomacy."

By ten o'clock that night the study carpet of 399 was neatly folded and deposited at the end of the corridor above, whence its origin would be difficult to trace. The entire region was steeped in an odor of turpentine, and the study floor of 399 was a shining black, except for four or five unpainted spots which Patty designated as "stepping-stones," and which were to be treated later. Every caller that had dropped in during the afternoon or evening had had a brush thrust into her hand and had been made to go down upon her knees and paint. Besides the floor, three bookcases and a chair had been transferred from mahogany to Flemish oak, and there was still half a can of paint left which Patty was anxiously trying to dispose of.

The next morning, in spite of the difficulty of getting about, the step-ladder had been reërected, and the business of tapestry-hanging was going forward with enthusiasm, when a knock suddenly interrupted the work.

Patty, all unconscious of impending doom, cheerily called, "Come in!"

The door opened, and the figure of Peters appeared on the threshold; and Priscilla basely fled, leaving her room-mate stranded on the ladder.

"Are you the young lady who borrowed my screw—" Peters stopped and looked at the floor, and his jaw dropped in astonishment. "Where is that there carpet?" he demanded, in a tone which seemed to imply that he thought it was under the paint.

"It's out in the hall," said Patty, pleasantly. "Please be careful and don't step on the paint. It's a great improvement, don't you think?"

"You oughter got permission—" he began, but his eye fell on the tapestry and he stopped again.

"Yes," said Patty; "but we knew you couldn't spare a man just now to paint it for us, so we didn't like to trouble you."

"It's against the rules to hang curtains on the walls."

"I have heard that it was," said Patty, affably, "and I think ordinarily it's a very good rule. But just look at the color of that wall-paper. It's pea-green. You have had enough experience with wall-paper, Mr. Peters, to know that *that* is impossible, especially when our window-curtains and portières are red."

Peters's eyes had traveled to the closet, bereft of its door. "Are you the young lady," he demanded gruffly, "who asked me to have that door taken off its hinges?"

"No," said Patty; "I think that must have been my room-mate. It was *very* heavy," she continued plaintively, "and we had a great deal of trouble getting it down, but of course we realized that you were awfully busy, and that it really wasn't your fault. That's what I wanted the screw-driver for," she added. "I'm sorry that I didn't get it back last night, but I was very tired, and I forgot."

Peters merely grunted. He was examining a corner cabinet hanging on the wall. "Didn't you know," he asked severely, "that it's against the rules to put nails in the plaster?"

"Those aren't nails," expostulated Patty. "They're hooks. I remembered that you didn't like holes, so I only put in two, though I am really afraid that three are necessary. What do you think, Mr. Peters? Does it seem solid?"

Peters shook it. "It's solid enough," he said sulkily. As he turned, his eye fell on the table in Priscilla's bedroom. "Is that a gas-stove in there?" he demanded.

Patty shrugged her shoulders. "An apology for one-be *careful*, Mr. Peters! *Don't* get against that bookcase. It's just painted."

Peters jumped aside, and stood like the Colossus of Rhodes, with one foot on one stepping-stone, and the other on another three feet away. It is hard for even a janitor to be dignified in such a position, and while he was gathering his scattered impressions Patty looked longingly around the room for some one to enjoy the spectacle with her. She felt that the silence was becoming ominous, however, and she hastened to interrupt it.

"There's something wrong with that stove; it won't burn a bit. I am afraid we didn't put it together just right. I shouldn't be surprised if *you* might be able to tell what's the matter with it, Mr. Peters." She smiled sweetly. "Men know such a lot about such things! Would you mind looking at it?"

Peters grunted again; but he approached the stove.

Five minutes later, when Priscilla stuck her head in to find out if, by chance, anything remained of Patty, she saw Peters on his knees on the floor of her bedroom, with the dismembered stove scattered about him, and heard him saying, "I don't know as I have any call to report you, for I s'pose, since they're up, they might as well stay"; and Patty's voice returning: "You're *very* kind, Mr. Peters. Of course if we'd *known* —" Priscilla shut the door softly, and retired around the corner to await Peters's departure.

"How in the world did you manage him?" she asked, bursting in as soon as the sound of his footsteps had died away down the corridor. "I expected to sing a requiem over your remains, and I found Peters on his knees, engaged in amicable conversation."

Patty smiled inscrutably. "You must remember," she said, "that Peters is not only a janitor: he is also a man."

Chapter II An Early Fright

I'll make the tea to-day," said Patty, graciously.

"As you please," said Priscilla, with a skeptical shrug.

Patty bustled about amid a rattle of china. "The cups are rather dusty," she observed dubiously.

"You'd better wash them," Priscilla returned.

"No," said Patty; "it's too much trouble. Just close the blinds, please, and we'll light the candles, and that will do as well. Come in," she called in answer to a knock.

Georgie Merriles, Lucille Carter, and the Bartlet Twin appeared in the doorway.

"Did I hear the two P's were going to serve tea this afternoon?" inquired the Twin.

"Yes; come in. I'm going to make it myself," answered Patty, "and you'll see how much more attentive a hostess I am than Priscilla. Here, Twin," she added, "you take the kettle out and fill it with water; and, Lucille, please go and borrow some alcohol from the freshmen at the end of the corridor; our bottle's empty. I'd do it myself, only I've borrowed such a lot lately, and they don't know you, you see. And-oh, Georgie, you're an obliging dear; just run down-stairs to the store and get some sugar. I think I saw some money in that silver inkstand on Priscilla's desk."

"We've got some sugar," objected Priscilla. "I bought a whole pound yesterday."

"No, my lamb; we haven't got it any more. I lent it to Bonnie Connaught last night. Just hunt around for the spoons," she added. "I think I saw them on the bottom shelf of the bookcase, behind Kipling."

"And what, may I ask, are *you* going to do?" inquired Priscilla.

"I?" said Patty. "Oh, I am going to sit in the arm-chair and preside."

Ten minutes later, the company being disposed about the room on cushions, and the party well under way, it was discovered that there were no lemons.

"Are you sure?" asked Patty, anxiously.

"Not one," said Priscilla, peering into the stein where the lemons were kept.

"I," said Georgie, "refuse to go to the store again."

"No matter," said Patty, graciously; "we can do very well without them." (She did not take lemon herself.) "The object of tea is not for the sake of the tea, but for the conversation which accompanies it, and one must not let accidents annoy him. You see, young ladies," she went on, in the tone of an instructor giving a lecture, "though I have just spilled the alcohol over the sugar, I appear not to notice it, but keep up an easy flow of conversation to divert my guests. A repose of manner is above all things to be cultivated." Patty leaned languidly back in her chair. "To-morrow is Founder's Day," she resumed in a conversational tone. "I wonder if many—"

"That reminds me," interrupted the Twin. "You girls needn't save any dances for my brother. I got a letter from him this morning saying he couldn't come."

"He hasn't broken anything, has he?" Patty asked sympathetically.

"Broken anything?"

"Ah-an arm, or a leg, or a neck. Accidents are so prevalent about Founder's time."

"No; he was called out of town on important business."

"Important business!" Patty laughed. "Dear man! why couldn't he have thought of something new?"

"I think myself it was just an excuse," the Twin acknowledged. "He seemed to have an idea that he would be the only man here, and that, alone and unaided, he would have to dance with all six hundred girls."

Patty shook her head sadly. "They're all alike. Founder's wouldn't be Founder's if half the guests didn't develop serious illness or important business or dead relations the last minute. The only safe way is to invite three men and make out one program."

"I simply can't realize that to-morrow is Founder's," said Priscilla. "It doesn't seem a week since we unpacked our trunks after vacation, and before we know it we shall be packing them again for Christmas."

"Yes; and before we know it we'll be unpacking them again, with examinations three weeks ahead," said Georgie the pessimist.

"Oh, for the matter of that," returned Patty the optimist, "before we know it we'll be walking up one side of the platform for our diplomas and coming down the other side blooming alumnæ."

"And then," sighed Georgie, "before we even have time to decide on a career, we'll be old ladies, telling our grandchildren to stand up straight and remember their rubbers."

"And," said Priscilla, "before any of us get any tea we'll be in our graves, if you don't stop talking and watch that kettle."

"It's boiling," said Patty.

"Yes," said Priscilla; "it's been boiling for ten minutes."

"It's hot," said Patty.

"I should think it might be," said Priscilla.

"And now the problem is, how to get it off without burning one's self."

"You're presiding to-day; you must solve your own problems."

"'Tis an easy matter," and Patty hooked it off on the end of a golf-club. "Young ladies," she said, with a wave of the kettle, "there is nothing like a college education to teach you a way out of every difficulty. If, when you are out in the wide, wide world —"

"Where, oh, where are the grave old seniors?"

chanted the Twin.

"Where, oh, where are they?"

The rest took it up, and Patty waited patiently.

"They've gone out of Cairnsley's ethics,
They've gone out of Cairnsley's ethics,
They've gone out of Cairnsley's ethics,
Into the wide, wide w-o-r-l-d."

"If you have finished your ovation, young ladies, I will proceed with my lecture. When, as I say, you are out in the wide, wide world, making five-o'clock tea some afternoon for one of the young men popularly supposed to be there, who have dropped in to make an afternoon call-Do you follow me, young ladies, or do I speak too fast? If, while you are engaged in conversation, the kettle should become too hot, do not put your finger in your mouth and shriek 'Ouch!' and coquettishly say to the young man, '*You* take it off,' as might a young woman who has not enjoyed your advantages; but, rather, rise to the emergency; say to him calmly, 'This kettle has become over-heated; may I trouble you to go into the hall and bring an umbrella?' and when he returns you can hook it off gracefully and expeditiously as you have seen me do, young ladies, and the young —"

"Patty, take care!" This from Priscilla.

"O-u-c-h!" in a long-drawn wail. This from Georgie.

Patty hastily set the kettle down on the floor. "I'm awfully sorry, Georgie. Does it hurt?"

"Not in the least. It's really a pleasant sensation to have boiling water poured over you."

The Bartlet Twin sniffed. "I smell burning rug."

Patty groaned. "I resign, Pris; I resign. Here, you preside. I'll never ask to make it again."

"I should like," observed the Twin, "to see Patty entertaining a young man."

"It's not such an unprecedented event," said Patty, with some warmth. "You can watch me to-morrow night if it will give you so much pleasure."

"To-morrow night? Are you going to have a man for the Prom?"

"That," said Patty, "is my intention."

"And you haven't asked me for a dance!" This in an aggrieved chorus from the entire room.

"I haven't asked any one," said Patty, with dignity.

"Do you mean you're going to have all of the twenty dances with him yourself?"

"Oh, no; I don't expect to dance more than ten with him myself—I haven't made out his card yet," she added.

"Why not?"

"I never do."

"Has he been here before, then?"

"No; that's the reason."

"The reason for what?"

"Well," Patty deigned to explain, "I've invited him for every party since freshman year."

"And did he decline?"

"No; he accepted, but he never came."

"Why not?"

"He was scared."

"Scared? Of the girls?"

"Yes," said Patty, "partly-but mostly of the faculty."

"The *faculty* wouldn't hurt him."

"Of course not; but he couldn't understand that. You see, he had a fright when he was young."

"A fright? What was it?"

"Well," said Patty, "it happened this way: It was while I was at boarding-school. He was at Andover then, and his home was in the South; and one time when he went through Washington he stopped off to call on me. As it happened, the butler had left two days before, and had taken with him all the knives and forks, and all the money he could find, and Nancy Lee's gold watch and two hat-pins, and my silver hair-brush, and a bottle of brandy, and a pie," she enumerated with a conscientious regard for details; "and Mrs. Trent-that's the principal-had advertised for a new butler."

"I should have thought the old one would have discouraged her from keeping butlers," said Georgie.

"You *would* think so," said Patty; "but she was a very persevering woman. On the day that Raoul-that's his name-came to call, nineteen people had applied for the place, and Mrs. Trent was worn out from interviewing them. So she told Miss Sarah-that's her daughter-to attend to those who came in the evening. Miss Sarah was tall and wore spectacles, and was-was —"

"A good disciplinarian," suggested the Twin.

"Yes," said Patty, feelingly, "an *awfully* good disciplinarian. Well, when Raoul got there he gave his card to Ellen and asked for me; but Ellen didn't understand, and she called Miss Sarah, and when Miss Sarah saw him in his evening clothes she —"

"Took him for a butler," put in Georgie.

"Yes, she took him for a butler; and she looked at the card he'd given Ellen, and said icily, 'What does this mean?'

"'It's —it's my name,' he stammered.

"'I see,' said Miss Sarah; 'but where is your recommendation?'

"'I didn't know it was necessary,' he said, terribly scared.

"'Of course it's necessary,' Miss Sarah returned. 'I can't allow you to come into the house unless I have letters from the places where you've been before.'

"'I didn't suppose you were so strict,' he said.

"'We have to be strict,' Miss Sarah answered firmly. 'Have you had much experience?'

"He didn't know what she meant, but he thought it would be safest to say he hadn't.

"'Then of course you won't do,' she replied. 'How old are you?'

"He was so frightened by this time that he couldn't remember. 'Nineteen,' he gasped —'I mean twenty.'

"Miss Sarah saw his confusion, and thought he had designs on some of the heiresses intrusted to her care. 'I don't see how you *dared* to come here,' she said severely. 'I should not think of having you in the house for a moment. You're altogether too young and too good-looking.' And with that Raoul got up and bolted.

"When Ellen told Miss Sarah the next day that he'd asked for me, she was terribly mortified, and she made me write and explain, and invite him to dinner; but wild horses couldn't have dragged him into the house again. He's been afraid to stop off in Washington ever since. He always goes straight through on a sleeper, and says he has nightmares even then."

"And is that why he won't come to the college?"

"Yes," said Patty; "that's the reason. I told him we didn't have any butlers here; but he said we had lady faculty, and that's as bad."

"But I thought you said he *was* coming to the Prom."

"He is this time."

"Are you sure?"

"Yes," said Patty, with ominous emphasis, "I'm sure. He knows," she added, "what will happen if he doesn't."

"What will happen?" asked the Twin.

"Nothing."

The Twin shook her head, and Georgie inquired, "Then why don't you make out his program?"

"I suppose I might as well. I didn't do it before because it sort of seemed like tempting Providence. I didn't want to be the cause of any really *serious* accident happening to him," she explained a trifle ambiguously as she got out pencil and paper. "What dances can you give me, Lucille? And you, Georgie, have you got the third taken?"

While this business was being settled, a knock unheeded had sounded on the door. It came again.

"What's that?" asked Priscilla. "Did some one knock? Come in."

The door opened, and a maid stood upon the threshold with a yellow envelope in her hand. She peered uncertainly around the darkened room from one face to another. "Miss Patty Wyatt?" she asked.

Patty stretched out her hand in silence for the envelop, and, propping it up on her desk, looked at it with a grim smile.

"What is it, Patty? Aren't you going to read it?"

"There's no need. I know what it says."

"Then I'll read it," said Priscilla, ripping it open.

"Is it a leg or an arm?" Patty inquired with mild curiosity.

"Neither," said Priscilla; "it's a collar-bone."

"Oh," murmured Patty.

"What is it?" demanded Georgie the curious. "Read it out loud."

"New Haven, November 29.

"Broke collar-bone playing foot-ball. Honest Injun. Terribly sorry. Better luck next time."

"Raoul."

"There will not," observed Patty, "*be* a next time."

Has the mail been around yet?" called Priscilla to a girl at the other end of the corridor.

"Don't believe so. It hasn't been in our room."

"There she comes now!" and Priscilla swooped down upon the mail-girl. "Got anything for 399?"

"Do you want Miss Wyatt's mail too?"

"Yes; I'll take everything. What a lot! Is that all for us?" And Priscilla walked down the corridor swinging her note-book by its shoe-string, and opening envelops as she went. She was presently joined by Georgie Merriles, likewise swinging a note-book by a shoe-string.

"Hello, Pris; going to English? Want me to help carry your mail?"

"Thank you," said Priscilla; "you may keep the most of it. Now, that," she added, holding out a blue envelop, "is an advertisement for cold cream which no lady should be without; and that"—holding out a yellow envelop—"is an advertisement for beef extract which no brain-worker should be without; and that"—holding out a white envelop—"is the worst of all, because it looks like a legitimate letter, and it's nothing but a 'Dear Madam' thing, telling me my tailor has moved from Twenty-second to Forty-third Street, and hopes I'll continue to favor him with my patronage.

"And here," she went on, turning to her room-mate's correspondence, "is a cold-cream and a beef-extract letter for Patty, and one from Yale; that's probably Raoul explaining why he couldn't come to the Prom. It won't do any good, though. No mortal man can ever make her believe he didn't have his collar-bone broken on purpose. And I don't know whom that's from," Priscilla continued, examining the last letter. "It's marked 'Hotel A——, New York.' Never heard of it, did you? Never saw the writing before, either."

Georgie laughed. "Do you keep tab on all of Patty's correspondents?"

"Oh, I know the most of them by this time. She usually reads the interesting ones out loud, and the ones that aren't interesting she never answers, so they stop writing. Hurry up; the bell's going to ring"; and they pushed in among the crowd of girls on the steps of the recitation-hall.

The bell did ring just as they reached the class-room, and Priscilla dropped the letters, without comment, into Patty's lap as she went past. Patty was reading poetry and did not look up. She had assimilated some ten pages of Shelley since the first bell rang, and as she was not sure which would be taken up in class, she was now swallowing Wordsworth in the same voracious manner. Patty's method in Romantic Poetry was to be very fresh on the first part of the lesson, catch the instructor's eye early in the hour, make a brilliant recitation, and pass the remainder of the time in gentle meditation.

To-day, however, the unwonted bulk of her correspondence diverted her mind from its immediate duty. She failed to catch the instructor's eye, and the recitation proceeded without her assistance. Priscilla watched her from the back seat as she read the Yale letter with a skeptical frown, and made a grimace over the blue and the yellow; but before she had reached the Hotel A——, Priscilla was paying attention to the recitation again. It was coming her way, and she was anxiously forming an opinion on the essential characteristics of Wordsworth's view of immortality.

Suddenly the room was startled by an audible titter from Patty, who hastily composed her face and assumed a look of vacuous innocence-but too late. She had caught the instructor's eye at last.

"Miss Wyatt, what do you consider the most serious limitations of our author?"

Miss Wyatt blinked once or twice. This question out of its context was not illuminating. It was a part of her philosophy, however, never to flunk flat; she always crawled.

"Well," she began with an air of profound deliberation, "that question might be considered in two ways, either from an artistic or a philosophic standpoint."

This sounded promising, and the instructor smiled encouragingly. "Yes?" she said.

"And yet," continued Patty, after still profounder deliberation, "I think the same reason will be found to be the ultimate explanation of both."

The instructor might have inquired, "Both what?" but she refrained and merely waited.

Patty thought she had done enough, but she plunged on desperately: "In spite of his really deep philosophy we notice a certain-one might almost say *dash* about his poetry, and a lack of-er-meditation which I should attribute to his immaturity and his a—rather wild life. If he had lived longer I think he might have overcome it in time."

The class looked dazed, and the corners of the instructor's mouth twitched. "It is certainly an interesting point of view, Miss Wyatt, and, as far as I know, entirely original."

As they were crowding out at the end of the recitation Priscilla pounced upon Patty. "What on earth were you saying about Wordsworth's youth and immaturity?" she demanded. "The man lived to be over eighty, and composed a poem with his last gasp."

"Wordsworth? I was talking about Shelley."

"Well, the class wasn't."

"How should I know?" Patty demanded indignantly. "She said 'our author,' and I avoided specific details as long as I could."

"Oh, Patty, Patty! and you said he was wild-the lamblike Wordsworth!"

"What were you laughing at, anyway?" demanded Georgie.

Patty smiled again. "Why, *this*" she said, unfolding the Hotel A—— letter. "It's from an Englishman, Mr. Todhunter, some one my father discovered last summer and invited out to stay with us for a few days. I'd forgotten all about him, and here he writes to know whether and when he may call, and, if so, will it be convenient for him to come to-night. That's a comprehensive sentence, isn't it? His train gets in at half-past five and he'll be out about six."

"He isn't going to take any chances," said Priscilla.

"No," said Patty; "but I don't mind. I invited him to come out to dinner some night, though I'd forgotten it. He's really very nice, and, in spite of what the funny papers say about Englishmen, quite entertaining."

"Intentionally or unintentionally?" inquired Georgie.

"Both," said Patty.

"What's he doing in America?" asked Priscilla. "Not writing a book on the American Girl, I hope."

"Not quite as bad as that," said Patty. "He's corresponding for a newspaper, though." She smiled dreamily. "He's very curious about college."

"Patty, I *hope* you were not guilty of trying to make an Englishman, a guest in your father's house, believe any of your absurd fabrications!"

"Of course not," said Patty; "I was most careful in everything I told him. But," she acknowledged, "he-he gets impressions easily."

"It is easy to get impressions when one is talking with you," observed Georgie.

"He asked me," Patty continued, ignoring this remark, "what we studied in college! But I remembered that he was an alien in a foreign land, and I curbed my natural instincts, and outlined the courses in the catalogue verbatim, and I explained the different methods of instruction, and described the library and laboratories and lecture-rooms."

"Was he impressed?" asked Priscilla.

"Yes," said Patty; "I think you might almost say dazed. He asked me apologetically if we ever did anything to relieve the strain,—had any amusements, you know,—and I said, oh, yes; we had a Browning and an Ibsen club, and we sometimes gave Greek tragedies in the original. He was positively afraid to come near me again, for fear I'd forget and talk to him in Greek instead of English."

In view of the facts, Patty's friends considered this last remark distinctly humorous, for she had flunked her freshman Greek three times, and had been advised by the faculty to take it over sophomore year.

"I hope, since he's a newspaper writer," said Priscilla, "that you'll do something to lighten his impression, or he'll never favor women's colleges in England."

"I hadn't thought of that," said Patty; "perhaps I ought."

They had reached the steps of the dormitory. "Let's not go in," said Georgie; "let's go down to Mrs. Muldoon's and get some chocolate cake."

"Thank you," said Priscilla; "I'm in training."

"Soup, then."

"Can't eat between meals."

"You come, then, Patty."

"Sorry, but I've got to take my white dress down to the laundry and have it pressed."

"Are you going to dress up for him to the extent of evening clothes?"

"Yes," said Patty; "I think I owe it to the American Girl."

"Well," sighed Georgie, "I'm hungry, but I suppose I might as well go in and dress that doll for the College Settlement Association. The show's to-night."

"Mine's done," said Priscilla; "and Patty wouldn't take one. Did you see Bonnie Connaught sitting on the back seat in biology this morning, hemming her doll's petticoat straight through the lecture?"

"Really?" laughed Patty. "It's a good thing Professor Hitchcock's near-sighted."

The College Settlement Association, by way of parenthesis, was in the habit of distributing three hundred dolls among the students every year before Christmas, to be dressed and sent to the settlement in New York. The dolls were supposed to be so well dressed that the East Side mothers could use them as models for the clothing of their own children, though it must be confessed that the tendency among the girls was to strive for effect and not for detail. On the evening before the dolls were to be shipped a doll show was regularly held, at which two cents admittance was charged (stamps accepted) to pay the expressage.

* * * * *

It was ten minutes past six, and Phillips Hall (such of it as was not late) was dining, when the maid arrived with Mr. Algernon Vivian Todhunter's card. Patty, radiant in a white evening gown, was trying, with much squirming, to fasten it in the middle of the back.

"Oh, Sadie," she called to the maid, "would you mind coming in here and buttoning my dress? I can't reach it from above or below."

"You look just beautiful, Miss Wyatt," said Sadie, admiringly.

Patty laughed. "Do you think I can uphold the honor of the nation?"

"To be sure, miss," said Sadie, politely.

Patty ran down the corridor to the door of the reception-room, and then swept slowly in with what she called an air of continental repose. The room was empty. She glanced about in some surprise, for she knew that the two reception-rooms on the other side of the hall were being used for the doll show. She tiptoed over and peered in through the half-open door. The room was filled with dolls in rows and tiers; every piece of furniture was covered with them; and in a far corner, at the end of a long vista of dolls, appeared Mr. Algernon Vivian Todhunter, gingerly sitting on the edge of a sofa, surrounded by flaxen-haired baby dolls, and awkwardly holding in his lap the three he had displaced.

Patty drew back behind the door, and spent fully three minutes in regaining her continental repose; then she entered the room and greeted Mr. Todhunter effusively. He carefully transferred the dolls to his left arm and stood up and shook hands.

"Let me take the little dears," said Patty, kindly; "I'm afraid they're in your way."

Mr. Todhunter murmured something about its being a pleasure and a privilege to hold them.

Patty plumped up their clothes and rearranged them on the sofa with motherly solicitude, while Mr. Todhunter watched her gravely, his national politeness and his reportorial instinct each struggling for the mastery. Finally he began tentatively: "I say, Miss Wyatt, do-er-the young ladies spend much time playing with dolls?"

"No," said Patty, candidly; "I don't think you could say they spend *too* much. I have never heard of but one girl actually neglecting her work for it. You mustn't think that we have as many dolls as this here *every* night," she went on. "It is rather an unusual occurrence. Once a year the girls hold what they call a doll show to see who has dressed her doll the best."

"Ah, I see," said Mr. Todhunter; "a little friendly rivalry."

"Purely friendly," said Patty.

As they started for the dining-room Mr. Todhunter adjusted his monocle and took a parting look at the doll show.

"I'm afraid you think us childish, Mr. Todhunter," said Patty.

"Not at all, Miss Wyatt," he assured her hastily. "I think it quite charming, you know, and so-er-unexpected. I had always been told that they played somewhat peculiar games at these women's colleges, but I never supposed they did anything so feminine as to play with dolls."

* * * * *

When Patty returned to her room that night, she found Georgie and Priscilla surrounded by grammars and dictionaries, doing German prose. Her appearance was hailed with a cry of indignant protest.

"When *I* have a man," said Priscilla, "I divide him up among my friends."

"*Especially* when he's a curiosity," added Georgie.

"And we dressed up in grand clothes, and stood in your way coming out of chapel," went on Priscilla, "and you never even looked at us."

"Englishmen are so bashful," apologized Patty; "I didn't want to frighten him."

Priscilla looked at her suspiciously. "Patty, I hope you didn't impose on the poor man's credulity."

"Certainly not!" said Patty, with dignity. "I explained everything he asked me, and was most careful not to exaggerate. But," she added with engaging frankness, "I cannot be responsible for any *impressions* he may have obtained. When an Englishman once gets an idea, you know, it's almost impossible to change it."

Chapter IV A Question of Ethics

Patty's class-room methods were the result of a wide experience in the professorial type of mind. By her senior year she had reduced the matter of recitation to a system, and could foretell with unvarying precision the day she would be called on and the question she would be asked. Her tactics varied with the subject and the instructor, and were the result of a penetration and knowledge of human nature that might have accomplished something in a worthier cause.

In chemistry, for example, her instructor was a man who had outlived any early illusions in regard to the superior conscientiousness of girls over boys. He was not by nature a suspicious person, but a long experience in teaching had inculcated an inordinate wariness which was sometimes out of season. He allowed no napping in his classes, and those who did not pay attention suffered. Patty discovered his weakness early in the year, and planned her campaign accordingly. As long as she did not understand the experiment in hand, she would watch him with a face beaming with intelligence; but when she did understand, and wished to recite, she would let her eyes wander to the window with a dreamy, far-away smile, and, being asked a question, would come back to the realities of chemistry with a start, and, after a moment of ostentatious pondering, make a brilliant recitation. It must be confessed that her moments of abstraction were rare; she was far too often radiantly interested.

In French her tactics were exactly opposite. The instructor, with all the native politeness of his race, called on those only who caught his eye and appeared willing and anxious to recite. This made the matter comparatively simple, but still required considerable finesse. Patty dropped her pen, spilled the pages from her note-book, tied her shoe-string, and even sneezed opportunely in order not to catch his eye at inconvenient moments. The rest of the class, who were not artists, contented themselves with merely lowering their eyes as he looked along the line—a method which in Patty's scornful estimation said as plainly as words, "Please don't call on me; I don't know."

But with Professor Cairnsley, who taught philosophy, it was more difficult to form a working hypothesis. He had grown old in the service of the college, and after thirty years' experience of girl-nature he was still as unsuspiciously trustful as he had been in the beginning. Taking it for granted that his pupils were as interested in the contemplation of philosophic truths as he himself, the professor conducted his recitations without a suspicion of guile, and based his procedure entirely upon the inspiration of the moment. The key to his method had always remained a mystery, and several generations of classes had searched for it in vain. Some averred that he called on every seventh girl; others, that he drew lots. Patty triumphantly announced early in the course that she had discovered the secret at last-that on Monday he called on the red-haired girls; on Tuesday, those with yellow hair; on Wednesday and Thursday, those with brown; and on Friday, those with black. But this solution, like the others, was found to break down in actual practice; and Patty, for one, discovered that it required all her ingenuity, and even a good deal of studying, to maintain her reputation for brilliancy in Professor Cairnsley's classes. And she cared about maintaining it, for she liked the professor and was one of his favorite pupils. She had known his wife before she entered college, and she often called upon them in their home, and, in short, exemplified the ideal relations between faculty and students.

Owing to the pressure of many interests, Patty's researches into philosophy were not as deep as the intentions of the course, but she had a very good working knowledge, which, in its details, would have astonished Professor Cairnsley could he have got behind the scenes. Though her knowledge was not based strictly on the text-book, her reputation in the class was good, and, as Patty admitted with a sigh, "It's a great strain on the imagination to keep up a reputation in philosophy."

It had been established, indeed, as far back as her sophomore year, when the psychology class was awed into silence by its first introduction to the abstractions of science, and Patty alone had dared to lift her voice. The professor, one morning, had been placidly lecturing along on the subject of sensation, and in the course of the lecture had remarked: "It is probable that the individual experiences all the primary sensations during the first few months of infancy, and that in after life there is no such thing as a new sensation."

"Professor Cairnsley," Patty piped up, "did you ever shoot the chutes?"

The ice was broken at last, and the class felt at home, even in the somewhat deep waters of philosophy; and Patty, however undeservedly, had gained the credit of having a deeper insight than most into matters psychical.

And so into her senior year, when she entered upon the study of ethics, she carried along an unearned and fragile reputation, built upon subterfuges and likely to crumble at the slightest touch. She had maintained it very creditably up to the Christmas vacation, and had argued upon the ultimate ground of moral obligation and the origin of conscience quite as intelligently as though she had previously read what the text-book had to say on the subject. But when they had commenced the study of specific theologies, based upon definite historical facts, Patty found her imagination of little use, and on several occasions it had been purely good luck that had saved her from exposure. Once the bell had rung at an opportune moment, and twice she had been able to avert a direct answer by leading the discussion into side issues. She realized, however, that fortune would not always favor her, and as the professor usually forgot to call the roll, she formed the nefarious practice of cutting class when she did not have her lesson.

For a week or so in particular, her pressure of work in other directions (not all of them scholastic) had prevented her from devoting her usual amount of energy to the task of maintaining her philosophy reputation, and she had, without conscience, cut ethics several days in succession, and had failed to comment upon the fact to the professor.

"What did he lecture about in ethics-those recitations I missed?" she inquired of Priscilla, one afternoon.

"Swedenborg."

"Swedenborg," repeated Patty, dreamily. "He got up a new religion, didn't he? Or was it a new system of gymnastics? I've heard about him, but I don't seem to remember any details."

"You'd better make him up; he's important."

"I dare say; but I've lived twenty-one years without knowing about him, and I can wait a month longer. I'm saving up Confucius and the Jesuits for examination-time, and I'll add Swedenborg to the list."

"You'd better not. Professor Cairnsley's fond of him, and is likely to pop a special examination at any moment."

"Not Professor Cairnsley," laughed Patty. "He doesn't want to waste the time. He's going to lecture straight on for two weeks-nice man; I see it in his eye. What I admire in a professor is a good, steady, plodding disposition that doesn't go in for sensational surprises."

"You'll find yourself mistaken some day," warned Priscilla.

"No danger, my dear Cassandra. I know Professor Cairnsley, and Professor Cairnsley thinks he knows me; and we just get along together beautifully. I wish there were more like him," Patty added with a sigh.

Professor Cairnsley began a lecture the next morning which was evidently calculated to extend through the hour, and Patty cast a triumphant glance at Priscilla as she unscrewed the top of her fountain-pen and settled down to work. In the course of the lecture, however, he had occasion to refer to Swedenborg, and, pausing a moment, he casually asked a girl on the front seat for a résumé of Swedenborg's philosophy. She, unfortunately confusing him with Schopenhauer, glibly attributed to him doctrines which would have outraged his soul could he have heard them. It is written that the worm will turn, and the professor's bland smile deserted him as he passed the question to a second girl without much better result. The class in general had evidently been laboring under Patty's delusion that the time had not come in which to learn back notes. Amazed and indignant, he pursued the matter with a persistency and a rancor he seldom showed. He began going straight through the class, growing more and more sarcastic with each recitation.

As she saw him finish with the row in front and begin on her row, Patty knew that she was doomed. She racked her brain for some memory of Swedenborg. He was a name to her and nothing more. He might have been an ancient Greek or a modern American, for all she knew. As Professor Cairnsley came along the line he was gradually eliciting from the terrified class the superficial points which were more or less common to all philosophers. Patty perceived that her imagination could not help her out, that for once the placid professor was on the war-path, and that Swedenborg, and nothing but Swedenborg, would serve. She cast an agonized glance up at Priscilla, and Priscilla grinned back with "I told you so" written on every feature.

Patty looked about desperately. The lecture-room was shaped like an amphitheater, with part of the seats on a level with the main floor, and the rest rising in tiers. Patty sat on the main floor, well toward the rear. She could barely see the professor's head, but he was coming irrevocably. She did not have to see very clearly to know that. The girl before her answered wildly; the professor frowned, and, looking down at his roll-book, slowly and deliberately made a zero.

When he raised his eyes again Patty's seat was empty. She was kneeling on the floor, with her head bowed behind the girl in front. The unconscious professor passed over her bent head and called on the girl on the other side, who coughed hysterically once or twice, and flunked flat; and while he was crediting the fact in his roll-book Patty resumed her seat. A ripple of laughter ran around the room; the professor frowned, and remarked that he saw no occasion for amusement. The bell rang, and the class somewhat sheepishly filed out.

That afternoon Patty burst into the study where Priscilla and Georgie Merriles were making tea. "Did you ever think I had much of a conscience?" she demanded.

"Never thought it was your strong point," said Georgie.

"Well, I've got a perfectly tremendous one! What do you think I've been doing?"

"Making up your ethics lectures," suggested Priscilla.

"Worse than that."

"You *haven't* been to gym, Patty!" said Georgie.

"Goodness, no! I'm not so far gone as that. Well, I'll tell you. I met Professor Cairnsley by the gate and walked in with him, and, if you please, he complimented me on my work in ethics!"

"That ought to have been embarrassing," said Georgie.

"It was," acknowledged Patty. "I told him I didn't really know as much as he thought I did."

"What did he say?"

"He said I was too modest. He's such a trustful old man, you know, that you sort of hate to deceive him. And what do you think? I told him about the seat!"

Priscilla smiled approvingly upon her usually recreant room-mate. "Well, Patty, you certainly are better than I gave you credit for!"

"Thank you," murmured Patty.

"I begin to believe you *have* got a conscience," said Georgie.

"An excellent one," said Patty, complacently.

"It pays in the end," said Priscilla.

"It does," agreed Patty. "Professor Cairnsley said he would explain Swedenborg to me himself, and he invited me over to dinner to-night!"

Chapter V The Elusive Kate Ferris

The mysterious Kate Ferris, who kept Priscilla on the verge of nervous prostration for a whole semester, entered upon her college career in an entirely unpremeditated and impromptu manner. It began one day away back in November. Georgie Merriles and Patty had just strolled home from the athletic field, where they had been witnessing the start of a paper-chase cross country, in which Priscilla was impersonating a fox. As they entered the study, Georgie stopped to examine some loose sheets of paper which were impaled upon the door.

"What's this, Patty?"

"Oh, that's the registration-list for the German Club. Priscilla's secretary, you know, and every one who wants to join comes here. The study has been so full of freshmen all the time that I told her to hang it on the door and let them join outside; it works beautifully." Patty turned the leaves and ran her eyes down the list of sprawling signatures. "It's a popular organization, isn't it? The freshmen are simply scrambling to get in."

"They're trying to show Fräulein Scherin how much interest they take in the subject," Georgie laughed.

Patty picked up the pencil. "Would you like to join? I know Priscilla would be gratified."

"No, thank you; I pay club dues enough already."

"I'm afraid I'm not exactly eligible myself, as I don't know any German. It's such a beautifully sharp pencil, though, that I hate not to write with it." Patty poised the pencil a moment, and abstractedly traced the name "Kate Ferris."

Georgie laughed. "If there should happen to be a Kate Ferris in college, she would be surprised to find herself a member of the German Club," and the incident was forgotten.

A few days later the two came in from class, to find Priscilla and the president of the German Club sitting on the divan with their heads together, frantically turning the leaves of the catalogue.

"She isn't a sophomore," the president announced. "She *must* be a freshman, Priscilla. Look again."

"I've gone over this list three times, and there isn't a single Ferris down."

Georgie and Patty exchanged glances and inquired the trouble.

"A girl named Kate Ferris has registered for the German Club, and we've gone through all the classes, and there simply isn't any such girl in college."

"Possibly a special," Patty suggested.

"Of course! Why didn't we think of that?" And Priscilla turned to the list of special students. "No; she isn't here."

"Let me look"; and Patty ran her eyes down the column. "You've mistaken the name," she remarked, handing the book back with a shrug.

Priscilla produced the registration-list, and triumphantly exhibited an unmistakable Kate Ferris.

"They forgot to put her in the catalogue."

"I never knew them to make such a mistake before," said the president, dubiously. "I don't believe we'd better put her in the roll-book till we find out who she is."

"Then you'll hurt her feelings," said Georgie. "Freshmen are terribly sensitive about being slighted."

"Oh, very well; it doesn't matter." And Kate Ferris was accordingly enrolled in the club records.

Several weeks later Priscilla was engaged in laboriously turning the minutes of the last meeting into grammatical German, and as she closed the dictionary and grammar with a sigh of relief, she remarked to Patty: "Do you know, it's very queer about that Kate Ferris. She hasn't paid her dues, and, as far as I can make out, she hasn't attended a single meeting. Wouldn't you take her name off the roll? I don't believe she's in college any more."

"You might as well," said Patty, and she listlessly watched Priscilla as she scratched out the name with a penknife. Patty never made the mistake of over-acting.

The next morning, as Priscilla came in from a class, she found a note on her door-block, written in the perpendicular characters of Kate Ferris. It ran:

> Dear Miss Pond: I came to pay my German Club dues, and as you are not in, I have left the money on the bookcase. Am sorry to have missed so many meetings, but have not been able to attend classes lately.
>
> Kate Ferris.

Priscilla exhibited the note to the president as a tangible proof that Kate Ferris still existed, and reinscribed the name in the roll-book.

A few weeks later she found a second note on her door-block:

> Dear Miss Pond: As I am very busy with my class work, I find that I have not time to attend the German Club meetings, and so have decided to resign. I left my letter of resignation on the bookcase.
>
> Kate Ferris.

As Priscilla scratched the name out of the roll-book again she remarked to Patty: "I am glad this Kate Ferris has left the club at last. She has caused me more trouble than all the rest of the members put together."

The next morning a third note appeared on the block:

> Dear Miss Pond: I happened to mention the fact of my having resigned from the German Club to Fräulein Scherin last night, and she said that the club would help me in my work, and advised me to stay in it. So I shall be much obliged if you will not present my letter at the meeting after all, as I have decided to follow her advice.
>
> Kate Ferris.

Priscilla tossed the note to Patty with a groan, and getting out the roll-book, she turned to the F's and reënrolled Kate Ferris.

Patty sympathetically watched the process over her shoulder. "The book is getting so thin in that spot," she laughed, "that Kate Ferris is actually coming through on the other side. If she changes her mind many more times there won't be anything left."

"I'm going to ask Fräulein Scherin about her," Priscilla declared. "She's made me so much trouble that I'm curious to see what she looks like."

She did ask Fräulein Scherin, but Fräulein denied all knowledge of the girl. "I have so many freshmen," she apologized, "I cannot all of them with their queer names remember."

Priscilla inquired about Kate Ferris from the freshmen she knew, but though all of them thought that the name sounded familiar, none of them could exactly place her. She was variously described as tall and dark and small and light, but further inquiry always proved that the girl they had in mind was some one else.

Priscilla kept hearing about the girl on all sides, but could never catch a glimpse of her. Miss Ferris called several times on business, but Priscilla always happened to be out. Her name was posted on the bulletin-board for having library books that were overdue. She even wrote a paper for one of the German Club meetings (Georgie was not a facile German scholar, and it had required a whole Saturday); but owing to the fact that she was suddenly called out of town, she did not read it in person.

A month or two after Kate Ferris's advent, Priscilla had friends visiting her from New York, for whom she gave a tea in the study.

"I am going to invite Kate Ferris," she announced. "I *insist* upon finding out what she looks like."

"Do," said Patty. "I should like to find out myself."

The invitation was despatched, and on the next day Priscilla received a formal acceptance.

"It's strange that she should send an acceptance for a tea," she remarked as she read it, "but I'm glad to get it, anyway. I like to feel sure that I'm to see her at last."

On the evening of the tea, after the guests had gone and the furniture had been moved back, the weary hostesses, in somewhat rumpled evening dresses (a considerable crush results when fifty are entertained in a room whose utmost capacity is fifteen), were reëntertaining one or two friends on the lettuce sandwiches and cakes the obliging guests had failed to consume. The company and the clothes having passed in review, the conversation flagged a little, and Georgie suddenly asked: "Was Kate Ferris here? I was so busy passing cakes that I didn't look, and I wanted to see her especially!"

"That's so!" Patty exclaimed. "I didn't see her, either. She's the most abnormally inconspicuous person I ever heard of. What did she look like, Pris?"

Priscilla knit her brows. "She couldn't have come. I kept watching for her all the evening. It's strange, isn't it?—when she was so careful to send an acceptance. I'm growing positively morbid over the girl; I begin to think she's invisible."

"I begin to think so myself," said Patty.

The next morning's mail brought a bunch of violets and an apology from Kate Ferris. "She had been unavoidably detained."

"It's positively uncanny!" Priscilla declared. "I shall go to the registrar and tell her that this Kate Ferris is neither down in the catalogue nor the college directory, and find out where she lives."

"Don't do anything reckless," Georgie pleaded. "Take what the gods send and be grateful."

But Priscilla was as good as her word, and she returned from the registrar's office flushed and defiant. "She insists that there isn't any such person in college, and that I must have made a mistake in the name! Did you ever hear anything so absurd?"

"That seems to me the only reasonable explanation," Patty agreed amicably. "Perhaps it is Harris instead of Ferris."

Priscilla faced her ominously. "You read the name yourself. It was as plain as printing."

"We're all liable to make mistakes," Patty murmured soothingly.

"Do you know," said Georgie, "I begin to think it's all a hallucination, and that there really isn't any Kate Ferris. It's strange, of course, but not any stranger than some of those cases you read about in psychology."

"Hallucinations don't send flowers," said Priscilla, hotly; and she stalked out of the room, leaving Patty and Georgie to review the campaign.

"I'm afraid it's gone far enough," said Georgie. "If she bothers the office very much there'll be an official investigation."

"I'm afraid so," sighed Patty. "It's been very entertaining, but she is really getting sensitive on the subject, and I don't dare mention Kate Ferris's name when we're alone."

"Shall we tell her?"

Patty shook her head. "Not just now—I shouldn't dare. She believes in corporal punishment."

A few days later Priscilla received another note directed in the hand she had come to dread. She threw it into the waste-basket unopened; but, curiosity prevailing, she drew it out again and read it:

> Dear Miss Pond: As I have been obliged to leave college on account of my health, I inclose my resignation to the German Club. I thank you very sincerely for your

kindness to me this year, and shall always look back upon our friendship as one of the happiest memories of my college life.

Yours sincerely,

Kate Ferris.

When Patty came in she found Priscilla silently and grimly scratching a hole into the roll-book where Kate Ferris's name had been.

"Changed her mind again?" Patty asked pleasantly.

"She's left college," Priscilla snapped, "and don't you ever mention her name to me again."

Patty sighed sympathetically and remarked to the room in general: "It's sort of pathetic to have your whole college life summed up in a hole in the German Club archives. I can't help feeling sorry for her!"

Chapter VI A Story with Four Sequels

It was Saturday, and Patty had been working ever since breakfast, with a brief pause for luncheon, on a paper entitled "Shakspere, the Man." At four o'clock she laid down her pen, pushed her manuscript into the waste-basket, and faced her room-mate defiantly.

"What do I care about Shakspere, the man? He's been dead three hundred years."

Priscilla laughed unfeelingly. "What do I care about a frog's nervous system, for the matter of that? But I am writing an interesting monograph on it, just the same."

"Ah, I dare say you are making a valuable addition to the subject."

"It's quite as valuable as your addition to Shaksperiana."

Patty dropped a voluble sigh and turned to the window to note that it was raining dismally.

"Oh, hand it in," said Priscilla, comfortingly. "You've worked on it all day, and it's probably no worse than the most of your things."

"No sense to it," said Patty.

"They're used to that," laughed Priscilla.

"What are you laughing at, anyway?" Patty asked crossly. "I don't see anything to laugh at in this beastly place. Always having to do what you don't want to do when you most don't want to do it. Just the same, day after day: get up by bells, eat by bells, sleep by bells. I feel like some sort of a delinquent living in an asylum."

Priscilla treated this outburst with the silence it deserved, and Patty turned back to her perusal of the rain-soaked campus.

"I wish something would happen," she said discontentedly. "I think I'll put on a mackintosh and go out in search of adventure."

"Pneumonia will happen if you do."

"What business has it to be raining, anyway, when it ought to be snowing?"

As this was unanswerable, Priscilla returned to her frogs, and Patty drummed gloomily on the window-pane until a maid appeared with a card.

"A caller?" cried Patty. "A missionary! A rescuer! A deliverer! Heaven send it's for me!"

"Miss Pond," said Sadie, laying the card on the table.

Patty pounced upon it. "'Mr. Frederick K. Stanthrope.' Who's he, Pris?"

Priscilla wrinkled up her brows. "I don't know; I never heard of him. What do you suppose it can be?"

"An adventure —I know it's an adventure. Probably your uncle, that you never heard of, has just died in the South Sea Islands, and left you a fortune because you're his namesake; or else you're a countess by rights, and were stolen from your cradle in infancy, and he's the lawyer come to tell you about it. I think it might have happened to me, when I'm so bored to death! But hurry up and tell me about it, at least; a second-hand adventure's better than no adventure at all. Yes, your hair is all right; never mind looking in the glass." And Patty pushed her room-mate out of the door, and, sitting down at her desk again, quite cheerfully pulled her discarded paper out of the waste-basket and began re-reading it with evident approval.

Priscilla returned before she had finished. "He didn't ask for me at all," she announced. "He asked for Miss McKay."

"Miss McKay?"

"That junior with the hair," she explained a trifle vaguely.

"How disgusting!" cried Patty. "I had it all planned how I was going to live with you in your castle up in the Hartz Mountains, and now it turns out that Miss McKay is the countess, and I don't even know her. What did the man look like, and what did he do?"

"Well, he looked rather frightened, and didn't do anything but stammer. There were two men in the reception-room, and of course I picked out the wrong one and begged his pardon and asked if he were Mr. Stanthrope. He said no; his name was Wiggins. So then the only thing left for me to do was to beg the other one's pardon.

"He was sitting in that high-backed green chair, with his eyes glued to his shoes, and holding his hat and cane in front of him like breastworks, as if he were preparing to repel an attack. He didn't look very approachable, but I boldly accosted him and asked if he were Mr. Stanthrope. He stood up and stammered and blushed and looked as if he wanted to deny it, but finally acknowledged that he was, and then stood politely waiting for me to state my business! I explained, and he stammered some more, and finally got out that he had called to see Miss McKay, and that the maid must have made a mistake. He was quite cross about it, you know, and acted as if I had insulted him; and the other man-the horrible Wiggins one-laughed, and then looked out of the window and pretended he hadn't. I apologized, —though I couldn't for the life of me see what there was to apologize for, —and told him I would send the maid for Miss McKay, and backed out."

"Is that all?" Patty asked disappointedly. "If I couldn't have a better adventure than that, I shouldn't have any."

"But the funny thing is that when I told Sadie, she *insisted* that he had asked for me."

"Ha! The plot thickens, after all. What does it mean? Did he look like a detective, or merely a pickpocket?"

"He looked like a very ordinarily embarrassed young man."

Patty shook her head dejectedly. "There's a mystery somewhere, but I don't see that it affords much entertainment. I dare say that when Miss McKay came he told her he hadn't asked for her at all; he had asked for Miss Higginbotham. The only explanation I can think of is that he is insane, and there are so many insane people in the world that it isn't even interesting."

Patty recounted the story of Priscilla's caller at the dinner-table that night.

"I know the sequel," said Lucille Carter. "The other man, the Mr. Wiggins, is Bonnie Connaught's cousin; and he told her about some young man who came out in the car with him, and asked for Miss Pond at the door, and then all of a sudden seemed to change his mind, and went tearing down the corridor after the maid, yelling, "Hi, there! Hi, there!" at the top of his voice; but he couldn't catch her, and when Miss Pond came he pretended he had asked for some one else."

"Is that all?" asked Patty. "I don't think it is much of a sequel. It just proves that there's a plot against Priscilla's life, and I already knew that. I intend to ask Miss McKay about him. I don't know her, except by sight, but in a case of life and death like this, I don't think it's necessary to wait for an introduction."

The next evening Patty announced: "Sequel number two! Mr. Frederick K. Stanthrope lives in New York, and is Miss McKay's brother's best friend. She has only met him once before, and doesn't know any of his past affiliations. But the queer thing is that he never mentioned to her anything about Priscilla. Shouldn't you naturally think he would have told her about such a funny mistake?

"In my opinion," Patty continued solemnly, "it was plainly premeditated. He is undoubtedly a villain in disguise, and he used his acquaintance with Miss McKay as a cloak to elude detection. My theory is this: He got Priscilla's name out of the catalogue, and came here intending to murder her for her *jools*; but when he saw how big she was he was scared and so abandoned his dastardly intent. Now if he had chosen me, my body would, at this moment, have been concealed behind the sofa, and my class-pin reposing in the murderer's pocket."

Patty shuddered. "Think what I escaped. And all the time I was grumbling because nothing ever happens here!"

A few days later she appeared at the table with a further announcement: "I have the pleasure of offering for your perusal, young ladies, the third and last sequel in the great Stanthrope-Pond-McKay mystery. And I hereby take the opportunity of apologizing to Mr. Stanthrope for my unworthy suspicions. He is not a burglar, nor a detective, nor a murderer, nor even a lawyer, but just a poor young man with a buried romance."

"How did you find out?" —in a chorus of voices.

"I just met Miss McKay in the hall, and she has been in New York, where her brother told her the particulars. It seems that three or four years ago Mr. Frederick K. Stanthrope was engaged to a girl here in college named Alice Pond-she is now Mrs. Hiram Brown, but that has nothing to do with the story.

"Being in town last Saturday on business, he decided to run out and call on Miss McKay, as he was such a friend of her brother's —and also for the sake of old times. He amused himself all the way out in the car by resurrecting his buried romance, and he kept getting more and more pensive with every mile. When he finally reached the door and handed his card to the maid, he abstractedly called for Miss Pond just as he used to do four years ago. He didn't realize at first what he had done. Then it came over him in a flash, but he couldn't catch Sadie. He knew, of course, that the other man had heard, and he sat there scared to death, trying to think of some plausible excuse, and momentarily expecting a strange Miss Pond to pop in and demand an explanation.

"Sure enough, the curtains parted, and a tall, beautiful, stately creature (I quote Miss McKay's brother) swept into the room, and, approaching the wrong man, asked him in haughty tones if he were Mr. Frederick K. Stanthrope. He very properly denied it, whereupon there was nothing for the right Mr. Stanthrope to do but stand up and acknowledge it like a man, which he did; but there he stuck. His imagination was numbed, paralyzed; so he turned it off on poor Sadie, and all the time he knew that the other man knew that he was lying. And that is all," Patty finished. "It's not much of a story, but such as it is, it's a blessing to have it concluded."

"Patty," called Priscilla, from the other end of the table, "have you been telling them that absurd story?"

"Why not?" asked Patty. "Having heard so many sequels, they naturally wanted to hear the last."

Priscilla laughed. "But yours doesn't happen to be the last. I know a still later one."

"Later than Patty's?" the table demanded.

"Yes, later than Patty's. It isn't really a sequel; it's just an appendix. I shouldn't tell you, only you'll find it out, so I might as well. Miss McKay has invited two men for the junior party, and both have accepted. As two men are hard to manage, she has (by request) asked me to take care of one of them-namely, Mr. Frederick K. Stanthrope."

Patty sighed. "I see a whole series of sequels stretching away into the future. It's worse than the Elsie Books!"

Chapter VII In Pursuit of Old English

"Hello, Patty! Have you read the bulletin-board this morning?" called Cathy Fair, as she caught up with Patty on the way home from a third-hour recitation.

"No," said Patty; "I think it's a bad habit. You see too many unpleasant things there."

"Well, there's certainly an unpleasant one to-day. Miss Skelling wishes the Old English class to be provided with writing materials this afternoon."

Patty stopped with a groan. "I think it's absolutely abominable to give an examination without a word of warning."

"Not an examination," quoted Cathy; "just a 'little test to see how much you know.'"

"I don't know a thing," wailed Patty—"not a blessed thing."

"Nonsense, Patty; you know more than any one else in the class."

"Bluff-it's all pure bluff. I come in strong on the literary criticism and the general discussions, and she never realizes that I don't know a word of the grammar."

"You've got two hours. You can cut your classes and review it up."

"Two hours!" said Patty, sadly. "I need two days. I've never learned it, I tell you. The Anglo-Saxon grammar is a thing no mortal can carry in his head, and I thought I might as well wait and learn it before examinations."

"I don't wish to appear unfeeling," laughed Cathy, "but I should say, my dear, that it serves you right."

"Oh, I dare say," said Patty. "You are as bad as Priscilla"; and she trailed gloomily homeward.

She found her friends reviewing biology and eating olives. "Have one?" asked Lucille Carter, who, provided with a hat-pin by way of fork, was presiding over the bottle for the moment.

"No, thanks," returned Patty, in the tone of one who has exhausted life and longs for death.

"What's the matter?" inquired Priscilla. "You don't mean to say that woman has given you another special topic?"

"Worse than that!" and Patty laid bare the tragedy.

A sympathetic silence followed; they realized that while she was, perhaps, not strictly deserving of sympathy, still her impending fate was of the kind that might overtake any one.

"You know, Pris," said Patty, miserably, "that I simply *can't* pass."

"No," said Priscilla, soothingly; "I don't believe you can."

"I shall flunk *flat* —absolutely *flat*. Miss Skelling will never have any confidence in me again, and will make me recite every bit of grammar for the rest of the semester."

"I should think you'd cut," ventured Georgie-that being, in her opinion, the most obvious method of escaping an examination.

"I can't. I just met Miss Skelling in the hall five minutes before the blow fell, and she knows I'm alive and able to be about; besides, the class meets again to-morrow morning, and I'd have to cram all night or cut that too."

"Why don't you go to Miss Skelling and frankly explain the situation," suggested Lucille the virtuous, "and ask her to let you off for a day or two? She would like you all the better for it."

"Will you listen to the guileless babe!" said Patty. "What is there to explain, may I ask? I can't very well tell her that I prefer not to learn the lessons as she gives them out, but think it easier to wait and cram them up at one fell swoop, just before examinations. That *would* ingratiate myself in her favor!"

"It's your own fault," said Priscilla.

Patty groaned. "I was just waiting to hear you say that! You always do."

"It's always true. Where are you going?" as Patty started for the door.

"I am going," said Patty, "to ask Mrs. Richards to give me a new room-mate: one who will understand and appreciate me, and sympathize with my afflictions."

Patty walked gloomily down the corridor, lost in meditation. Her way led past the door of the doctor's office, which was standing invitingly open. Three or four girls were sitting around the room, laughing and talking and waiting their turns. Patty glanced in, and a radiant smile suddenly lightened her face, but it was instantly replaced by a look of settled sadness. She walked in and dropped into an arm-chair with a sigh.

"What's the matter, Patty? You look as if you had melancholia."

Patty smiled apathetically. "Not quite so bad as that," she murmured, and leaned back and closed her eyes.

"Next," said the doctor from the doorway; but as she caught sight of Patty she walked over and shook her arm. "Is this Patty Wyatt? What is the matter with you, child?"

Patty opened her eyes with a start. "Nothing," she said; "I'm just a little tired."

"Come in here with me."

"It's not my turn," objected Patty.

"That makes no difference," returned the doctor.

Patty dropped limply into the consulting-chair.

"Let me see your tongue. Um-m —isn't coated very much. Your pulse seems regular, though possibly a trifle feverish. Have you been working hard?"

"I don't think I've been working any harder than usual," said Patty, truthfully.

"Sitting up late nights?"

Patty considered. "I was up rather late twice last week," she confessed.

"If you girls persist in studying until all hours of the night, I don't know what we doctors can do."

Patty did not think it necessary to explain that it was a Welsh-rabbit party on each occasion, so she merely sighed and looked out of the window.

"Is your appetite good?"

"Yes," said Patty, in a tone which belied the words; "it seems to be very good."

"Um-m," said the doctor.

"I'm just a little tired," pursued Patty, "but I think I shall be all right as soon as I get a chance to rest. Perhaps I need a tonic," she suggested.

"You'd better stay out of classes for a day or two and get thoroughly rested."

"Oh, no," said Patty, in evident perturbation. "Our room is so full of girls all the time that it's really more restful to go to classes; and, besides, I can't stay out just now."

"Why not?" demanded the doctor, suspiciously.

"Well," said Patty, a trifle reluctantly, "I have a good deal to do. I've got to cram for an examination, and —"

The word "cram" was to the doctor as a red rag to a bull. "Nonsense!" she ejaculated. "I know what I shall do with you. You are going right over to the infirmary for a few days —"

"Oh, doctor!" Patty pleaded, with tears in her eyes, "there's *truly* nothing the matter with me, and I've *got* to take that examination."

"What examination is it?"

"Old English-Miss Skelling."

"I will see Miss Skelling myself," said the doctor, "and explain that you cannot take the examination until you come out. And now," she added, making a note of Patty's case, "I will have you put in the convalescent ward, and we will try the rest cure for a few days, and feed you up on chicken-broth and egg-nog, and see if we can get that appetite back."

"Thank you," said Patty, with the resigned air of one who has given up struggling against the inevitable.

"I like to see you take an interest in your work," added the doctor, kindly; "but you must always remember, my dear, that health is the first consideration."

Patty returned to the study and executed an impromptu dance in the middle of the floor.

"What's the matter?" exclaimed Priscilla. "Are you crazy?"

"No," said Patty; "only ill." And she went into her bedroom and began slinging things into a dress-suit case.

Priscilla stood in the doorway and watched her in amazement. "Are you going to New York?" she asked.

"No," said Patty; "to the infirmary."

"Patty Wyatt, you're a wretched little hypocrite!"

"Not at all," said Patty, cheerfully. "I didn't ask to go, but the doctor simply insisted. I told her I had an examination, but she said it didn't make any difference; health must be the first consideration."

"What's in that bottle?" demanded Priscilla.

"That's for my appetite," said Patty, with a grin; "the doctor hopes to improve it. I didn't like to discourage her, but I don't much believe she can." She dropped an Old English grammar and a copy of "Beowulf" into her suit-case.

"They won't let you study," said Priscilla.

"I shall not ask them," said Patty. "Good-by. Tell the girls to drop in occasionally and see me in my incarceration. Visiting hour from five to six." She stuck her head in again. "If any one wants to send violets, I think they might cheer me up."

* * * * *

The next afternoon Georgie and Priscilla presented themselves at the infirmary, and were met at the door by the austere figure of the head nurse. "I will see if Miss Wyatt is awake," she said dubiously, "but I am afraid you will excite her; she's to be kept very quiet."

"Oh, no; we'll do her good," remonstrated Georgie; and the two girls tiptoed in after the nurse.

The convalescent ward was a large, airy room, furnished in green and white, with four or five beds, each surrounded with brass poles and curtains. Patty was lying in one of the corner beds near a window, propped up on pillows, with her hair tumbled about her face, and a table beside her covered with flowers and glasses of medicine. This elaborate paraphernalia of sickness created a momentary illusion in the minds of the visitors. Priscilla ran to the bedside and dropped on her knees beside her invalid room-mate.

"Patty dear," she said anxiously, "how do you feel?"

A seraphic smile spread over Patty's face. "I've been able to take a little nourishment to-day," she said.

"Patty, you're a scandalous humbug! Who gave you those violets? 'With love, from Lady Clara Vere de Vere'—that blessed freshman!—and you've borrowed every drop of alcohol the poor child ever thought of owning. And whom are those roses from? Miss Skelling! Patty, you ought to be ashamed."

Patty had the grace to blush slightly. "I was a trifle embarrassed," she admitted; "but when I reflected upon how sorry she would have been to find out how little I knew, and how glad she will be to find out how much I know, my conscience was appeased."

"Have you been studying?" asked Georgie.

"Studying!" Patty lifted up the corner of her pillow and exhibited a blue book. "Two days more of this, and I shall be the chief authority in America on Anglo-Saxon roots."

"How do you manage it?"

"Oh," said Patty, "when the rest-hour begins I lie down and shut my eyes, and they tiptoe over and look at me, and whisper, 'She's asleep,' and softly draw the curtains around the bed; and I get out the book and put in two solid hours of irregular verbs, and am still sleeping when they come to look at me. They're perfectly astonished at the amount I sleep. I heard the nurse telling the doctor that she didn't believe I'd had any sleep for a month. And the worst of it is," she added, "that I *am* tired, whether you believe it or not, and I should just love to stay over here and sleep all day if I weren't so beastly conscientious about that old grammar."

"Poor Patty!" laughed Georgie. "She will be imposing on herself next, as well as on the whole college."

Friday morning Patty returned to the world.

"How's Old English?" inquired Priscilla.

"Very well, thank you. It was something of a cram, but I think I know that grammar by heart, from the preface to the index."

"You're back in all your other work. Do you think it paid?"

"That remains to be seen," laughed Patty.

She knocked on Miss Skelling's door, and, after the first polite greetings, stated her errand: "I should like, if it is convenient for you, to take the examination I missed."

"Do you feel able to take it to-day?"

"I feel much better able to take it to-day than I did on Tuesday."

Miss Skelling smiled kindly. "You have done very good work in Old English this semester, Miss Wyatt, and I should not ask you to take the examination at all if I thought it would be fair to the rest of the class."

"Fair to the rest of the class?" Patty looked a trifle blank; she had not considered this aspect of the question, and a slow red flush crept over her face. She hesitated a moment, and rose uncertainly. "When it comes to that, Miss Skelling," she confessed, "I'm afraid it wouldn't be quite fair to the rest of the class for me to take it."

Miss Skelling did not understand. "But, Miss Wyatt," she expostulated in a puzzled tone, "it was not difficult. I am sure you could pass."

Patty smiled. "I am sure I could, Miss Skelling. I don't believe you could ask me a question that I couldn't answer. But the point is that it's all learned since Tuesday. The doctor was laboring under a little delusion-very natural under the circumstances-when she sent me to the infirmary, and I spent my time there studying."

"But, Miss Wyatt, this is very unusual. I shall not know how to mark you," Miss Skelling murmured in some distress.

"Oh, mark me zero," said Patty, cheerfully. "It doesn't matter in the least—I know such a lot that I'll get through on the finals. Good-by; I'm sorry to have troubled you." And she closed the door and turned thoughtfully homeward.

"Did it pay?" asked Priscilla.

Patty laughed and murmured softly:

> "'The King of France rode up the hill with full ten thousand men;
> The King of France did gain the top, and then rode down again.'"

"What are you talking about?" demanded Priscilla.

"Old English," said Patty, as she sat down at her desk and commenced on the three days' work she had missed.

Chapter VIII The Deceased Robert

It was ten o'clock, and Patty, having just read her ethics over for the third time without comprehending it, had announced sleepily, "I shall have to be good by inspiration; I can't seem to grasp the rule," when a knock sounded on the door and a maid appeared with the announcement, "Mrs. Richards wishes to see Miss Wyatt."

"At this hour!" Patty cried in dismay. "It must be something serious. Think, Priscilla. What have I been doing lately that would outrage the warden sufficiently to call me up at ten o'clock? You don't suppose I'm going to be suspended or rusticated or expelled or anything like that, do you? I *honestly* can't think of a thing I've done."

"It's a telegram," the maid said sympathetically.

"A telegram?" Patty's face turned pale, and she left the room without a word.

Priscilla and Georgie sat on the couch and looked at each other with troubled faces. All ordinary telegrams came directly to the students. They knew that something serious must have happened to have it sent to the warden. Georgie got up and walked around the room uncertainly.

"Shall I go away, Pris?" she asked. "I suppose Patty would rather be alone if anything has happened. But if she's going home and has to pack her trunk to-night, come and tell me and I will come down and help."

They stood at the door a few moments talking in low tones, and as Georgie started to turn away, Patty's step suddenly sounded in the corridor. She came in with a queer smile on her lips, and sat down on the couch.

"The warden has certainly reduced the matter of scaring people to a fine art," she said. "I was never more frightened in my life. I thought that the least that had happened was an earthquake which had engulfed the entire family."

"What was the matter?" Georgie and Priscilla asked in a breath.

Patty spread out a crumpled telegram on her knee, and the girls read it over her shoulder:

> Robert died of an overdose of chloroform at ten this morning. Funeral to-morrow.
>
> Thomas M. Wyatt.

"Thomas M. Wyatt," said Patty, grimly, "is my small brother Tommy, and Robert is short for Bobby Shafto, which was the name of Tommy's bull pup, the homeliest and worst-tempered dog that was ever received into the bosom of a respectable family."

"But why in the world did he telegraph?"

"It's a joke," said Patty, shaking her head dejectedly. "Joking runs in the family, and we've all inherited the tendency. One time my father-but, as my friend Kipling says, that's another story. This dog, you see-this Robert Shafto-has cast a shadow over my vacations for more than a year. He killed my kitten, and ate my Venetian lace collar-it didn't even give him indigestion. He went out and wallowed in the rain and mud and came in and slept on my bed. He stole the beefsteak for breakfast and the rubbers and door-mats for blocks around. Property on the street appreciably declined, for prospective purchasers refused to purchase so long as Tommy Wyatt kept a dog. Robert was threatened with death time and again, but Tommy always managed to conceal him from impending justice until the trouble had blown over. But this time I suppose he committed some supreme enormity-probably chewed up the baby or one of my father's Persian rugs, or something like that. And Tommy, knowing how I detested the beast, evidently thought it would be a good joke to telegraph, though wherein lies the point I can't make out."

"Ah, I see," said Georgie; "and Mrs. Richards thought that Robert was a relation. What did she say?"

"She said, 'Come in, Patty dear,' when I knocked on the door. Usually when I have had the honor of being received by her she has somewhat frigidly called me 'Miss Wyatt.' I opened the door with my knees shaking when I heard that 'Patty dear,' and she took my hand and said, 'I am sorry to have to tell you that I have heard bad news from your brother.'

"'Tommy?' I gasped.

"'No; Robert.'

"I was dazed. I racked my brains, but I couldn't remember any brother Robert.

"'He is very ill,' she went on. 'Yes, I must tell you the truth, Patty; poor little Robert passed away this morning'; and she laid the telegram before me. Then, when it flashed over me what it meant, I was so relieved that I put my head down on her desk and simply laughed till I cried; and she thought I was crying all the time, and kept patting my head and quoting Psalms. Well, then I didn't dare to tell her, after she had expended all that sympathy; so as soon as I could stop laughing (which wasn't very soon, for I had got considerable momentum) I raised my head and told her-trying to be truthful and at the same time not hurt her feelings-that Robert was not a brother, but just a sort of friend. And, do you know, she immediately jumped to the conclusion that he was a fiancé, and began stroking my hair and murmuring that it was sometimes harder to lose friends than relatives, but that I was still young, and I must not let it blast my life, and that maybe in the future when time had dulled the pain-and then, remembering that it wouldn't do to advise me to adopt a second fiancé before I had buried my first, she stopped suddenly and asked if I wished to go home to the funeral.

"I told her no, that I didn't think it would be best; and she said perhaps not if it hadn't been announced, and she kissed me and told me she was glad to see me bearing up so bravely."

"Patty!" Priscilla exclaimed in horror, "it's dreadful. How could you let her think it?"

"How could I help it?" Patty demanded indignantly. "What with being frightened into hysterics first, and then having a strange fiancé thrust at me without a moment's notice, I think that I carried off the situation with rare delicacy and finesse. Do you think it would have been tactful to tell her it was nothing but a bull pup she was quoting Scripture about?"

"I don't see how it was exactly your fault," Georgie acknowledged.

"Thank you," said Patty. "If you had a brother like Tommy Wyatt you would know how to sympathize with me. I suppose I ought to be grateful to know that the dog is dead, but I should like to have had the news broken a little less gently."

"Patty," exclaimed Priscilla, as a sudden thought struck her, "do you happen to remember that you are on the reception committee of the Dramatic Club cotillion to-morrow night? What will Mrs. Richards think when she sees you in evening dress, receiving at a party, on the very day your fiancé has been buried?"

"I wonder?" said Patty, doubtfully. "Do you really think I ought to stay away? After working like a little buzz-saw making tissue-paper favors for the thing, I hate to have to miss it just because my brother's bull pup, that I never even *liked*, is dead.

"I'll go," she added, brightening, "and receive the guests with a forced and mechanical smile; and every time I feel the warden's eyes upon me I shall with difficulty choke back the tears, and she will say to herself:

"'Brave girl! How nobly she is struggling to present a composed face to the world! None would dream, to look at that seemingly radiant creature, that, while she is outwardly so gay, she is in reality concealing a great sorrow which is gnawing at her very vitals.'"

Chapter IX Patty the Comforter

It was on the eve of the mid-year examinations, and a gloom had fallen over the college. The conscientious ones who had worked all the year were working harder than ever, and the frivolous ones who had played all the year were working with a desperate frenzy calculated to render their minds a blank when the crucial hour should have arrived. But Patty was not working. It was a canon of her college philosophy, gained by three and a half years' of personal experience, that the day before examinations is not the time to begin to study. One has impressed the instructor with one's intelligent interest in the subject, or one has not, and the result is as sure as if the marks were already down in black and white in the college archives. And so Patty, who at least lived up to her lights, was, with the exception of a few points which she intended to learn for this period only, conscientiously neglecting the "judicious review" recommended by the faculty.

Her friends, however, who, though perhaps equally philosophic, were less consistent, were subjecting themselves to what was known as a "regular freshman cram"; and as no one had any time to talk to Patty, or to make anything to eat, she found it an unprofitable period. Her own room-mate even drove her from the study because she laughed out loud over the book she was reading; and, an exile, she wandered around to the studies of her friends, and was confronted by an "engaged" on every door. She was sitting on a window-sill in the corridor, pondering on the general barrenness of things, when she suddenly remembered her friends the freshmen in study 321. She had not visited them for some time, and freshmen are usually interesting at this period. She accordingly turned down the corridor that led to 321, and found a "positively engaged to every one!!" in letters three inches high, across the door. This promised a richness of entertainment within, and Patty heaved a disappointed sigh loud enough to carry through the transom.

The turning of leaves and rustling of paper ceased; evidently they were listening, but they gave no sign. Patty wrote a note on the door-block with reverberating punctuation-points, and then retired noisily, and tiptoed back a moment later, and leaned against the wall. Curiosity prevailed; the door opened, and a face wearing a hunted look peered out.

"Oh, Patty Wyatt, was that you?" she asked. "We thought it was Frances Stoddard coming down to have geometry explained, and so we kept still. Come in."

"Goodness, no; I wouldn't come in over an 'engaged' like that for anything. I'm afraid you're busy."

The freshman grasped her by the arm. "Patty, if you love us come in and cheer us up. We're so scared we don't know what to do."

Patty consented to be drawn across the threshold. "I don't want to interrupt you," she remonstrated, "if you have anything to do." The study was occupied by three girls. Patty smiled benignly at the two haggard faces before her. "Where's Lady Clara Vere de Vere?" she asked. "She surely isn't wasting these precious last moments in anything frivolous."

"She's in her bedroom, with a geometry in one hand and a Greek grammar in the other, trying to learn them both at once."

"Tell her to come out here; I want to give her some good advice"; and Patty sat down on the divan and surveyed the dictionary-bestrewn room with an appreciative smile.

"Oh, Patty, I'm so glad to see you!" Lady Clara exclaimed, appearing in the doorway. "The sophomores have been telling us the most *dreadful* stories about examinations. They aren't true, are they?"

"Mercy, no! Don't believe a word those sophomores tell you. They were freshmen themselves last year, and if the examinations were as bad as they say, they wouldn't have passed them, either."

A relieved expression stole over the three faces.

"You're such a comfort, Patty. Upper-classmen take things easily, don't they?"

"One gets inured to almost anything in time," said Patty. "Examinations are even entertaining, if you know the right answers."

"But we won't know the right answers!" one of the freshmen wailed, her terror returning. "We simply don't know *anything*, and Latin comes to-morrow, and geometry the next day."

"Oh, well, in that case you can't get through anyway, so don't worry. You must take it philosophically, you know." Patty settled herself among the cushions and smiled upon her frightened auditors with easy nonchalance. "As an example of the uselessness of studying at the eleventh hour when you haven't done anything through the term, I will tell you my experience with freshman Greek. I was badly prepared when I came, I didn't study through the term, and, without exaggeration, I didn't know anything. Three days before examinations I suddenly comprehended the situation, and I began swallowing that grammar in chunks. I drank black coffee to keep awake, and worked till two in the morning, and scarcely stopped cramming irregular verbs for meals. I simply thought in Greek and dreamed in Greek. And, if you will believe it, after all that work I flunked in Greek! It shook my faith in studying for examinations. I've never done it since, and I've never flunked since. I believe that it's just a matter of fate whether you get through or not, so I never bother any more."

The freshmen looked at one another disconsolately. "If it's all decided beforehand, we're lost."

Patty smiled reassuringly.

"A little flunking now and then
 Will happen to the best of men."

"But I've heard they send people home, drop them, you know, if they flunk more than a certain amount. Is that so?" Lady Clara inquired in hushed tones.

"Oh, yes," said Patty; "they have to. I've known some of the brightest girls in college to be dropped."

Lady Clara groaned. "I'm awfully shaky in geometry, Patty. Do they flunk many girls in that?"

"Many!" said Patty. "The mere clerical labor of writing out the notes occupies the department two days."

"Is the examination terribly hard?"

"I don't remember much about it. It's been such a long time since I was a freshman, you see. They picked out the hardest theorems, I know-things you couldn't even draw, let alone demonstrate: the pyramid that's cut in slices, for one, —I don't remember its name, —and that sprawling one that looks like a snail crawling out of its shell: the devil's coffin, I believe it's called technically. And-oh, yes! they give you originals —*frightful* originals, like nothing you've ever had before; and they put a little note at the top of the page telling you to do them first, and you get so muddled trying to think fast that you can't think at all. I know a girl who spent all the two hours trying to think out an original, and just as she got ready to write it down the bell rang and she had to hand in her paper."

"And what happened?"

"Oh, she flunked. You couldn't really blame the instructor, you know, for not reading between the lines, for there weren't any lines to read between; but it was sort of a pity, for the girl really knew an awful lot-but she couldn't express it."

"That's just like me."

"Ah, it's like a good many people." A silence ensued, and the freshmen looked at one another dejectedly. "But you can live, even if you should flunk math," Patty continued reassuringly. "Other people have done it before you."

"If it were only geometry-but we're scared over Latin."

"Oh, Latin! There's no use studying for that, for you can't possibly read it all over, and if you just pick out a part, it's sure not to be the same part *they* pick out. The best way is to say incantations over the book, and open it with your eyes blindfolded, and study the page it opens to; then, in case you don't pass, —and you probably won't, —you can throw the blame on fate. My freshman year, if I remember right, they gave us for prose composition one of Emerson's essays to translate into Latin, and we couldn't even tell what it meant in English."

The three looked at one another again.

"I couldn't do anything like that."

"Nor I."

"Nor I."

"Nor any one else," said Patty.

"We can flunk Latin and math; but if we flunk any more we're gone."

"I believe so," said Patty.

"And I'm awfully shaky in German."

"And I in French."

"And I in Greek."

"I don't know anything about German," said Patty. "Never had it myself. But I remember hearing Priscilla say that the printed examination papers didn't come but in time, and Fräulein Scherin, who writes a frightful hand, wrote the questions on the board in German script, and they couldn't even read them. In French I believe the first question was to write out the 'Marseillaise'; there are seven verses, and no one had learned them, and the 'Marseillaise,' you know, is a thing that you simply *can't* make up on the spur of the moment. As for Greek, I told you my own experience; I am sure nothing could be worse than that."

The freshmen looked at one another hopelessly. "There's only English and hygiene and Bible history left."

"English is something you can't tell anything about," said Patty. "They're as likely as not to ask you to write a heroic poem in iambic pentameters, if you know what they are. You have to depend on inspiration; you can't study for it."

"I hope," sighed Lady Clara, "to get through hygiene and Bible history, though, as they only count one hour apiece, I suppose it isn't much."

"You mustn't be too sanguine," said Patty. "It all depends on chance. The class in hygiene is so big that the professor hasn't time to read the papers; he just goes down the list and flunks every thirteenth girl. I'm not sure about Bible history, but I think he does the same, because I know, freshman year, that I made a mistake and handed in my map of the Holy Lands done in colored chalk to the hygiene professor, and my chart of the digestive system to the Bible professor, and neither of them noticed it. They did look a good deal alike, but not so much but what you could tell them apart. All I have to say is that I hope none of you will be number thirteen."

The freshmen stared at one another in speechless horror, and Patty rose. "Well, good-by, my children, and, above all things, don't worry. I'm glad if I've been able to cheer you up a little, for so much depends on not being nervous. Don't believe any of the silly stories the sophomores tell," she called back over her shoulder; "they're just trying to frighten you."

Chapter X "Per l'Italia"

College is a more or less selfish place. Everybody is so busy with her own affairs that she has no time to give to her neighbor, unless her neighbor has something to give in return. Olivia Copeland apparently had nothing to give in return. She was quiet and inconspicuous, and it took a second glance to realize that her face was striking and that there was a look in her eyes that other freshmen did not have. By an unfelicitous chance she was placed in the same study with Lady Clara Vere de Vere and Emily Washburn. They thought her foreign and queer, and she thought them crude and boisterous, and after the first week or two of politely trying to get acquainted the effort was dropped on both sides.

The year wore on, and nobody knew, or at least no one paid any attention to the fact, that Olivia Copeland was homesick and unhappy. Her room-mates thought that they had done their duty when they occasionally asked her to play golf or go skating with them (an invitation they were very safe in giving, as she knew how to do neither). Her instructors thought that they had done their duty when they called her up to the desk after class and warned her that her work was not as good as it had been, and that if she wished to pass she must improve in it.

The English class was the only one in which she was not warned; but she had no means of knowing that her themes were handed about among the different instructors and that she was referred to in the department as "that remarkable Miss Copeland." The department had a theory that if they let a girl know she was doing good work she would immediately stop and rest upon her reputation; and Olivia, in consequence, did not discover that she was remarkable. She merely discovered that she was miserable and out of place, and she continued to drip tears of homesickness before a sketch of an Italian villa that hung above her desk.

It was Patty Wyatt who first discovered her. Patty had dropped into the freshmen's room one afternoon on some errand or other (probably to borrow alcohol), and had idly picked up a pile of English themes that were lying on the study table.

"Whose are these? Do you care if I look at them?" she asked.

"No; you can read them if you want to," said Lady Clara. "They're Olivia's, but she won't mind."

Patty carelessly turned the pages, and then, as a title caught her eye, she suddenly looked up with a show of interest. "'The Coral-fishers of Capri'! What on earth does Olivia Copeland know about the coral-fishers of Capri?"

"Oh, she lives somewhere near there-at Sorrento," said Lady Clara, indifferently.

"Olivia Copeland lives at Sorrento!" Patty stared. "Why didn't you tell me?"

"I supposed you knew it. Her father's an artist or something of the sort. She's lived in Italy all her life; that's what makes her so queer."

Patty had once spent a sunshiny week in Sorrento herself, and the very memory of it was intoxicating. "Where is she?" she asked excitedly. "I want to talk to her."

"I don't know where she is. Out walking, probably. She goes off walking all by herself, and never speaks to any one, and then when we ask her to do something rational, like golf or basket-ball, she pokes in the house and reads Dante in Italian. Imagine!"

"Why, she must be interesting!" said Patty, in surprise, and she turned back to the themes. "I think these are splendid!" she exclaimed.

"Sort of queer, I think," said Lady Clara. "But there's one that's rather funny. It was read in class-about a peasant that lost his donkey. I'll find it"; and she rummaged through the pile.

Patty read it soberly, and Lady Clara watched her with a shade of disappointment.

"Don't you think it's pretty good?" she asked.

"Yes; I think it's one of the best things I ever read."

"You never even smiled!"

"My dear child, it isn't funny."

"Isn't funny! Why, the class simply roared over it."

Patty shrugged. “Your appreciation must have gratified Olivia. And here it’s February, and I’ve barely spoken to her.”

The next afternoon Patty was strolling home from a recitation, when she spied Olivia Copeland across the campus, headed for Pine Bluff and evidently out for a solitary walk.

“Olivia Copeland, wait a moment,” Patty called. “Are you going for a walk? May I come too?” she asked, as she panted up behind.

Olivia assented with evident surprise, and Patty fell into step beside her. “I just found out yesterday that you live in Sorrento, and I wanted to talk to you. I was there myself once, and I think it’s the most glorious spot on earth.”

Olivia’s eyes shone. “Really?” she gasped. “Oh, I’m so glad!” And before she knew it she was telling Patty the story of how she had come to college to please her father, and how she loved Italy and hated America; and what she did not tell about her loneliness and homesickness Patty divined.

She realized that the girl *was* remarkable, and she determined in the future to take an interest in her and make her like college. But a senior’s life is busy and taken up with its own affairs, and for the next week or two Patty saw little of the freshman beyond an occasional chat in the corridors.

One evening she and Priscilla had returned late from a dinner in town, to be confronted by a dark room and an empty match-safe.

“Wait a moment and I’ll get some matches,” said Patty; and she knocked on a door across the corridor where a freshman lived with whom they had a borrowing acquaintance. She found within her own freshman friends, Lady Clara Vere de Vere and Emily Washburn. It was evident by the three heads close together, and the hush that fell on the group as she entered, that some momentous piece of gossip had been interrupted. Patty forgot her room-mate waiting in the dark, and dropped into a chair with the evident purpose of staying out the evening.

“Tell me all about it, children,” she said cordially.

The freshmen looked at one another and hesitated.

“A new president?” Patty suggested, “or just a class mutiny?”

“It’s about Olivia Copeland,” Lady Clara returned dubiously; “but I don’t know that I ought to say anything.”

“Olivia Copeland?” Patty straightened up with a new interest in her eyes. “What’s Olivia Copeland been doing?”

“She’s been flunking and—”

“Flunking!” Patty’s face was blank. “But I thought she was so bright!”

“Oh, she is bright; only, you know, she hasn’t a way of making people find it out; and, besides,” Lady Clara added with meaning emphasis, “she was scared over examinations.”

Patty cast a quick look at her. “What do you mean?” she asked.

Lady Clara was fond of Patty, but she was only human, and she had been frightened herself. “Well,” she explained, “she had heard a lot of stories from-er-upper-classmen about how hard the examinations are, and the awful things they do to you if you don’t pass, and being a stranger, she believed them. Of course Emily and I knew better; but she was just scared to death, and she went all to pieces, and—”

“Nonsense!” said Patty, impatiently. “You can’t make me believe that.”

“If it had been a sophomore that had tried to frighten us,” pursued Lady Clara, “we shouldn’t have minded so much: but a senior!”

“Now, Patty, aren’t you sorry that you told us all those things?” asked Emily.

Patty laughed. ”For the matter of that, I never say anything I’m not sorry for half an hour later. I’m going to get out a book some day entitled ’Things I Wish I Hadn’t Said: A Collection of *Faux Pas*,’ by Patty Wyatt.”

”I think it’s more than a *faux pas* when you frighten a girl so she—”

“I suppose you think you’re rubbing it in,” said Patty, imperturbably; “but girls don’t flunk because they’re frightened: they flunk because they don’t know.”

"Olivia knew five times as much geometry as I did, and I got through and she didn't."

Patty examined the carpet in silence.

"She thinks she's going to be dropped, and she's just crying terribly," pursued Emily, with a certain relish in the details.

"Crying!" said Patty, sharply. "What's she crying for?"

"Because she feels bad, I suppose. She'd been out walking, and got caught in the rain, and she didn't get back in time for dinner, and then found those notes waiting for her. She's up there lying on the bed, and she's got hysterics or Roman fever or something like that. She told us to go away and let her alone. She's awfully cross all of a sudden."

Patty rose. "I think I'll go and cheer her up."

"Let her alone, Patty," said Emily. "I know the way you cheer people up. If you hadn't cheered her up before examinations she wouldn't have flunked."

"I didn't know anything about her then," said Patty, a trifle sulkily; "and, anyway," she added as she opened the door, "I didn't say anything that affected her passing, one way or the other." She turned toward Olivia's room, however, with a conscience that was not quite comfortable. She could not remember just what she *had* told those freshmen about examinations, but she had an uneasy feeling that it might not have been of a reassuring nature.

"I wish I could ever learn when it is time for joking and when it is not," she said to herself as she knocked on the study door.

No one answered, and she turned the knob and entered. A stifled sob came from one of the bedrooms, and Patty hesitated.

She was not in the habit of crying herself, and she always felt uncomfortable when other people did it. Something must be done, however, and she advanced to the threshold and silently regarded Olivia, who was stretched face downward on the bed. At the sound of Patty's step she raised her head and cast a startled glance at the intruder, and then buried her face in the pillows again. Patty scribbled an "engaged" sign and pinned it on the study door, and drawing up a chair beside the bed, she sat down with the air of a physician about to make a diagnosis.

"Well, Olivia," she began in a business-like tone, "what is the trouble?"

Olivia opened her hands and disclosed some crumpled papers. Patty spread them out and hastily ran her eyes over the official printed slips:

> Miss *Copeland* is hereby informed that she has been found deficient in *German* (*three* hours).

> Miss *Copeland* is hereby informed that she has been found deficient in *Latin prose* (*one* hour).

> Miss *Copeland* is hereby informed that she has been found deficient in *geometry* (*four* hours).

Patty performed a rapid calculation,—"three and one are four and four are eight,"—and knit her brows.

"Will they send me home, Patty?"

"Mercy, no, child; I hope not. A person who's done as good work as you in English ought to have the right to flunk every other blessed thing, if she wants to."

"But you're dropped if you flunk eight hours; you told me so yourself."

"Don't believe anything I told you," said Patty, reassuringly. "I don't know what I'm talking about more than half the time."

"I'd hate to be sent back, and have my father know I'd failed, when he spent so much time preparing me; but"—Olivia began to cry again—"I want to go back so much that I don't believe I care."

"You don't know what you're talking about," said Patty. She put her hand on the girl's shoulder. "Mercy, child, you're sopping wet, and you're shivering! Sit up and take those shoes off."

Olivia sat up and pulled at the laces with ineffectual fingers, and Patty jerked them open and dumped the shoes in a squashy heap on the floor.

"Do you know what's the matter with you?" she asked. "You're not crying because you've flunked. You're crying because you've caught cold, and you're tired and wet and hungry. You take those wet clothes off this minute and get into a warm bath-robe, and I'll get you some dinner."

"I don't want any dinner," wailed Olivia, and she showed signs of turning back to the pillows again.

"Don't act like a baby, Olivia," said Patty, sharply; "sit up and be a—a man."

Ten minutes later Patty returned from a successful looting expedition, and deposited her spoils on the bedroom table. Olivia sat on the edge of the bed and watched her apathetically, a picture of shivering despondency.

"Drink this," commanded Patty, as she extended a steaming glass.

Olivia obediently raised it to her lips, and drew back. "What's in it?" she asked faintly.

"Everything I could find that's hot-quinine and whisky and Jamaica ginger and cough syrup and a dash of red pepper, and-one or two other things. It's my own idea. You can't take cold after *that*."

"I—I don't believe I want any."

"Drink it-every drop," said Patty, grimly; and Olivia shut her eyes and gulped it down.

"Now," said Patty, cheerfully bustling about, "I'll get dinner. Have you a can-opener? And any alcohol, by chance? That's nice. We'll have three courses,—canned soup, canned baked beans, and preserved ginger,—all of them hot. It's mighty lucky Georgie Merriles was in New York or she'd never have lent them to me."

Olivia, to her own astonishment, presently found herself laughing (she had thought that she would never smile again) as she sipped mulligatawny soup from a tooth-mug and balanced a pin-trayful of steaming baked beans on her knee.

"And now," said Patty, as, the three courses disposed of, she tucked the freshman into bed, "we'll map out a campaign. While eight hours are pretty serious, they are not of necessity deadly. What made you flunk Latin prose?"

"I never had any before I came, and when I told Miss—"

"Certainly; she thought it her duty to flunk you. You shouldn't have mentioned the subject. But never mind. It's only one hour, and it won't take you a minute to work it off. How about German?"

"German's a little hard because it's so different from Italian and French, you know; and I'm sort of frightened when she calls on me, and—"

"Pretty stupid, on the whole?" Patty suggested.

"I'm afraid I am," she confessed.

"Well, I dare say you deserved to flunk in that. You can tutor it up and pass it off in the spring. How about geometry?"

"I thought I knew that, only she didn't ask what I expected and—"

"An unfortunate circumstance, but it will happen. Could you review it up a little and take a reëxamination right away?"

"Yes; I'm sure I could, only they won't give me another chance. They'll send me home first."

"Who's your instructor?"

"Miss Prescott."

Patty frowned, and then she laughed. "I thought if it were Miss Hawley I could go to her and explain the matter and ask her to give you a reëxamination. Miss Hawley's occasionally human. But Miss Prescott! No wonder you flunked. I'm afraid of her myself. She's the only woman that ever got a degree at some German university, and she simply hasn't a thought in the world beyond mathematics. I don't believe the woman has any soul. If one of those mediums should come here and dematerialize her, all that would be left would be an equilateral triangle."

Patty shook her head. "I'm afraid there's not much use in arguing with a person like that. If she once sees a truth, you know, she sees it for all time. But never mind; I'll do the best I can. I'll tell her you're an undiscovered mathematical genius; that it's latent, but if she'll examine you again she'll find it. That ought to appeal to her. Good-night. Go to sleep and don't worry; I'll manage her."

"Good night; and thank you, Patty," called a tolerably cheerful voice from under the covers.

Patty closed the door, and stood a moment in the hall, pondering the situation. Olivia Copeland was too valuable to throw away. The college must be made to realize her worth. But that was difficult. Patty had tried to make the college realize things before. Miss Prescott was the only means of salvation that she could think of, and Miss Prescott was a doubtful means. She did not at all relish the prospect of calling on her, but there seemed to be nothing else to do. She made a little grimace and laughed. "I'm acting like a freshman myself," she thought. "Walk up, Patty, and face the guns"; and without giving herself time to hesitate she marched up-stairs and knocked on Miss Prescott's door. She reflected after she had knocked that perhaps it would have been more politic to have postponed her business until the morrow. But the door opened before she had time to run away, and she found herself rather confusedly bowing to Miss Prescott, who held in her hand, not a book on calculus, but a common, every-day magazine.

"Good evening, Miss Wyatt. Won't you come in and sit down?" said Miss Prescott, in a very cordially human tone.

As she sank into a deep rush chair Patty had a blurred vision of low bookcases, pictures, rugs, and polished brass thrown into soft relief by a shaded lamp which stood on the table. Before she had time to mentally shake herself and reconstruct her ideas she was gaily chatting to Miss Prescott about the probable outcome of a serial story in the magazine.

Miss Prescott did not seem to wonder in the least at this unusual visit, but talked along easily on various subjects, and laughed and told stories like the humanest of human beings. Patty watched her, fascinated. "She's *pretty*," she thought to herself and she began to wonder how old she was. Never before had she associated any age whatever with Miss Prescott. She had regarded her much in the same light as a scientific truth, which exists, but is quite irrespective of time or place. She tried to recall some story that had been handed about among the girls her freshman year. She remembered vaguely that it had in it the suggestion that Miss Prescott had once been in love. At the time Patty had scoffingly repudiated the idea, but now she was half willing to believe it.

Suddenly, in the midst of the conversation, the ten-o'clock bell rang, and Patty recalled her errand with a start.

"I suppose," she said, "you are wondering why I came."

"I was hoping," said Miss Prescott, with a smile, "that it was just to see me, without any ulterior motive."

"It will be the next time-if you will let me come again; but to-night I had another reason, which I'm afraid you'll think impertinent-and," she added frankly, "I don't know just what's the best way to tell it so that you *won't* think it impertinent."

"Tell it to me any way you please, and I will try not to think so," said Miss Prescott, kindly.

"Don't you think sometimes the girls can tell more of one another's ability than the instructors?" Patty asked. "I know a girl," she continued, "a freshman, who is, in some ways, the most remarkable person I have ever met. Of course I can't be sure, but I should say that she is going to be very good in English some day-so good, you know, that the college will be proud of her. Well, this girl has flunked such a lot that I am afraid she is in danger of being sent home, and the college simply can't afford to lose her. I don't know anything about your rules, of course, but what seems to me the easiest way is for you to give her another examination in geometry immediately,—she really knows it,—and then tell the faculty about her and urge them to give her another trial."

Patty brought out this astounding request in the most matter-of-fact way possible, and the corners of Miss Prescott's mouth twitched as she asked: "Of whom are you speaking?"

"Olivia Copeland."

Miss Prescott's mouth grew firm, and she looked like the instructor in mathematics again.

"Miss Copeland did absolutely nothing on her examination, Miss Wyatt, and what little she has recited during the year does not betoken any unusual ability. I am sorry, but it would be impossible."

"But, Miss Prescott," Patty expostulated, "the girl has worked under such peculiar disadvantages. She's an American, but she lives abroad, and all our ways are new to her. She has never been to school a day in her life. Her father prepared her for college, and, of course, not in the same way that the other girls have been prepared. She is shy, and not being used to reciting in a class, she doesn't know how to show off. I am sure, Miss Prescott, that if you would take her and examine her yourself, you would find that she understands the work-that is, if you would let her get over being afraid of you first. I know you're busy, and it's asking a good deal," Patty finished apologetically.

"It is not that, Miss Wyatt, for of course I do not wish to mark any student unjustly; but I cannot help feeling that you have overestimated Miss Copeland's ability. She has really had a chance to show what is in her, and if she has failed in as many courses as you say-The college, you know, must keep up the standard of its work, and in questions like this it is not always possible to consider the individual."

Patty felt that she was being dismissed, and she groped about wildly for a new plea. Her eye caught a framed picture of the old monastery of Amalfi hanging over the bookcase.

"Perhaps you've lived in Italy?" she asked.

Miss Prescott started slightly. "No," she said; "but I've spent some time there."

"That picture of Amalfi, up there, made me think of it. Olivia Copeland, you know, lives near there, at Sorrento."

A gleam of interest flashed into Miss Prescott's eye.

"That's how I first came to notice her," continued Patty; "but she didn't interest me so much until I talked to her. It seems that her father is an artist, and she was born in Italy, and has only visited America once when she was a little girl. Her mother is dead, and she and her father live in an old villa on that road along the coast leading to Sorrento. She has never had any girl friends; just her father's friends-artists and diplomats and people like that. She speaks Italian, and she knows all about Italian art and politics and the church and the agrarian laws and how the people are taxed; and all the peasants around Sorrento are her friends. She is so homesick that she nearly dies, and the only person here that she can talk to about the things she is interested in is the peanut man down-town.

"The girls she rooms with are just nice exuberant American girls, and are interested in golf and basket-ball and Welsh rabbit and Richard Harding Davis stories and Gibson pictures-and she never even *heard* of any of them until four months ago. She has a water-color sketch of the villa, that her father did. It's white stucco, you know, with terraces and marble balustrades and broken statues, and a grove of ilex-trees with a fountain in the center. Just think of *belonging* to a place like that, Miss Prescott, and then being suddenly plunged into a place like this without any friends or any one who even knows about the things you know-think how lonely you would be!"

Patty leaned forward with flushed cheeks, carried away by her own eloquence. "You know what Italy's like. It's a sort of disease. If you once get fond of it you'll never forget it, and you just can't be happy till you get back. And with Olivia it's her home, besides. She's never known anything else. And it's hard at first to keep your mind on mathematics when you're dreaming all the time of ilex groves and fountains and nightingales and-and things like that."

She finished lamely, for Miss Prescott suddenly leaned back in the shadow, and it seemed to Patty that her face had grown pale and the hand that held the magazine trembled.

Patty flushed uncomfortably and tried to think what she had said. She was always saying things that hurt people's feelings without meaning to. Suddenly that old story from her freshman year flashed into her mind. He had been an artist and had lived in Italy and had died of Roman fever; and Miss Prescott had gone to Germany to study mathematics, and had never cared for anything else since. It sounded rather made up, but it might be true. Had she stumbled on a forbidden subject? she wondered miserably. She had, of course; it was just her way.

The silence was becoming unbearable; she struggled to think of something to say, but nothing came, and she rose abruptly.

"I'm sorry to have taken so much of your time, Miss Prescott. I hope I haven't bored you. Good night."

Miss Prescott rose and took Patty's hand. "Good night, my dear, and thank you for coming to me. I am glad to know of Olivia Copeland. I will see what can be done about her geometry, and I shall be glad, besides, to know her as-as a friend; for I, too, once cared for Italy."

Patty closed the door softly and tiptoed home through the dim corridors.

"Did you bring the matches?" called a sleepy voice from Priscilla's bedroom.

Patty started. "Oh, the matches!" she laughed. "No; I forgot them."

"I never knew you to accomplish anything yet that you started out to do, Patty Wyatt."

"I've accomplished something to-night, just the same," Patty retorted, with a little note of triumph in her voice; "but I haven't an idea how I happened to do it," she added frankly to herself.

And she went to bed and fell asleep, quite unaware of how much she *had* accomplished; for unconsciously she had laid the foundation of a friendship which was to make happy the future of a lonely freshman and an equally lonely instructor.

Chapter XI "Local Color"

The third senior table had discovered a new amusement with which to enlighten the tedium of waiting while Maggie was in the kitchen foraging for food. The game was called "local color," in honor of Patty Wyatt's famous definition in English class, "Local color is that which makes a lie seem truthful." The object of the game was to see who could tell the biggest lie without being found out; and the one rule required that the victims be disillusionized before they left the table.

Patty was the instigator, the champion player, and the final victim of the game. Baron Münchhausen himself would have blushed at some of her creations, and her stories were told with such an air of ingenuous honesty that the most outrageous among them obtained credence.

The game in its original conception may have been innocent enough, but the rule was not always as carefully observed as it should have been, and the most unaccountable scandals began to float about college. The president of "Christians" had been called up for cutting chapel. The shark of the class had flunked her ethics, and even failed to get through on the "re." Cathy Fair was an own cousin of Professor Hitchcock's, and called him "Tommy" to his face. These, and far worse, were becoming public property; and even personal fabrications in regard to the faculty, intended solely for undergraduate consumption, were reaching the ears of the faculty themselves.

One day Patty dropped into an under-classman's room on some committee work, and she found the children, in the manner of their elders, regaling themselves on dainty bits of college gossip.

"I heard the funniest thing about Professor Winters yesterday," piped up a sophomore.

"Tell it to us. What was it?" cried a chorus of voices.

"I'd like to hear something funny about Professor Winters; he's the solemnest-looking man I ever saw," remarked a freshman.

"Well," resumed the sophomore, "it seems he was going to get married last week, and the invitations were all out, and the presents all there, when the bride came down with the mumps."

"Really? How funny!" came in a chorus from the delighted auditors.

"Yes-on both sides; and the clergyman had never had it, so the ceremony had to be postponed."

Patty's blood froze. She recognized the tale. It was one of her own offspring, only shorn of its unessential adornments.

"Where in the world did you hear any such absurd thing as that?" she demanded severely.

"I heard Lucille Carter tell it at a fudge party up in Bonnie Connaught's room last night," answered the sophomore, stoutly, sure that the source was a reputable one.

Patty groaned. "And I suppose that every blessed one of that dozen girls has told it to another dozen by this time, and that it's only bounded by the boundaries of the campus. Well, there's not a word of truth in it. Lucille Carter doesn't know what she is talking about. That's a likely story, isn't it?" she added with fine scorn. "Does Professor Winters look like a man who'd ever dare propose to a girl, let alone marry her?" And she stalked out of the room and up to the single where Lucille lived.

"Lucille," said Patty, "what do you mean by spreading that story about Professor Winters's bride's mumps?"

"You told it to me yourself," answered Lucille, with some warmth. She was a believing creature with an essentially literal mind, and she had always been out of her element in the lofty imaginative realms of local color.

"I told it to you!" said Patty, indignantly. "You goose, you don't mean to tell me you believed it? I was just playing local color."

"How should I know that? You told it as if it were true."

"Of course," said Patty; "that's the game. You wouldn't have believed me if I hadn't."

"But you never said it wasn't true. You don't follow the rule."

"I didn't think it was necessary. I never supposed any one would believe any such absurd story as that."

"I don't see how it was my fault."

"Of course it was your fault. You shouldn't be spreading malicious tales about the faculty; it's irreverent. The story's all over college by this time, and Professor Winters has probably heard it himself. He'll flunk you on the finals to pay for it; see if he doesn't." And Patty went home, leaving a conscience-smitten and thoroughly indignant Lucille behind her.

* * * * *

About a month before the introduction of local color, Patty had entered upon a new activity, which she referred to impartially as "molding public opinion" and "elevating the press." The way of it was this:

The college, which was a modest and retiring institution craving only to be unmolested in its atmosphere of academic calm, had been recently exploited by a sensational newspaper. The fact that none of the stories was true did not mitigate the annoyance. The college was besieged by reporters who had heard rumors and wished to have them corroborated for exclusive publication in the "Censor" or "Advertiser" or "Star." And they would also like a photograph of Miss Bentley as she appeared in the character of Portia; and since she refused to give it to them, they stated their intention of "faking" one, which, they gallantly assured her, would be far homelier than the original.

The climax was reached when Bonnie Connaught was unfortunate enough to sprain her ankle in basket-ball. Something more than a life-size portrait of her, clothed in a masculine-looking sweater, with a basket-ball under her arm, appeared in a New York evening paper, and scare-heads three inches high announced in red ink that the champion athlete and most popular society girl in college was at death's door, owing to injuries received in basket-ball.

Bonnie's eminently respectable family descended upon the college in an indignant body for the purpose of taking her home, and were with difficulty soothed by an equally indignant faculty. The alumnæ wrote that in their day such brutal games as basket-ball had not been countenanced, and that they feared the college had deteriorated. Parents wrote that they would remove their daughters from college if they were to be subjected to such publicity; and the poor president was, of course, quite helpless before the glorious American privilege of free speech.

Finally the college hit upon a partially protective measure-that of furnishing its own news; and a regularly organized newspaper corps was formed among the students, with a member of the faculty at the head. The more respectable of the papers were very glad to have a correspondent from the inside whose facts needed no investigation, and the less respectable in due time betook themselves to more fruitful fields of scandal and happily forgot the existence of the college.

Patty, having the reputation of being an "English shark," had been duly empaneled and presented with a local paper. At first she had been filled with a fit sense of the responsibility of the position, and had conscientiously neglected her college work for its sake; but in time the novelty wore off, and her weekly budgets became more and more perfunctory in character.

The choice of Patty for this particular paper perhaps had not been very far-sighted, for the editor wished a column a week of what he designated as "chatty news," whereas it would have been wiser to have given her a city paper which required only a brief statement of important facts. Patty's own tendencies, it must be confessed, had a slightly yellow tinge, and, with a delighted editor egging her on, it was hard for her to suppress her latent love for "local color." The paper, however, had a wide circulation among the faculty, which circumstance tended to have a chastening effect.

The day following Patty's bride-with-the-mumps contretemps with Lucille happened to be Friday, and she was painfully engaged in her weekly molding of public opinion. It had been a barren week, and there was nothing to write about.

She reviewed at length a set of French encyclopedias which had been given to the library, and spoke with enthusiasm of a remarkable collection of jaw-bones of the prehistoric cow which had been presented to the department of paleontology. She gave in full the list of the seventeen girls who had been honored with scholarships, laboriously writing out their full names, with "Miss" attached to each, and the name of the town and the State in its unabbreviated length. And still it only mounted up to ten pages, and it took eighteen of Patty's writing to make a column.

She strolled down to examine the bulletin-board again, and discovered a new notice which she had overlooked before:

> Friday, January 17. Professor James Harkner Wallis of the Lick Observatory will lecture in the auditorium, at eight o'clock, upon "Theories of the Sidereal System."

Patty regarded the notice without emotion. It did not look capable of expansion, and she did not feel the remotest interest in the sidereal system. The brief account of the lecturer, however, which was appended to the notice, stated that Professor Wallis was one of the best known of living astronomers, and that he had conducted important original investigations.

"If I knew anything about astronomy," she thought desperately, "I might be able to spread him out over two pages."

An acquaintance of Patty's strolled up to the bulletin-board.

"Did you ever hear of that man?" asked Patty, pointing to the notice.

"Never; but I'm not an astronomer."

"I'm not, either," said Patty. "I wonder who he is?" she added wistfully. "It seems he's very famous, and I'd really like to know something about him."

The girl opened her eyes in some surprise at this thirst for gratuitous information; it did not accord with Patty's reputation: and ever after, when it was affirmed in her presence that Patty Wyatt was brilliant but superficial, she stoutly maintained that Patty was deeper than people thought. She pondered a moment, and then returned, "Lucille Carter takes astronomy; she could tell you about him."

"So she does. I'd forgotten it"; and Patty swung off toward Lucille's room.

She found a number of girls sitting around on the various pieces of furniture, eating fudge and discussing the tragedies of one Maeterlinck.

"What's this?" said Patty. "A party?"

"Oh, no," said Lucille; "just an extra session of the Dramatic Theory class. Don't be afraid; there's your room-mate up on the window-seat."

"Hello, Pris. What are you doing here?" said Patty, dipping out some fudge with a spoon. (There had been a disagreement as to how long it should boil.)

"Just paying a social call. What are you doing? I thought you were going to hurry up and get through so you could go down-town to dinner."

"I am," said Patty, vaguely; "but I got lonely."

The conversation drifting off to Maeterlinck again, she seized the opportunity to inquire of Lucille: "Who's this astronomy man that's going to lecture to-night? He's quite famous, isn't he?"

"Very," said Lucille. "Professor Phelps has been talking about him every day for the last week."

"Where's the Lick Observatory, anyway?" pursued Patty. "I can't remember, for the life of me, whether it's in California or on Pike's Peak."

Lucille considered a moment. "It's in Dublin, Ireland."

"Dublin, Ireland?" asked Patty, in some surprise. "I could have sworn that it was in California. Are you sure you know where it is, Lucille?"

"Of course I'm sure. Haven't we been having it for three days steady? California! You must be crazy, Patty. I think you'd better elect astronomy."

"I know it," said Patty, meekly. "I was going to, but I heard that it was terribly hard, and I thought senior year you have a right to take something a little easy. But, you know, that's the funniest thing about the Lick Observatory, for I really know a lot about it-read an article on it just a little while ago; and I don't know how I got the impression, but I was almost sure it was in the United States. It just shows that you can never be sure of anything."

"No," said Lucille; "it isn't safe."

"Is it connected with Dublin University?" asked Patty.

"I believe so," said Lucille.

"And this astronomy person," continued Patty, warming to her work—"I suppose he's an Irishman, then."

"Of course," said Lucille. "He's very noted."

"What's he done?" asked Patty. "It said on the bulletin-board he'd made some important discoveries. I suppose, though, they're frightful technicalities that no one ever heard of."

"Well," said Lucille, considering, "he discovered the rings of Saturn and the Milky Way."

"The rings of Saturn! Why, I thought those had been discovered *ages* ago. He must be a terribly old man. I remember reading about them when I was an infant in arms."

"It was a good while ago," said Lucille. "Eight or nine years, at least."

"And the Milky Way!" continued Patty, with a show of incredulity. "I don't see how people could have helped discovering that long ago. I could have done it myself, and I don't pretend to know anything about astronomy."

"Oh, of course," Lucille hastened to explain, "the phenomenon had been observed before, but had never been accounted for."

"I see," said Patty, surreptitiously taking notes. "He must really be an awfully important man. How did he happen to do all this?"

"He went up in a balloon," said Lucille, vaguely.

"A balloon! What fun!" exclaimed Patty, her reportorial instinct waking to the scent. "They use balloons a lot more in Europe than they do here."

"I believe he has his balloon with him here in America," said Lucille. "He never travels without it."

"What's the good of it?" inquired Patty. "I suppose," she continued, furnishing her own explanation, "it gets him such a lot nearer to the stars."

"That's without doubt the reason," said Lucille.

"I wish he'd send it up here," sighed Patty. "Do you know any more interesting details about him?"

"N—no," said Lucille; "I can't think of any more at present."

"He's certainly the most interesting professor I ever heard of," said Patty, "and it's strange I never heard of him before."

"There seem to be a good many things you have never heard of," observed Lucille.

"Yes," acknowledged Patty; "there are."

"Well, Patty," said Priscilla, emerging from the discussion on the other side of the room, "if you're going to dinner with me, you'd better stop fooling with Lucille, and go home and get your work done."

"Very well," said Patty, rising with obliging promptitude. "Good-by, girls. Come and see me and I'll give you some fudge that's done. Thank you for the information," she called back to Lucille.

* * * * *

The Monday afternoon following, Patty and Priscilla, with two or three other girls, came strolling back from the lake, jingling their skates over their arms.

"Come in, girls, and have some hot tea," said Priscilla, as they reached the study door.

"Here's a note for Patty," said Bonnie Connaught, picking up an envelop from the table. "Terribly official-looking. Must have come in the college mail. Open it, Patty, and let's see what you've flunked."

"Dear me!" said Patty, "I thought that was a habit I'd outgrown freshman year."

They crowded around and read the note over her shoulder. Patty had no secrets.

The Observatory, January 20.

Miss Patty Wyatt.

Dear Miss Wyatt: I am informed that you are the correspondent for the "Saturday Evening Post-Despatch," and I take the liberty of calling your attention to a rather grave error which occurred in last week's issue. You stated that the Lick Observatory is in Dublin, Ireland, while, as is a matter of general information, it is situated near San Francisco, California. Professor James Harkner Wallis is not an Irishman; he is an American. Though he has carried on some very important investigations, he is the discoverer of neither the rings of Saturn nor the Milky Way.

Very truly yours,

Howard D. Phelps.

"It's from Professor Phelps-what can he mean?" said the Twin, in bewilderment.

"Oh, Patty," groaned Priscilla, "you don't mean to say that you actually believed all that stuff?"

"Of course I believed it. How could I know she was lying?"

"She wasn't lying. Don't use such reckless language."

"I'd like to know what you call it, then?" said Patty, angrily.

"Local color, my dear, just local color. The worm will turn, you know."

"Why didn't you tell me?" wailed Patty.

"Never supposed for a moment you believed her. Thought you were joking all the time."

"What's the matter, Patty? What have you done?" the others demanded, divided between a pardonable feeling of curiosity and a sense that they ought to retire before this domestic tragedy.

"Oh, tell them," said Patty, bitterly. "Tell every one you see. Shout it from the dome of the observatory. You might as well; it'll be all over college in a couple of hours."

Priscilla explained, and as she explained the funny side began to strike her. By the time she had finished they were all-except Patty-reduced to hysterics.

"The poor editor," gurgled Priscilla. "He's always after a scoop, and he's certainly got one this time."

"Where is it, Patty-the paper?" gasped Bonnie.

"I threw it away," said Patty, sulkily.

Priscilla rummaged it out of the waste-basket, and the four bent over it delightedly.

> Ireland's eminent astronomer spending a few weeks in America lecturing at the principal colleges-His famous discovery of the rings of Saturn made during a balloon ascension three thousand feet in the air-Though this is his first visit to the States, he speaks with only a slight brogue-Loyal son of old Erin

"Patty, Patty! And you, of all people, to be so gullible!"

"Professor James Harkner Wallis's parents will be writing to Prexy next to say that their son can't lecture here any more if he is to be subjected to this sort of thing."

"It's disgusting!" said Bonnie Connaught, feelingly.

"When you've got through laughing, I wish you'd tell me what to do."

"Tell Professor Phelps it was a slip of the pen."

"A slip of the pen to the extent of half a column is good," said the Twin.

"I think you girls are beastly to laugh when I am probably being expelled this minute."

"Faculty meeting doesn't come till four," said Bonnie.

Patty sat down by the desk and buried her head in her arms.

"Patty," said Priscilla, "you aren't crying, are you?"

"No," said Patty, savagely; "I'm thinking."

"You will never think of anything that will explain that."

Patty looked up with the air of one who has received an inspiration. "I'm going to tell him the truth."

"Don't do anything so rash," pleaded the Twin.

"That is, of course, the only thing you can do," said Priscilla. "Sit down and write him a note, and I'll promise not to laugh till you get through."

Patty stood up. "I think," she said, "I'll go and see him."

"Oh, no. Write him a note. It's loads easier."

"No," said Patty, with dignity; "I think I owe him a personal explanation. Is my hair all right? If you girls reveal this to a single person before I come back, I'll not tell you a thing he says," she added as she closed the door.

Patty returned half an hour later, just as they were finally settling down to tea. She peered around the darkening room; finding only four expectant faces, she leisurely seated herself on a cushion on the floor and stretched out her hand for a steaming cup.

"What did he say? What kept you so long?"

"Oh, I stopped in the office to change my electives, and it delayed me."

"You don't mean to tell me that man made you elect astronomy?" Priscilla asked indignantly.

"Certainly not," said Patty. "I shouldn't have done it if he had."

"Oh, Patty, I know you like to tease, but I think it's odious. You know we're in suspense. Tell us what happened."

"Well," said Patty, placidly gathering her skirts about her, "I told him exactly how it was. I didn't hide anything-not even the bride with the mumps."

"Was he cross, or did he laugh?"

"He laughed," said Patty, "till I thought he was going to fall off his chair, and I looked anxiously around for some water and a call-bell. He really has a surprising sense of humor for a member of the faculty."

"Was he nice?"

"Yes," said Patty; "he was a dear. When he got through discussing Universal Truth, I asked him if I might elect astronomy, and he said I would find it pretty hard the second semester; but I told him I was willing to work, and he said I really showed a remarkable aptitude for explaining phenomena, and that if I were in earnest he would be glad to have me in the class."

"I think a man as forgiving as that *ought* to be elected," said Priscilla.

"You certainly have more courage than I gave you credit for," said Bonnie. "I never could have gone over and explained to that man in the wide world."

Patty smiled discreetly. "When you have to explain to a woman," she said in the tone of one who is stating a natural law, "it is better to write a note; but when it is a man, always explain in person."

Chapter XII The Exigencies of Etiquette

"If I had been the one to invent etiquette," said Patty, "I should have made party calls payable one year after date, and then should have allowed three days' grace at the end."

"In which case," said Priscilla, "I suppose you would get out of calling on Mrs. Millard altogether."

"Exactly," said Patty.

Mrs. Millard-more familiarly referred to as Mrs. Prexy-annually invited the seniors to dinner in parties of ten. Patty, whose turn had come a short time before, owing to an untoward misfortune, had been in the infirmary at the time; but, though she had missed the fun, she now found it necessary to pay the call.

"Of course," she resumed, "I can see why you should be expected to call if you attend the function and partake of the food; but what I *can't* understand is why a peaceable citizen who desires only to gang his ain gait should, upon the reception of an entirely unsolicited invitation, suddenly find it incumbent upon him to put on his best dress and his best hat and gloves in order to call upon people he barely knows."

"Your genders," said Priscilla, "are a trifle mixed."

"That," said Patty, "is the fault of the language. The logic, I think, you will find correct. You can see what would happen," she pursued, "if you carry it out to its logical conclusion. Suppose, for instance, that every woman I have ever met in this town should suddenly take it into her head to invite me to a dinner. Here I—perfectly unsuspicious and innocent of any evil, because of a purely arbitrary law which I did not help to make-would not only have to sit down and write a hundred regrets, but would have to pay a hundred calls within the next two weeks. It makes me shudder to think of it!"

"I don't believe you need worry about it, Patty; of course we know you're popular, but you're not as popular as that."

"No," said Patty; "I didn't mean that I thought I really *should* get that many invitations. It's only that one is open to the constant danger."

During the progress of this conversation Georgie Merriles had been lounging on the couch by the window, reading the "Merchant of Venice" in a critically unimpassioned way that the instructor in Dramatic Theory could not have praised too much. The room finally having become too dark for reading, she threw down the book with something like a yawn. "It would have been a joke on Portia," she remarked, "if Bassanio had chosen the wrong casket"; and she turned her attention to the campus outside. Groups of girls were coming along the path from the lake, and the sound of their voices, mingled with laughter and the jingling of skates, floated up through the gathering dusk. Across the stretches of snow and bare trees lights were beginning to twinkle in the other dormitories, while nearer at hand, and more clearly visible, rose the irregular outline of the president's house.

"Patty," said Georgie, with her nose against the pane, "if you really want to get that call out of the way, now's your chance. Mrs. Millard has just gone out."

Patty dashed into her bedroom and began jerking out bureau drawers. "Priscilla," she called in an agonized tone, "do you remember where I keep my cards?"

"It's ten minutes of six, Patty; you can't go now."

"Yes, I can. It doesn't matter what time it is, so long as she's out. I'll go just as I am."

"Not in a golf-cape!"

Patty hesitated an instant. "Well," she admitted, "I suppose the butler might tell her. I'll put on a hat"—this with the air of one who is making a really great concession. Some more banging of bureau drawers, and she appeared in a black velvet hat trimmed with lace, with the brown jacket of her suit over her red blouse, and a blue golf-skirt and very muddy boots showing below.

"Patty, you're a disgrace to the room!" cried Priscilla. "Do you mean to tell me that you are going to Mrs. Millard's in a short skirt and those awful skating-shoes?"

"The butler won't look at my feet; I'm so beautiful above"; and Patty banged the door behind her.

Georgie and Priscilla flattened themselves against the window to watch the progress of the call.

"Look," gasped Priscilla. "There's Mrs. Millard going in at the back door."

"And there's Patty. My, but she looks funny!"

"Call her back," cried Priscilla, wildly trying to open the window.

"Let her alone," laughed Georgie; "it will be such fun to gloat over her."

The window came up with a jerk. "Patty! Patty!" shrieked Priscilla.

Patty turned and waved her hand airily. "Can't stop now-will be back in a moment"; and she sped on around the corner.

The two stood watching the house for several minutes, vaguely expecting an explosion of some sort to occur. But nothing happened. Patty was swallowed as if by the grave, and the house gave no sign. They accordingly shrugged their shoulders and dressed for dinner with the philosophy which a life fraught with alarms and surprises gives.

* * * * *

Dinner was half over, and the table had finished discussing Patty's demise, when that young lady trailed placidly in, smiled on the expectant faces, and inquired what kind of soup they had had.

"Bean soup; it wasn't any good," said Georgie, impatiently. "What happened? Did you have a nice call?"

"No, Maggie, I don't care for any soup to-night. Just bring me some steak, please."

"Patty!" in a pleading chorus, "what happened?"

"Oh, I beg your pardon," said Patty, sweetly. "Yes, thank you, I had a very pleasant call. May I trouble you for the bread, Lucille?"

"Patty, I think you're obnoxious," said Georgie. "Tell us what happened."

"Well," began Patty, in a leisurely manner, "I said to the butler, 'Is Mrs. Millard in?' and he said to me (without even a smile), 'I am not sure, miss; will you please step into the drawing-room and I'll see.' I was going to tell him that he needn't bother, as I knew she was out; but I thought that perhaps it would look a little better if I waited and let him find out for himself. So I walked in and sat down in a pink-and-white embroidered *Louis-Quatorze* chair. There was a big mirror in front of me, and I had plenty of time to study the effect, which, I will acknowledge, was a trifle mixed."

"A trifle," Georgie assented.

"I was beginning," pursued Patty, "to feel nervous for fear some of the family might drop in, when the man came back and said, 'Mrs. Millard will be down in a minute.'

"If I had seen you at that moment, Georgie Merriles, there would have been battle, murder, and sudden death. My first thought was of flight; but the man was guarding the door, and Mrs. Prexy had my card. While I was frenziedly trying to think of a valid excuse for my costume the lady came in, and I rose and greeted her graciously, one might almost say gushingly. I talked very fast and tried to hypnotize her, so that she would keep her eyes on my face; but it was no use: I saw them traveling downward, and pretty soon I knew by the amused expression that they had arrived at my shoes.

"Concealment was no longer possible," pursued Patty, warming to her subject. "I threw myself upon her mercy and confessed the whole damning truth. What kind of ice-cream is that?" she demanded, leaning forward and gazing anxiously after a passing maid. "*Don't* tell me they're giving us raspberry again!"

"No; it's vanilla. Go on, Patty."

"Well, where was I?"

"You'd just told her the truth."

"Oh, yes. She said she'd always wanted to meet the college girls informally and know them just as they are, and she was very glad of this opportunity. And there I sat, looking like a kaleidoscope and feeling like a fool, and she taking it for granted that I was being perfectly natural. Complimentary, wasn't it? At this point dinner was announced, and she invited me to stay-quite insisted, in fact, to make up, she said, for the one I had missed when I was ill in the infirmary." Patty looked around the table with a reminiscent smile.

"What did you say? Did you refuse?" asked Lucille.

"No; I accepted, and am over there at present, eating *pâté de foie gras.*"

"No, really, Patty; what did you say?"

"Well," said Patty, "I told her that this was ice-cream night at the college, and that I sort of hated to miss it; but that to-morrow would be mutton night, which I didn't mind missing in the least; so if she would just as leave transfer her invitation, I would accept for to-morrow with pleasure."

"Patty," exclaimed Lucille, in a horrified tone, "you didn't say that!"

"Just a little local color, Lucille," laughed Priscilla.

"But," objected Lucille, "we'd promised not to play local color any more."

"Have you not learned," said Priscilla, "that Patty can no more live without local color than she can live without food? It's ingrained in her nature."

"Never mind," said Patty, good-naturedly; "you may not believe me now, but to-morrow night, when I'm all dressed up in beautiful clothes, swapping stories with Prexy and eating lobster salad, while you are over here having mutton, *then* maybe you'll be sorry."

Chapter XIII A Crash Without

"I love the smell of powder," said Patty.

"Gunpowder or baking-powder?"

As Patty at the moment had her nose buried in a box of face-powder she thought it unnecessary to answer.

"It brings back my youth," she pursued. "The best times of my life have been mixed up with powder and rouge-Washington's Birthday nights, and minstrel shows, and masquerades, and plays at boarding-school, and even Mother Goose tableaux when I was a—"

Patty's reminiscences were interrupted by Georgie, who was anxiously pacing up and down the wings. "It's queer some of the cast don't come. I told them to be here early, so we could get them all made up and not have a rush at the end."

"Oh, there's time enough," said Patty, comfortably. "It isn't seven yet, and if they're going to dress in their rooms it won't take any time over here just to make them up and put on their wigs. It's a comparatively small cast, you see. Now, on the night of the Trig. ceremonies, when we had to make up three whole ballets and only had one box of make-up, we *were* rushed. I thought I'd never live to see the curtain go down. Do you remember the suit of chain-mail we made for Bonnie Connaught out of wire dish-cloths? It took sixty-three, and the ten-cent store was terribly dubious about renting them to us; and then, after working every spare second for three days over the thing, we found, the last minute, that we hadn't left a big enough hole for her to get into, and—"

"Oh, do keep still, Patty," said Georgie, nervously; "I can't remember what I have to do when you talk all the time."

A manager on the eve of producing a new play, with his reputation at stake, may be excused for being a trifle irritable. Patty merely shrugged her shoulders and descended through the stage-door to the half-lighted hall, where she found Cathy Fair strolling up and down the center aisle in an apparently aimless manner.

"Hello, Cathy," said Patty; "what are you doing over here?"

"I'm head usher, and I wanted to see if those foolish sophomores had mixed up the numbers again."

"It strikes me they're a trifle close together," said Patty, sitting down and squeezing in her knees.

"Yes, I know; but you can't get eight hundred people into this hall any other way. When we once get them packed they'll have to sit still, that's all. What are you doing over here yourself?" she continued. "I didn't know you were on the committee. Or are you just helping Georgie?"

"I'm in the cast," said Patty.

"Oh, are you? I saw the program to-day, but I'd forgotten it. I've often wondered why you haven't been in any of the class plays."

"Fortune and the faculty are against it," sighed Patty. "You see, they didn't discover my histrionic ability before examinations freshman year, and after examinations, when I was asked to be in the play, the faculty thought I could spend the time to better advantage studying Greek. At the time of the sophomore play I was on something else and couldn't serve, and this year I had just been deprived of my privileges for coming back late after Christmas."

"But I thought you said you were in it?"

"Oh," said Patty, "it's a minor part, and my name doesn't appear."

"What sort of a part is it?"

"I'm a crash."

"A crash?"

"Yes, 'a crash without.' Lord Bromley says, 'Cynthia, I will brave all for your sake. I will follow you to the ends of the earth.' At this point a crash is heard without. I," said Patty, proudly, "am the crash. I sit behind a moonlit balcony in a space about two feet square, and drop a lamp-chimney into a box. It may not sound like a very important part, but it is the pivot upon which the whole plot turns."

"I hope you won't be taken with stage-fright," laughed Cathy.

"I'll try not," said Patty. "There comes the butler and Lord Bromley and Cynthia. I've got to go and make them up."

"Why are you making people up, if you are not on the committee?"

"Oh, once, during a period of mental weakness, I took china-painting lessons, and I'm supposed to know how. Good-by."

"Good-by. If you get any flowers I'll send them in by an usher."

"Do," said Patty. "I'm sure to get a lot."

Behind the scenes all was joyful confusion. Georgie, in a short skirt, with her shirt-waist sleeves rolled up and a note-book in her hand, was standing in the middle of the stage directing the scene-shifters and distracted committee. Patty, in the "green-room," was presiding over the cast, with a hare's foot in one hand and the other daubed with red and blue grease-paints.

"Oh, Patty," remonstrated Cynthia, with a horrified glance in the mirror, "I look more like a soubrette than a heroine."

"That's the way you ought to look," returned Patty. "Here, hold still till I put another dab on your chin."

Cynthia appealed to the faithful Lord Bromley, who was sitting in the background, politely letting the ladies go first. "Look, Bonnie, don't you think I'm too red? I know it'll all come off when you kiss me."

"If it comes off as easily as that, you'll be more fortunate than most of the people I make up"; and Patty smiled knowingly as she remembered how Priscilla had soaked half the night on the occasion of a previous play, and then had appeared at breakfast the next morning with lowering eyebrows and a hectic flush on each cheek. "You must remember that foot-lights take a lot of color," she explained condescendingly. "You'd look ghastly if I let you go the way you wanted to at first. Next!

"No," said Patty, as the butler presented himself; "you don't come till the second act. I'll take the Irate Parent first." The Irate Parent was dragged from a corner where he had been anxiously mumbling over his lines. "What's the matter?" asked Patty, as she began daubing in wrinkles with a liberal hand; "are you afraid?"

"N-no," said the Parent; "I'm not afraid, only I'm afraid that I will be afraid."

"You'd just better change your mind, then," said Patty, sternly. "We aren't going to allow any stage-fright to-night."

"Patty, you can manage Georgie Merriles; make her let me go on without any wig," cried Cynthia, returning and holding up to view a mass of yellow curls of a shade that was never produced in the course of nature.

Patty looked at the wig critically. "It is, perhaps, a trifle golden for the part."

"Golden!" said Cynthia. "It's positively *orange*. Wait till you see how it lights up. He calls me his dark-eyed beauty: and I'm sure no one with dark eyes, or any other kind of eyes, would have hair like that. My own looks a great deal better."

"Why don't you wear your own, then? Wrinkle up your forehead, Parent, and let me see which way they run."

"Georgie paid two dollars for renting it, and she's bound to get the money's worth of wear out of it, even if she makes me look like a fright and spoils the play."

"Nonsense," said Patty, pushing away the Parent and giving her undivided attention to the question. "Your own hair does look better. Just mislay the wig and keep out of Georgie's way till the curtain goes up. The audience are beginning to come," she announced to the room in general, "and you've got to keep still back there. You're making an awful racket, and they can hear you all over the house. Here, what are you making such a noise for?" she demanded of Lord Bromley, who came clumping up with footfalls which reverberated through the flies.

"I can't help it," he said crossly. "Look at these boots. They're so big that I can step out of them without unlacing them."

"It's not my fault. I haven't anything to do with the costumes."

"I know it; but what can I do?"

"Never mind," said Patty, soothingly; "they don't look so awfully bad. You'll have to try and walk without raising your feet."

She went out on the stage, where Georgie was giving her last directions to the scene-shifters. "The minute the curtain goes down on the first act change this forest to the drawing-room scene, and don't make any noise hammering. If you have to hammer, do it while the orchestra's playing. How does it look?" she asked anxiously, turning to Patty.

"Beautiful," said Patty. "I'd scarcely recognize it."

The "forest scene" had served in every outdoor capacity for the last four years, and it was usually hailed with a groan on the part of the audience.

"I was just coming in to see if the cast were ready," said Georgie.

"They're all made up, and are sitting in the green-room getting stage-fright. What shall I do now?"

"Let me see," said Georgie, consulting her book. "One of the committee is to prompt, one is to stay with the men and see that they manage the curtain and the lights in the right places, one is to give the cues, and two are to help change costumes. Cynthia has to change from a riding-habit to a ball-gown in four minutes. I think you'd better help her, too."

"Anything you please," said Patty, obligingly. "I'll stand on a stool with the ball-gown in the air ready to drop it over her head the moment she appears, like a harness on a fire-horse. Is everything out here done? What time is it?"

"Yes; everything's done, and it's five minutes of eight. We can begin as soon as the audience is ready."

They peered through the folds of the heavy velvet curtain at the sea of faces in front. Eight hundred girls in light evening-gowns were talking and laughing and singing. Snatches of song would start up in one corner and sweep gaily over the house, and sometimes two would meet and clash in the center, to the horror of those who preferred harmony to volume.

"Here come the old girls!" said Patty, as a procession of some fifty filed into reserved seats near the front. "There are loads of last year's class back. What are the juniors doing? Look; I believe they are going to serenade them."

The juniors rose in a body, and, turning to their departed sister class, sang a song notable for its sentiment rather than its meter.

"I do hope it will be a success," sighed Georgie. "If it doesn't come up to last year's senior play I shall *die*."

"Oh, it will," said Patty, reassuringly. "Anything would be better than that."

"Now the glee club's going to sing two songs," said Georgie. "Thank heaven, they're new!" she added fervently. "And the orchestra plays an overture, and then the curtain goes up. Run and tell them to come out here, ready for the first act."

Lord Bromley was standing in the wings disgustedly viewing the banquet-table. "See here, Patty," he called as she hurried past. "Look at this stuff Georgie Merriles has palmed off on us for wine. You can't expect me to drink any such dope as *that*."

Patty paused for an instant. "What's the matter with it?" she inquired, pouring out some in a glass and holding it up to the light.

"Matter? It's made of currant jelly and water, with cold tea mixed in."

"I made it myself," said Patty, with some dignity. "It's a beautiful color."

"But I have to drain my glass at a draught," expostulated the outraged lord.

"I'm sure there's nothing in currant jelly or tea to hurt you. You can be thankful it isn't poisonous." And Patty hurried on.

The glee club sang the two new songs, punctuated with the appreciative applause of a long-suffering audience, and the orchestra commenced the overture.

"Everybody clear the stage," said Georgie, in a low tone, "and you keep your eyes on the book," she added sternly to the prompter; "you lost your place twice at the dress rehearsal."

The overture died down; a bell tinkled, and the curtain parted in the middle, discovering Cynthia sitting on a garden-seat in the castle park (originally the Forest of Arden).

As the curtain fell at the end of the act, and the applause gave way to an excited buzz in the audience, Patty hugged Georgie gleefully. "It's fifty times better than last year!"

"Heaven send Theo Granby is out there!" piously ejaculated Georgie. (Theo Granby had been the chairman of last year's senior play.)

* * * * *

The curtain had risen on the fourth act, and Patty squeezed herself into the somewhat close quarters behind the balcony. There was fortunately-or rather unfortunately—a window in the rear of the building at this point, and Patty opened it and perched herself at one end of the sill, with the lamp-chimney ready for use at the other end. The crash was not due for some time, and Patty, having lately elected astronomy, whiled away the interval by examining the stars.

On the stage matters were approaching a climax. Lord Bromley was making an excellent lover, as was proved by the fact that the audience was taking him seriously instead of laughing through the love scenes as usual.

"Cynthia," he implored, "say that you will be mine, and I will brave all for your sake. I will follow you to the ends of the earth." He gazed tenderly into her eyes, and waited for the crash. A silence as of the tomb prevailed, and he continued to gaze tenderly, while a grin rapidly spread over the audience.

"Hang Patty!" he murmured savagely. "Might have known she'd do something like this.—What was that? Did you hear a noise?" he asked aloud.

"No," said Cynthia, truthfully; "I did not hear anything."

"Pretend you did," he whispered, and they continued to improvise. After some five minutes of hopeless floundering, the prompter got them back on the track again, and the act proceeded, with the audience happily unaware that anything was missing.

Ten minutes later Lord Bromley was declaiming: "Cynthia, let us flee this place. Its dark rooms haunt me; its silence oppresses me—" And the crash came.

For the first moment the audience was too startled to notice that the actors were also taken by surprise. Then Lord Bromley, who was getting used to emergencies, pulled himself together and ejaculated, "Hark! What was that sound?"

"I think it was a crash," said Cynthia.

He grasped her hand and ran back toward the balcony. "Give us our lines," he said to the prompter, as he went past.

The prompter had dropped the book, and couldn't find the place.

"Make them up," came in a piercing whisper from behind the balcony.

A silence ensued while the two dashed back and forth, looking excitedly up and down the stage. Then the despairing Lord Bromley stretched out his arms in a gesture of supplication. "Cynthia," he burst out in tones of realistic longing, "I cannot bear this horrible suspense. Let us flee." And they fled, fully three pages too early, forgetting to leave the letter which should have apprised the Irate Parent of the circumstance.

Georgie was tramping up and down the wings, wringing her hands and lamenting the day that ever Patty had been born.

"Hurry up that Parent before they stop clapping," said Lord Bromley, "and they'll never know the difference."

The poor old man, with his wig over one ear, was unceremoniously hustled on to the stage, where he raved up and down and swore never to forgive his ungrateful daughter in so realistic a manner that the audience forgot to wonder how he found it out. In due time the runaways returned from the notary's, overcame the old man's harshness, received the parental blessing, and the curtain fell on a scene of domestic felicity that delighted the freshmen in the gallery.

Patty crawled out from under the balcony and fell on her knees at Georgie's feet.

Lord Bromley raised her up. "Never mind, Patty. The audience doesn't know the difference; and, anyway, it was all for the best. My mustache wouldn't have stayed on more than two minutes longer."

They could hear some one shouting in the front, "What's the matter with Georgie Merriles?" and a hundred voices replied, "She's all right!"

"Who's all right?"

"G-e-o-r-g-i-e M-e-r-r-i-l-e-s."

"What's the matter with the cast?"

"They're all right!"

The stage-door burst open and a crowd of congratulatory friends burst in and gathered around the disheveled actors and committee. "It's the best senior play since we've been in college." "The freshmen are simply crazy over it." "Lord Bromley, your room will be full of flowers for a month." "Patty," called the head usher, over the heads of the others, "let me congratulate you. I was in the very back of the room, and never heard a thing but your crash. It sounded *fine*!"

"Patty," demanded Georgie, "what in the world were you doing?"

"I was counting the stars," said the contrite Patty, "and then I remembered too late, and I turned around suddenly, and it fell off. I am terribly sorry."

"Never mind," laughed Georgie; "since it turned out well, I'll forgive you. All the cast and committee," she said, raising her voice, "come up to my room for food. I'm sorry I can't invite you all," she added to the girls crowded in the doorway, "but I live in a single."

Chapter XIV The Mystery of the Shadowed Sophomore

Oh, I say, Bonnie-Bonnie Connaught! Priscilla! Wait a minute," called a girl from across the links, as the two were strolling homeward one afternoon, dragging their caddie-bags behind them. They turned and waited while Bonnie's sophomore cousin, Mildred Connaught, dashed up. She grasped them excitedly, and at the same time glanced over her shoulder with the air of a criminal who is being tracked.

"I want to tell you something," she panted. "Come in here where no one will see us"; and she dived into a clump of pine-trees growing by the path.

Priscilla and Bonnie followed more leisurely, and dropped down on the soft needles with an air of amused tolerance.

"Well, Mildred, what's the matter?" Bonnie inquired mildly.

The sophomore lowered her voice to an impressive whisper, although there was not a person within a hundred yards. "I am being *followed*," she said solemnly.

"Followed!" exclaimed Bonnie, in amazement. "Are you crazy, child? You act like a boy who's been reading dime novels."

"Listen, girls. You mustn't tell a soul, because it's a great secret. We're going to plant the class tree to-night, and I am chairman of the ceremonies. Everything is ready-the costumes are finished and the plans all arranged so that the class can get out to the place without being seen. The freshmen haven't a suspicion that it's going to be to-night. But they have found out that I'm chairman of the committee, and, if you please,"—Mildred's eyes grew wide with excitement,—"they've been *tracking* me for a week. They have *relays* of girls appointed to watch me, and I can't stir without a freshman tagging along behind. When I went down to order the ice-cream, there was one right at my elbow, and I had to pretend that I'd come for soda-water. I have simply had to let the rest of the committee do all of the work, because I was so afraid the freshmen would find out the time. It was funny at first, but I am getting nervous. It's horrible to think that you're being watched all the time. I feel as if I'd committed a murder, and keep looking over my shoulder like-like Macbeth."

"It's *awful*," Bonnie shuddered. "I'm thrilled to the bone to think of the peril a member of my family is braving for the sake of her class."

"You needn't laugh," said Mildred. "It's a serious matter. If those freshmen come to our tree ceremonies, we'll never hear the last of it. But they are not going to come," she added with a meaning smile. "They have another engagement. We chose to-night because there's a lecture before the Archæological Society by some alumna person who's been digging up remains in Rome. The freshmen have been told to go and hear her on account of their Latin. Imagine their feelings when they are cooped up in the auditorium, trying to look intelligent about the Roman Forum, and listening to our yells outside!"

Priscilla and Bonnie smiled appreciatively. It was not so long, after all, since they themselves were sophomores, and they recalled their own tree ceremonies, when the freshmen had *not* been cooped up.

"But the trouble is," pursued Mildred, "that it's more important for me to get there than any one else, because I have to dig the hole,—Peters is really going to dig it, you know; I just take out the first shovelful,—but I can't get there on account of that beastly scout. As soon as she saw me acting suspicious, she'd run and warn the class."

"I see," said Bonnie; "but what have Priscilla and I to do with it?"

"Well," said Mildred, tentatively, "you're both pretty big, you know, and you're our sister class, and you ought to help us."

"Certainly," acquiesced Bonnie; "but in just what way?"

"Well, my idea was this. If you would just stroll down by the lake after chapel, and loiter sort of inconspicuously among the trees, you know, I would come that way a little later, and then, when the detective person came along after me, you could just nab her and—"

"Chuck her in the lake?" asked Bonnie.

"No, of course not. Don't use any force. Just politely detain her till you hear us yelling-take her for a walk. She'd feel honored."

Bonnie laughed. The program struck her as entertaining. "I don't see anything very immoral in delaying a freshman who is going where she has no business to go. What do you say, Pris?"

"It's not exactly a Sunday-school excursion," acknowledged Priscilla, "but I don't see why it isn't as legitimate for us to play detective as for them."

"By all means," said Bonnie. "Behold Sherlock Holmes and his friend Dr. Watson about to solve the Mystery of the Shadowed Sophomore."

"You've saved my life," said Mildred, feelingly. "Don't forget. Right after chapel, by the lake." She peered warily out through the branches. "I've got to get the keys to the gymnasium, so the refreshments can be put in during chapel. Do you see anybody lurking about? I guess I can get off without being seen. Good-by"; and she sped away like a hunted animal.

Bonnie looked after her and laughed. "'Youth is a great time, but somewhat fussy,'" she quoted; and the two took their homeward way.

They found Patty, who was experiencing a periodical fit of studying, immersed in dictionaries and grammars. It was under protest that she allowed herself to be interrupted long enough to hear the story of their proposed adventure.

"You babies!" she exclaimed. "Haven't you grown up yet? Don't you think it's a little undignified for seniors-one might almost say alumnæ-to be kidnapping freshmen?"

"We're not kidnapping freshmen," Bonnie remonstrated; "we're teaching them manners. It's my duty to protect my little cousin."

"You can come with us and help detect," said Priscilla, generously.

"Thank you," said Patty, loftily. "I haven't time to play with you children. Cathy Fair and I are going to do Old English to-night."

That evening, as Patty, keyed to the point of grappling with and throwing whole pages of "Beowulf," stood outside the chapel door waiting for Cathy to appear, the professor of Latin came out with a stranger.

"Oh, Miss Wyatt!" she exclaimed in a relieved tone, pouncing upon Patty. "I wish to present you to Miss Henderson, one of our alumnæ who is to lecture to-night before the Archæological Society. She has not been back for several years, and wishes to see the new buildings. Have you time to show her around the campus a little before the lecture begins?"

Patty bowed and murmured that she would be most happy, and cast an agonized glance back at Cathy as she led the lecturer off. As they strolled about, Patty poured out all the statistics she knew about the various buildings, and Miss Henderson received them with exclamations of delighted surprise. She was rather young and gushing for a Ph.D. and an archæologist, Patty decided, and she wondered desperately how she could dispose of her and get back to "Beowulf" and Cathy.

They rounded the top of a little hill, and Miss Henderson exclaimed delightedly, "There is the lake, just as it used to be!"

Patty stifled a desire to remark that lakes had a habit of staying where they used to be, and asked politely if Miss Henderson would like to take a row.

Miss Henderson thought that it would be pleasant; but she had forgotten her watch, and was afraid there would not be time.

Patty glanced about vaguely for some further object of interest, and spied Mildred Connaught sauntering toward the lake. She had forgotten all about the Sherlock Holmes adventure, and she suddenly had an inspiration. Be it said to her credit that she hesitated a moment; but the lecturer's next remark led to her own undoing. She was murmuring something about feeling like a stranger, and wishing that she might know the students informally and see a little of the real college life.

"It would be a pity not to gratify her when I can do it so easily," Patty told herself; and she added out loud, "I am sure we have time for a little row, Miss Henderson. You walk on, and I will run back and get my watch; it won't take a minute."

"I wouldn't have you do that; it is too much trouble," remonstrated Miss Henderson.

"It's no trouble whatever," Patty protested kindly. "I can take a cross cut, and meet you at the little summer-house where the boats are moored. It's straight down this path; you can't miss it. Just follow that girl over there"; and she darted away.

The lecturer gazed dubiously after her a moment, and then started on after the girl, who cast a look over her shoulder and quickened her pace. It was growing quite dusky under the trees, and the lecturer hurried on, trying to keep the girl in sight; but she unexpectedly turned a corner and disappeared, and at the same moment two strange girls suddenly dropped into the path, apparently from the tree-tops.

"Good evening," they said pleasantly. "Are you taking a walk?"

The lecturer started back with an exclamation of surprise; but as soon as she could regain her composure, she replied politely that she was strolling about and looking at the campus.

"Perhaps you would like to stroll with us?" they inquired.

"Thank you, you are very kind; but I have an engagement to row with one of the students."

Priscilla and Bonnie exchanged delighted glances. They had evidently caught a resourceful young person.

"Oh, no; it's too late for a row. You might get malaria," Priscilla remonstrated. "Come and sit on the fence with us and admire the stars; it's a lovely night."

The lecturer cast an alarmed glance toward the fence, which appeared to have an unusually narrow top rail. "You are very kind," she stammered, "but I really can't stop. The girl will be waiting."

"Who is the girl?" they inquired.

"I don't know that I remember her name."

"Mildred Connaught?" Bonnie suggested.

"No; I don't think that is it, but I really can't say. I have only just met her."

Miss Henderson was growing more and more puzzled. In her day the students had not been in the habit of way-laying strangers with invitations to go walking and sit on fences.

"Ah, *do* stay with us," Bonnie begged, laying a hand on her arm. "We're lonely and want some one to talk to-we'll tell you a secret if you do."

"I am sorry," Miss Henderson murmured confusedly, "but—"

"We'll tell you the secret anyway," said Bonnie, generously, "and I'm sure you'll be interested. The sophomores are going to have their tree ceremonies to-night!"

"And you know," Priscilla broke in, "that the freshmen really ought to attend them too-it doesn't matter if they aren't invited. But where do you suppose the freshmen are to-night? They're attending a foolish little lecture on the Roman Forum."

"And though we don't wish to seem insistent," Bonnie added, "we should really like to have your company until the lecture is over."

"Until the lecture is over! But I am the lecturer," gasped Miss Henderson.

Bonnie grinned delightedly. "I am happy to meet you," she said, with a bow. "And perhaps you do not recognize us. I am Mr. Sherlock Holmes, and this is my friend Dr. Watson."

Dr. Watson bowed, and remarked that it was an unexpected pleasure. He had often heard of the famous lecturer, but had never hoped to meet her.

Miss Henderson, who was not very conversant with recent literature, looked more dazed than ever. It flashed across her mind that there was an insane asylum in the neighborhood, and the thought was not reassuring.

"We'll not handcuff you," said Bonnie, magnanimously, "if you'll come with us quietly."

The lecturer, in spite of fervid protestations that she was a lecturer, presently found herself sitting on the fence, with a girl on either side grasping an elbow. A light was beginning to break upon her, together with a poignant realization of the fact that she was seeing more of the real college life than she cared for.

"What time is it?" she asked anxiously.

"Ten minutes past eight by my watch, but I think it's a little slow," said Bonnie.

"I am afraid you're going to be late for your lecture," said Priscilla. "It seems a pity to waste it. Suppose you tell it to us instead."

"Yes, do," urged Bonnie. "I just dote on the Roman Forum."

The lecturer preserved a dignified silence, which was broken only by the croaking of the frogs and the occasional remarks of the two detectives. She had relinquished all hope of ever seeing the Archæological Society, and had philosophically resigned herself to the prospect of sitting on the fence all night, when suddenly there burst out from across the campus a song of victory, mingled with cheers and inarticulate yells.

At the first sound, Bonnie and Priscilla tumbled down from the fence, bringing the lecturer with them, and, each grasping her by a hand, they started to run. "Come on and see the fun," they laughed. "You're perfectly welcome; it's no secret any more." And, in spite of breathless protestations that she much preferred to walk, Miss Henderson found herself dashing across the campus in the direction of the sounds.

Heads suddenly appeared in the dormitory windows, doors banged, and girls came running from every quarter with excited exclamations: "The sophomores are having their tree ceremonies!" "Where are the freshmen?" "Why didn't they get there?"

A crowd quickly gathered in the shadow of the trees and watched the scene with laughing interest. A wide circle of colored lanterns swayed in the breeze, and, within, a line of white-robed figures wound and unwound about a tiny tree to the music of a solemn chant.

"Isn't it pretty? Aren't you glad we brought you?" Bonnie demanded as they pushed through the crowd.

The lecturer did not answer, for she caught sight of the Latin professor hurrying toward them.

"Miss Henderson! I was afraid you were lost. It is nearly half-past eight. The audience has been waiting, and we have been filling in the time with reports."

For a moment the lecturer was silent, being occupied with an amused scrutiny of the faces of her captors; and then she rose to the occasion like a lady and a scholar, and delivered a masterly apology, with never a reference to her sojourn on the fence.

Bonnie and Priscilla stared at each other without a word, and as Miss Henderson was led away to the remnants of her audience Patty suddenly appeared.

"Good evening, Mr. Sherlock Holmes and Dr. Watson. Did you solve your mystery?" she asked sweetly.

Priscilla turned her to the light and scrutinized her face.

Patty smiled back with wide-open, innocent eyes.

Priscilla knew the expression, and she shook her. "You little wretch!" she exclaimed.

Patty squirmed out from under her grasp. "If you remember," she murmured, "I once said that the Lick Observatory was in Dublin, Ireland. It was a very funny mistake, of course, but I know of others that are funnier."

"What do you mean?" Bonnie demanded.

"I mean," said Patty, "that I wish you never to mention the Lick Observatory again."

Chapter XV Patty and the Bishop

The dressing-bell rang for Sunday morning service, and Patty laid down her book with a sigh and went and stood by the open window. The outside world was a shimmering green and yellow, the trees showed a feathery fringe against the sky, and the breeze was redolent of violets and fresh earth.

"Patty," called Priscilla, from her bedroom, "you'll have to hurry if you want me to fasten your dress. I have to go to choir rehearsal."

Patty turned back with another sigh, and began slowly unhooking her collar. Then she sat down on the edge of the couch and stared absently out of the window.

A vigorous banging of bureau drawers in Priscilla's room was presently followed by Priscilla herself in the doorway. She surveyed her room-mate suspiciously. "Why aren't you dressing?" she demanded.

"I'll fasten my own dress; you needn't wait," said Patty, without removing her eyes from the window.

"Bishop Copeley's going to preach to-day, and he's such an old dear; you mustn't be late."

Patty elevated her chin a trifle and shrugged her shoulders.

"Aren't you going to chapel?"

Patty brought her gaze back from the window and looked up at Priscilla beseechingly. "It's such a lovely day," she pleaded, "and I'd so much rather spend the time out of doors; I'm sure it would be a lot better for my spiritual welfare."

"It's not a question of spiritual welfare; it's a question of cuts. You've already over-cut twice. What excuse do you intend to give when the Self-Government Committee asks for an explanation?"

"'Sufficient unto the day,'" laughed Patty. "When the time comes I'll think of a beautiful new excuse that will charm the committee."

"You ought to be ashamed to evade the rules the way you do."

"Where is the fun of living if you are going to make yourself a slave to all sorts of petty rules?" asked Patty, wearily.

"I don't know why you have a right to live outside of rules any more than the rest of us."

Patty shrugged. "I take the right, and every one else can do the same."

"Every one else can't," returned Priscilla, hotly, "for there wouldn't be any law left in college if they did. I should a good deal rather play out of doors myself than go to chapel, but I've used up all my cuts and I can't. You couldn't either if you had a shred of proper feeling left. The only way you can get out of it is by lying."

"Priscilla dear," Patty murmured, "people in polite society don't put things quite so baldly. If you would be respected in the best circles, you must practise the art of equivocation."

Priscilla frowned impatiently. "Are you coming, or are you not?" she demanded.

"I am not."

Priscilla closed the door-not quite as softly as a door should be closed-and Patty was left alone. She sat thinking a few minutes with slightly flushed cheeks, and then as the chapel bell rang she shook herself and laughed. Even had she wished to go it was too late now, and all feeling of responsibility vanished. As soon as the decorous swish of Sunday silks had ceased in the corridor outside, she caught up a book and a cushion, and, creeping down by the side stairs, set gaily out across the sunlit lawn, with the deliciously guilty thrill of a truant little boy who has run away from school.

From the open windows of the chapel she could hear the college chanting: "Lord, have mercy upon us, and incline our hearts to keep this law." She laughed happily to herself; she was not keeping laws to-day. They might stay in there in the gloom, if they wanted to, with their commandments and their litanies. She was worshiping under the blue sky, to the jubilant chanting of the birds.

She was the only person alive and out that morning, and the spring was in her blood, and she felt as though she owned the world. The campus had never seemed so radiant. She paused on the little rustic bridge to watch the excited swirling of the brook, and she nearly lost her balance while trying to launch a tiny boat made of a piece of bark. She dropped pebbles into the pool in order to watch the startled frogs splash back into the water, and she threw her cushion at a squirrel, and laughed aloud at its angry chattering. She raced up the side of Pine Bluff, and dropped down panting on the fragrant needles in the shadow of a tall pine.

Below her the ivy-covered buildings of the college lay clustered among the trees; and in the Sunday quiet, with the sunlight shining on the towers, it looked like some medieval village sleeping in the valley. Patty gazed down dreamily with half-shut eyes, and imagined that presently a band of troubadours and ladies would come riding out on milk-white mules. But the sight of Peters, strolling to the gateway in his Sunday clothes, spoiled the illusion, and she turned to her book with a smile. Presently she closed it, however. This was not the time for reading. One could read in winter and when it rained, and even in the college library with every one else turning pages; but out here in the open, with the real things of life happening all about, it was a waste of opportunity.

Her eyes wandered back to the campus again, and she suddenly grew sober as the thought swept over her that in a few weeks more it would be hers no longer. This happy, irresponsible community life, which had come to be the only natural way of living, was suddenly at an end. She remembered the first day of being a freshman, when everything but herself had looked so big, and she had thought desperately, "Four years of this!" It had seemed like an eternity; and now that it was over it seemed like a minute. She wanted to clutch the present and hold it fast. It was a terrible thing-this growing old.

And there were the girls. She would have to say good-by, with no opening day in the fall-and Priscilla lived in California and Georgie in South Dakota and Bonnie in Kentucky and she in New England, and they were the only people in the world she particularly cared to talk to. She would have to get acquainted with her mother's friends-with chronically grown-up people, who talked about husbands and children and servants. And there would be men. She had never had time to know many men; but some day she would probably be marrying one of them, and then all *would* be over; and before she had time to think, she would be an old lady, telling her grandchildren stories about when she was a girl.

Patty gazed mournfully down on the campus, almost on the verge of tears over her lost youth, when a step suddenly sounded on the gravel path, and she looked up with a startled glance to see a churchly figure rounding the hill. Involuntarily she prepared for flight; but the bishop had spied her, together with a little rustic seat under a tree, and he smiled upon the one and dropped down upon the other with a sigh of content.

"A beautiful view," he gasped; "but a very steep hill."

"It is steep," Patty agreed politely; and as there seemed to be no chance of escape, she resumed her seat and added, with a laugh: "I have just run away from you, Bishop Copeley, and here you come following along behind like an accusing conscience."

The bishop chuckled. "I've run away myself," he returned; "I knew I should have to be introduced to a hundred or so of you after service, so I just slipped out the back way for a quiet stroll."

Patty eyed him appreciatively, with a new sense of fellow-feeling.

"I should like to have run away from church as well," he confessed, with a twinkle in his eye. "Out of doors is the best church on a day like this."

"That's what I think," said Patty, cordially; "but I had no idea that bishops were so sensible."

They chatted along in a friendly manner on various subjects, and exchanged lay opinions on the college and the clergy.

"It's a funny thing about this place," said Patty, ruminatingly, "that, though we have a different preacher every Sunday, we always have the same sermon."

"The same sermon?" inquired the bishop, somewhat aghast.

"Practically the same," said Patty. "I've heard it for four years, and I think I could almost preach it myself. They all seem to think, you know, that because we come to college we must be monsters of reason, and they urge us to remember that reason and science are not the only things that count in the world-that feeling is, after all, the main factor; and they quote a little poem about the flower being beautiful, I know not why. That wasn't what yours was about?" she asked anxiously.

"Not this time," said the bishop; "I preached an old one."

"It's the best way," said Patty. "We're human beings, if we do come to college. I remember once we had a man from Yale or Harvard or some such place, and he preached an old sermon: he urged us to become more manly. It was very refreshing."

The bishop smiled. "Do you run away from church very often?" he inquired mildly.

"No; I don't have a chance when I room with Priscilla. But obligatory chapel makes you want to run away," she added. "It's not the chapel I object to; it's the obligatoriness."

"But you have a system of-er-cuts," he suggested.

"Three a month," said Patty, sadly. "Evening chapel counts as one, but Sunday morning church as two."

"So you expended two cuts to escape me?" he asked with a smile.

"Oh, it wasn't you," Patty remonstrated hastily. "It was just-the obligatoriness. And besides," she added frankly, "my legitimate cuts were used up days ago, and when I once begin over-cutting, I am reckless."

"And may I ask what happens when you over-cut?" the bishop inquired.

"Well," said Patty, "there are proctors, you know, that mark you when you are absent; and then, if they find that you've over-cut, the Self-Government Committee calls you up and asks the reason. If you can't produce a good excuse you are deprived of your privileges for a month, and you can't be on committees or in plays or get leave of absence to go out of town."

"I see," said the bishop; "and will you have to suffer all of those penalties?"

"Oh, no," said Patty, comfortably; "I shall produce a good excuse."

"What will you say?" he inquired.

"I don't know, exactly; I shall have to depend on the inspiration of the moment."

The bishop regarded her quizzically. "Do you mean," he asked, "that, having broken the rule, you intend to evade the penalty by-to put it flatly—a falsehood?"

"Oh, no, bishop," said Patty, in a shocked tone. "Of course I shall tell the truth, only"—she looked up in the bishop's face with an irresistible smile—"the committee probably won't understand it."

For an instant the bishop's face relaxed, and then he grew grave again. "By a subterfuge?" he asked.

"Y-yes," acknowledged Patty; "I suppose you *might* call it a subterfuge. I dare say I am pretty bad," she added, "but you have to have a reputation for something in a place like this or you get overlooked. I can't compete in goodness or in athletics or in anything like that, so there's nothing left for me but to surpass in badness—I have quite a gift for it."

The corners of the bishop's mouth twitched. "You don't look like one with a criminal record."

"I'm young yet," said Patty. "It hasn't commenced to show."

"My dear little girl," said the bishop, "I have already preached one sermon to-day, which you didn't come to hear, and I can't undertake to preach another for your benefit,"—Patty looked relieved,—"but there is one question I should like to ask you. In after years, when you are through college and the question is asked of some of your class-mates, 'Did you know—' You have not told me your name."

"Patty Wyatt."

"'Did you know Patty Wyatt, and what sort of a girl was she?' will the answer be what you would wish?"

Patty considered. "Ye-yes; I think, on the whole, they'd stand by me."

"This morning," the bishop continued placidly, "I asked a professor in an entirely casual way about a young woman —a class-mate of your own-who is the daughter of an old friend of mine. The answer was immediate and unhesitating, and you can imagine how much it gratified me. 'There is not a finer girl in college,' he replied. 'She is honest in work and honest in play, and thoroughly conscientious in everything she does.' "

"Um-m," said Patty; "that must have been Priscilla."

"No," smiled the bishop, "it was not Priscilla. The young woman of whom I am speaking is the president of your Student Association, Catherine Fair."

"Yes, it's true," said Patty, critically. "Cathy Fair hits straight from the shoulder."

"And wouldn't you like to go out with that reputation?"

"I'm really not *very* bad," pleaded Patty, "that is, as badness goes. But I couldn't be as good as Cathy; it would be going against nature."

"I am afraid," suggested the bishop, "that you do not try very hard. You may not think that it matters what people think now that you are young, but how will it be when you grow older? And it will not be long," he added. "Age slips upon you before you realize it."

Patty looked sober.

"You will soon be thirty, and then forty, and then fifty."

Patty sighed.

"And do you think that a woman of that age is attractive if she deals in subterfuges and evasions?"

Patty squirmed a trifle, and dug a little hole in the pine-needles with her toe.

"You must remember that you cannot form your character in a moment, my dear. Character is a plant of slow growth, and the seeds must be planted early."

The bishop rose, and Patty scrambled to her feet with a look of relief. He took the pillow and the book under his arm, and they started down the hill. "I have preached you a sermon, after all," he said apologetically; "but preaching is my trade, and you must forgive an old man for being prosy."

Patty held out her hand with a smile as they stopped before the door of Phillips Hall. "Good-by, bishop," she said, "and thank you for the sermon; I guess I needed it —I *am* getting old."

She climbed the stairs slowly, and, hesitating a moment outside her own room, where the sound of laughing voices through the transom betokened that the clan was gathered, she kept on to the door of a single at the end of the corridor.

"Come in," a voice called in response to her knock.

Patty turned the knob and stuck her head in. "Hello, Cathy! Are you busy?"

"Of course not. Come in and talk to me."

Patty shut the door and leaned with her back against it. "This isn't a social call," she announced impressively. "I've come to see you officially."

"Officially?"

"You're president of students, I believe?"

"I believe I am," sighed Cathy; "and if the President of the United States has half as much trouble with his subjects as I have with mine, he has my sincerest sympathy."

"I suppose we are a great deal of trouble," said Patty, contritely.

"Trouble! My dear," said Cathy, solemnly. "I've spent the entire week running around to the different cottages making speeches to those blessed freshmen. They *won't* hand in chapel excuses, and they *will* run off with library books, and, altogether, they're an immoral lot."

"They can afford to be; they're young," sighed Patty, enviously. "But I," she added, "am getting old, and it's time I was getting good. I've called to tell you that I've over-cut four times, and I haven't any excuse."

"What are you talking about?" asked Cathy, in amazement.

"Chapel excuses. I've over-cut four times, —I think it's four, though I've rather lost count, — and I haven't any excuse."

"But, Patty, don't tell me that. You must have some excuse, some reason for —"

"Not the shadow of one. Just stayed away because I didn't feel like going."

"But you must give me *some* reason," remonstrated Cathy, in distress, "or I'll have to report it to the committee and you'll be deprived of your privileges. You can't afford that, you know, for you're chairman of the Senior Prom."

"But I didn't have any excuse, and I can't make one up," said Patty. "I will soon be thirty, and then forty, and then fifty. Do you think a woman of that age is attractive if she deals in subterfuges and evasions? Character," she added solemnly, "is a plant of slow growth, and the seeds must be planted early."

Cathy looked puzzled. "I don't know what you're talking about," she said, "but I suppose you do. Anyway," she added, "I'm sorry about the chairmanship; but I'm—well, I'm sort of glad, too." She laid a hand on Patty's shoulder. "Of course I've always liked you, Patty,—everybody does,—but I don't believe I've ever appreciated you, and I'm glad to find it out before we leave college."

Patty's face flushed a trifle and she drew away half sheepishly. "You'd best postpone your felicitations until to-morrow," she laughed, "for I may think of some good excuse in the night. Good-by."

She was greeted in the study with a cry of welcome.

"Well, Patty," said Priscilla, "I hear you've been taking a walk with the bishop. Did you tell him you'd cut chapel?"

"I did; and he said he wished he might have cut, too."

"She's incorrigible," sighed Georgie; "she's even been corrupting the bishop."

"You'd better be careful, Patty Wyatt," warned Bonnie Connaught. "Self-Government will get you if you don't watch out, and *then* you'll be sorry when they take you off the Senior Prom."

Patty sobered for a moment, but she hastily assumed a nonchalant air. "They have got me," she laughed, "and I'm already off-or, at least, I shall be as soon as they have a meeting."

"Patty!" cried the room, in a horrified chorus. "What do you mean?"

Patty shrugged. "Just what I say: deprived of my privileges for cutting chapel."

"It's a shame!" said Georgie, indignantly. "That Self-Government Committee is going a little too far when it takes a senior's privileges away without even hearing her case." She grasped Patty by the arm and started toward the door. "Come on and tell Cathy Fair about it. She will fix it all right."

Patty hung back and disengaged her wrist from Georgie's grasp. "Let me alone," she said sulkily. "There's nothing to be done. I told her myself I hadn't any excuse."

"You told her?" Georgie stared her incredulity, and Bonnie Connaught laughed.

"Patty reminds me of the burglar who crawled out the back window with the silver, and then rang the front door-bell and handed it back."

"What's the matter, Patty?" Priscilla asked solicitously. "Don't you feel well?"

Patty sighed. "I'm getting old," she said.

"You're getting what?"

"Old. Soon I'll be thirty, and then forty, and then fifty; and do you think any one will love me then if I deal in subterfuges and evasions? Character, my dear girls, is a plant of slow growth, and the seeds must be planted early."

"You went and told the committee voluntarily,—of your own accord,—without even waiting to be called up?" Georgie persisted, determined to get at the facts of the case.

"I'm getting old," repeated Patty. "It's time I was getting good. As I said before, character is a plant—"

Georgie looked at the others and shook her head in bewilderment, and Bonnie Connaught laughed and murmured to the room in general: "When Patty gets to heaven I'm afraid the Recording Angel will have some trouble in balancing his books."

Printed in Dunstable, United Kingdom

70711913R00092